Developing Advanced Primary Teaching Skills

Do you believe that continuous improvement in teaching is essential?
Do you wish to enhance your understanding of how children learn?
Are you eager to become a well-informed professional?

From the author of the hugely respected *Foundations of Primary Teaching*, this advanced textbook explores the essential elements of teaching and learning, and the process of becoming a caring and competent teacher. It introduces a wide range of education issues, challenges and requirements with the intention of promoting advanced classroom practice, both for individuals and within teams. The book offers insights, ideas, hints and thought-provoking education topics for individual reflection and team discussion.

With a focus on understanding the teaching and learning processes and the factors that impact upon providing a high-quality education for every pupil, this book discusses in detail key learning skills, dilemmas and challenges for primary teachers and themes in continuing professional development. It covers issues in teaching and learning including:

- the nature–nurture debate
- motivation
- emotional and moral development
- raising boys' achievement levels
- gender and teachers
- accelerated learning
- reflective practice.

Incorporating action points, hints and challenges, this book will be of interest to trainee teachers, postgraduates, experienced qualified teachers, deputy head teachers and head teachers who wish to be more consistently effective and make a positive impact on the lives of children in their primary classroom.

Denis Hayes is an education writer and speaker. He was Professor of Primary Education at the Faculty of Education, University of Plymouth after spending seventeen years teaching across primary, middle and secondary schools. He has authored *Foundations of Primary Teaching*, *The Guided Reader to Teaching and Learning* and *Encyclopedia of Primary Education*, all published by Routledge.

Developing Advanced Primary Teaching Skills

By Denis Hayes

Routledge
Taylor & Francis Group

LONDON AND NEW YORK

First published 2012
by Routledge
2 Park Square, Milton Park, Abingdon, Oxon OX14 4RN

Simultaneously published in the USA and Canada
by Routledge
711 Third Avenue, New York, NY 10017

Routledge is an imprint of the Taylor & Francis Group, an informa business

British Library Cataloguing in Publication Data
A catalogue record for this book is available from the British Library

Library of Congress Cataloging in Publication Data
Hayes, Denis, 1949–
    Developing advanced primary teaching skills / By Denis Hayes.
        p.cm
    Includes bibliographical references and index.
    1. Education, Elementary – Great Britain. 2. Effective teaching – Great
Britain. I. Title.
    LB1556.7.G7H387 2012
    372.941 – dc23
            2011045208

ISBN: 978-0-415-51653-2 (hbk)
ISBN: 978-0-415-51654-9 (pbk)
ISBN: 978-0-203-12419-2 (ebk)

Typeset in Plantin and Helvetica
by Taylor & Francis Books

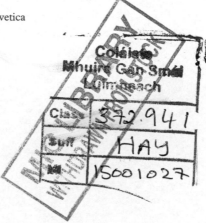

Contents

Introduction

Teachers matter. Children matter. Excellence in teaching matters. This book is written for experienced trainee teachers, postgraduates and qualified teachers wishing to advance their understanding of education through dedicated study. It builds on the contents of *Foundations of Primary Teaching* (Routledge, 2012), which explores the basic elements of teaching, learning and the process of becoming a caring, competent teacher. *Developing Advanced Primary Teaching Skills* is not a book for excellent practitioners (e.g. advanced skills teachers) but, rather, for good teachers who aspire to be excellent. As such, it introduces a wide range of education issues, challenges and requirements with the intention of promoting advanced classroom practice, both for individuals and within teams. If you are looking for a book to extend your thinking, develop your pedagogy and help colleagues to do the same, and yet that is free from the baggage of dense academic theory, *Developing Advanced Primary Teaching Skills* will provide you with insights, ideas, hints, strategies and thought-provoking education issues for personal reflection, classroom implementation and discussion with colleagues.

At heart, this book is for thinking teachers who want to better understand the teaching and learning process and the factors that impact upon providing a high-quality education for every pupil. *Developing Advanced Primary Teaching Skills* is for teachers, new and nearly-new, who long to be more consistently effective; for those who are eager to do well in the job but have yet to 'break free' and realise their true potential; for those who are dissatisfied with merely conforming to the basic requirements; and for those who want to make a positive impact in the lives of children so that they blossom intellectually, socially and emotionally. The book is not for people who want easy answers or simplistic solutions to complex issues.

The words of Palmer (2005: 1) are highly relevant when he declares:

> If you are a teacher who never has had bad days or who has them but does not care, this book is not for you. This book is for teachers who have good days and bad, and whose bad days bring the suffering that comes only from something one loves. It is for teachers who refuse to harden their hearts – because they love learners, learning and the teaching life.

So, *Developing Advanced Primary Teaching Skills* will assist all those who:

- believe that continuous improvement in teaching is of fundamental importance;
- are eager to become well-informed professionals;
- want to learn more about how to teach effectively;
- are curious to find out about how education issues affect classroom practice;
- want to gain ideas and insights from research, written sources and experienced professionals to enhance understanding of how children learn.

The book begins with a Prelude, which consists of two elements: 'Change in education' and 'Excellence in teaching', which in turn is sub-divided into four parts:

- Effective communication
- Meaningful connection with pupils
- Closely monitoring pupil progress
- Skilful pedagogy.

The remainder of the book is divided into four chapters:

- Chapter 1: Key learning skills
- Chapter 2: Teaching and learning issues
- Chapter 3: Professional themes
- Chapter 4: Challenges for teachers.

This book is not saturated with references, complex theories and complicated arguments that leave you more perplexed than enlightened. It does, however, invite you to engage with many of the factors that influence classroom practice and affect decisions that teachers like you have to make on a daily basis.

Reference

Palmer, P.J. (2005) *The Courage to Teach: Exploring the Inner Landscape of a Teacher's Life*, San Francisco: Jossey-Bass.

Prelude

Change in education

It is astonishing how rapidly things change in education. Governments and Education Ministers come and go; their policies are enthusiastically heralded to a waiting world, amended and, in some cases, quietly discarded. The latest documents and associated themes, ideas and terminology are discussed, analysed and seized upon by this or that interest group wishing to promote its own agenda. Education 'buzz' words and phrases are introduced and dominate teacher discourse for a time until a new selection of terms is promoted by policymakers for us all to understand and digest. It is hard for people who work in school to keep pace with what seems like a constant whirlwind of innovation. Many teachers are resentful about what they perceive as external interference in the way they conduct their professional lives.

Over the past fifteen years, there have also been major changes in the way that schools are run and the education they are expected to provide. For instance, there has been:

- a series of workplace reforms, a consequence of which has been a large increase in the number of teaching assistants;
- an emphasis on the educational and social requirements of children, notably through the inclusion of pupils with special needs into mainstream schools;
- a major expansion in numbers and range of pupils from overseas, for whom English is not their principal language;
- an acceleration of information and communication technology (ICT), with an accompanying expansion of specialist facilities;
- greater sensitivity about safeguarding children, through the introduction of a national system of checks for all personnel; increased security systems; and regulations governing pupil activities in and out of school;
- a considerable expansion in the amount of paperwork, not least in recording assessments of pupil progress;
- national limits on class sizes of thirty for children aged from five to seven years;
- closer parental involvement in school decision-making through the school governing body and a variety of consultation procedures;
- a plethora of government policies, not only on what is taught but also how it is taught: for example, the use of phonics in teaching reading;

- an increase in the significance of school inspections as a means of formally identifying the level of each school's success;
- the use of national test results as the indicator of a school's overall competence, with consequent funding implications;
- internal monitoring of staff performance through appraisal and, in the case of teachers, lesson observations;
- greater involvement of the local community in contributing to key decisions that affect the school and local residents;
- an increase in the number of specialist and 'free' schools.

The decision to integrate education and social services provision as a means of facilitating close liaison between them has altered the landscape of child welfare. Arrangements through the local or regional authority have increased access to health professionals, psychological services, special needs teaching services, early years support teachers, and teachers for hearing- or visually impaired children. Some schools work actively alongside external specialist agencies to support subjects such as physical education and school sport, drama and environmental studies.

A characteristic of the past twenty years or so has been the way in which successive Governments have increasingly promoted their views about pedagogy in the form of 'recommended' teaching approaches. Most notably, the so-called 'literacy hour' (introduced in 1998) and 'numeracy hour' (1999) sought to promote the notion that a three-part lesson – teacher introduction, followed by tasks and activities, and concluded by means of a lesson review in the form of a 'plenary' – would result in higher standards of academic achievement, duly reflected in formal tests. Alongside this mantra was the dark threat that teachers whose pupils failed to meet the arbitrarily imposed standards of attainment were failing and would be 'named and shamed'; in reality, the schools and not individual teachers were exposed in this way. Naturally, head teachers and school governors ensured that their staffs complied with the external guidelines, not least because the Office for Standards in Education, Children's Services and Skills (Ofsted) inspections used the degree of compliance as an informal yardstick by which to judge the leadership team's competence at managing learning in the school and promoting teachers' professional growth through in-service training opportunities. However, growing concerns over the way in which pupil and teacher motivation was eroded as a result of the ubiquitous use of such a systematic approach led to a rush of glossy pamphlets extolling the value of *enjoyment* and *creativity*. Teachers were informed that, after all, the official guidance could be reinterpreted in the light of specific school circumstances. It was not surprising that a degree of bewilderment ensued as educators at every level tried to make sense of the apparent contradiction, namely, 'teach formulaically but do so imaginatively'.

One of the many paradoxes thrown up by the interaction of interventionist policy and school innovativeness is that inspection data began to reveal that the best performing schools with regard to test results were also the most creative in their teaching methods and imaginative approach to learning. The Government's experiment of imposing a rigidly controlled form of teaching method as a means of ensuring consistency across schools, 'driving up' standards and identifying poor schools (i.e. those that failed to implement Government recommendations), was seen to be flawed.

A second key theme was that the discourse became heavily weighted towards 'learning and teaching' instead of 'teaching and learning'. This reversal was more than dabbling in semantics; it revealed a belief that teachers must first examine how children learn best and adjust their teaching accordingly, rather than using a teaching approach favoured by the teacher on the basis of which children had to learn. The change of direction resulted in increasing attention being paid to children's brain functions and so-called 'learning styles', of which a popular format was represented by the acronym, VAK: visual, auditory and kinaesthetic (see Chapter 2, Teaching and learning issue 14). Subsequently, the concept of a 'personalised' curriculum, tailor-made for each child; an emphasis on individual learning needs or 'individualisation'; plus ways to develop and enhance a child's stronger areas (sometimes referred to as 'personalisation') have saturated the literature, set the agenda for courses and dominated discourse in staffrooms up and down the country (see Chapter 3, Professional theme 16).

A changed Government in 2010 set about introducing fresh ideas about what constitutes effective teaching. The new National Curriculum (2012) focuses on every primary teacher being a teacher of reading, which is rather stating the obvious but reflects a view that too many children move on to secondary education with underdeveloped reading skills and, as a result, fall behind in their studies.

Publication of the *Independent Review of Teachers' Standards* (TDA 2011) was based on the view that 'the quality of an education system cannot exceed the quality of its teachers'. This premise led to what is described in the review as 'a relentless focus on high-quality teachers and teaching [that] requires a clear and universal understanding of the basic elements of good teaching'. As a result, the new standards explicitly define expectations of professional practice and, in the words of the review, 'set the benchmark for excellent teaching and exemplary personal conduct', something to which trainee teachers must aspire and that qualified teachers should embody. According to the standards, a teacher must:

- set high expectations which inspire, motivate and challenge pupils;
- promote good progress and outcomes by pupils;
- demonstrate good subject and curriculum knowledge;
- plan and teach well structured lessons;
- adapt teaching to respond to the strengths and needs of all pupils;
- make accurate and productive use of assessment;
- manage behaviour effectively to ensure a good and safe learning environment;
- fulfil wider professional responsibilities.

(TDA 2011)

A glance at the above bullet points shows that the new standards for teachers prioritise the importance of: (a) classroom practice; (b) subject knowledge; and (c) child welfare.

Over a generation, therefore, education practice has moved from what might be described as 'uninformed spontaneity' in the middle years of the twentieth century, to 'uninformed structure' in the latter part of the twentieth/early twenty-first century, towards the 'informed prescription' that characterises teaching today. See Cunningham (2001) for an overview of the role and nature of primary education in the twentieth century and suggestions about educational priorities for the present century (Chapter 1 of the Aldrich book, reference below).

References

Cunningham, P. (2001) 'Primary education', in R. Aldrich (ed.) *A Century of Education*, Abingdon: RoutledgeFalmer.

TDA –Training and Development Agency for Schools (2011) *Independent Review of Teachers' Standards*, London: Crown Copyright.

Excellence in teaching

Excellence as a teacher is not an attribute that some members of the profession possess and others do not. Achieving excellence is a process that has to continue throughout your working life and can fluctuate depending on circumstances such as level of responsibility, health, well-being, enthusiasm for the job, desire for promotion and quality of team membership. It is a curious fact that a teacher who blossoms in one school sometimes struggles to make an impact in a different but similar one; nevertheless, the pursuit of excellence is the responsibility of every teacher, and excellence should be eagerly sought.

Despite the importance of qualifications, the number possessed by a teacher does not necessarily equate with excellence; neither does position in the school hierarchy; nor even reputation. In fact, excellence is measured by a teacher's effectiveness in elevating pupils' enthusiasm such that they have a burning desire to learn, behave responsibly and achieve the best learning outcomes they can. Excellent teachers are characterised by knowing how to motivate pupils and influence the way that they see themselves as learners; how they view the significance and relevance of the subject matter; and how worthwhile they feel it is to strive for high standards. Children are more likely to fulfil their potential if teachers show a positive attitude towards learning, celebrate success, commiserate with failure, enthuse about discoveries, specify alternatives and offer uncomplaining help and guidance.

Excellence relies to an extent on the basic procedures of planning and organising for learning, but it is possible to produce impressive plans and spend hours organising and resourcing your lessons, yet never achieve top teacher status. The reason for this anomaly is that, while these procedures *facilitate* effective teaching, they do not of themselves bring it about. To ensure that children learn well and fulfil their potential, you must pay close attention to four aspects of classroom practice:

- effective communication
- meaningful connection with pupils
- closely monitoring pupil progress
- skilful pedagogy.

Effective communication

Excellent teachers must first and foremost be outstanding communicators, not only with pupils but also with colleagues, as they seek to play their role as part of a learning community (see under Chapter 3, Professional theme 32). Put simply, effective communication depends in the first instance on knowing what you are doing, what children should be doing and how best it is done. Transmitting this information requires an ability to construct careful explanations that employ terminology appropriate to the age range. It also requires sensitivity about the way in which what is said is being received and understood by the children, as the most carefully crafted and eloquent exposition is like water poured on sand unless the information is absorbed and inwardly digested by the recipients. Furthermore, as the rabbi and family therapist, Edwin Friedman (1932–96), is said to have declared:

> Communication does not depend on syntax or eloquence or rhetoric or articulation but on the *emotional context* in which the message is being heard. People can only hear you when they are moving toward you – and they are not likely to when your words are pursuing them. Even the choicest words lose their power when they are used to overpower. Attitudes are the real figures of speech.
>
> (source unspecified)

Strong communicators take careful account of the audience and simplify complex ideas without reducing their significance and impact. In particular, the use of carefully framed questions to interrogate the depth of children's knowledge is a crucial component of the communication process and deserves close attention by every teacher who seeks for excellence. Good questions transcend language and cultural barriers by giving close attention to pace of delivery, careful use of vocabulary and judicious use of body language, which is significant in education because the teacher's non-verbal communication can have an impact on pupil behaviour and conduct and thereby on the quality of learning.

Robertson (1996) argues that a teacher's gestures are valuable unless used to excess, as they constitute an integral part of the adult's relationship with the learner and help to clarify the message being conveyed. The author argues that teachers are performers – not in the same way as a stage artist who wants to receive public acclaim – but rather as professionals who aim to improve their teaching by practising and rehearsing essential skills that positively affect the 'audience'. Variations in body language can increase pupil response rate, create enthusiasm and help to excite a more vibrant learning environment. It is estimated that children learn a lot more through the teacher's tone of voice, facial expressions and gestures than they do from the words alone; consequently, excellent teachers combine the four elements (words, tone, facial expression and gesture) to convey meaning. Effective communication necessarily relies on pupils' willingness and capacity to listen carefully, so time spent in developing these skills in children pays dividends.

Reference

Robertson, J. (1996) *Effective Classroom Control*, London: Hodder & Stoughton.

Top tip

Your principal task as a teacher is to be an *effective communicator* in every possible way. Everything else pales into insignificance by comparison. So concentrate on communicating to pupils your: (a) expectations; (b) explanations; (c) personality; (d) concern for their welfare; (e) interest in their ideas and experiences; (f) refusal to countenance bad behaviour; (g) sympathy for their distress; (h) delight at their achievements; (i) determination to do your best for them; (j) reliability and trustworthiness as an adult.

Activate your thinking!

Communication skills work in three directions, namely: adult to pupil; pupil to adult; and pupil to pupil. Teachers must learn to listen closely to children; in turn, children must learn to listen closely to the teacher and to one another. To develop listening skills in children, teachers must create and foster a learning environment in which children's questions, views and opinions are invited and valued, if properly expressed (see also Chapter 2, Teaching and learning issue 29).

Meaningful connection with pupils

Excellent teachers make pupils' learning their priority, so they are not afraid to employ imaginative methods and strategies to engage, motivate and enthral them. Every study shows that the most popular teachers are personable and willing to explain things patiently. They give children time to say what they need to convey and try hard to accommodate their comments and ideas and even their extravagances. In addition, however, children like teachers who speak with authority, maintain order and insist on high standards. Contrary to a popular myth among uninformed people, children do not enjoy working with passive, feeble or sycophantic teachers (see Chapter 2, Teaching and learning issue 23). Excellent teachers strive to stimulate each pupil by paying heed to the child's particular learning needs and preferences. Such teachers constantly evaluate their teaching performance with reference to the pupils in their class and refuse to be blown this way and that way by the latest pronouncement of the 'best' way to teach. Instead, they thoughtfully evaluate new ideas and suggestions about teaching, gradually introducing elements that are likely to enhance their effectiveness. These teachers do their utmost to inspire in children a desire to do their very best and not to give up, regardless of struggles and setbacks. They impress the need for understanding that surpasses the mere acquisition of facts. Excellent teachers engage in an almost mystical way with their pupils, though in fact the secret lies in relationships, not in wizardry!

Top tip

Demonstrate that you care as much about children's welfare as about their academic achievements. For instance, whenever possible, stand by the door as children leave the room so that you can monitor their exit and offer words of encouragement.

Activate your thinking!

How do you come across to the pupils in your class? What do they say about you to their parents after school? How do you know? Are the majority of children pleased to have you as their teacher? Does it matter?

Closely monitoring pupil progress

Teachers have always monitored pupils' progress by observing their reactions, listening to their comments, noting their responses to questions and reviewing their work output. In the past, however, the emphasis has tended to be more upon task-completion than on what children have learned. It is relatively easy to allocate a grade or mark for a piece of work; it is more challenging to take account of the circumstances under which the task was done. For example, a child might have been paired with a slower worker; or had little time using key resources; or left the room for specialist tuition; or been absent on a preceding day when the topic was being introduced. Unfortunately, the use of a descriptor such as 'tried hard' is now interpreted as meaning 'inadequate', rather than being a commendation for effort, so you might need to find other ways of commending genuine effort.

An excellent teacher develops and uses assessments of pupils' work to continuously improve their learning experiences in line with stated course objectives but is also alert to related avenues of knowledge that a pupil may explore. In other words, assessments are made on the basis of the things that children *actually* learn and not solely on the basis of a predetermined check list. Desirable learning outcomes for pupils form an essential part of lesson plans, but they should act as a guide not a blueprint.

Top teachers not only monitor and assess pupil progress but they also employ a systematic approach to assess their own teaching, strive to keep the material fresh and engaging and make changes to their methods on the basis of feedback from tutors, colleagues and children. In this way the monitoring process is not unidirectional (teacher to pupil), but also welcomes and accommodates children's perspectives, ideas and suggestions. A highly competent teacher encourages children to recognise, confront and benefit from their limitations and errors, rather than using them as an excuse for inaction or negativity (see Chapter 2, Teaching and learning issue 28).

Finally, to be among the very best practitioners, you will always prioritise deep and meaningful learning over achieving results in a narrowly focused way. Such learning involves opportunities for children to reflect, exchange ideas and benefit from their classmates' insights, though it is worth noting that such a fluid and interactive environment cannot take place without first establishing a high standard of discipline.

Top tip

Have a digital camera available for regular use in recording key moments, such as completion of a model, map or chart, or effective use of play equipment. You might want to encourage pupils to use the camera, in which case maintain strict control over who, when, where and for what purpose.

Activate your thinking!

Constructive and sensitive feedback that results from monitoring is more likely to act as an encouragement and stimulus to pupils as they grapple with concepts and master skills if you promote a comfortable working relationship. Your monitoring and assessment should not be perceived by pupils as an attempt to 'catch them out', as this attitude leads to defensiveness and possibly a degree of resentment. Invite pupils to be self-critical and evaluate their own or other pupil's work through peer assessment as an important contribution to the sense of shared endeavour.

Skilful pedagogy

Pedagogy can be loosely defined as the method and practice of teaching and, in a real sense, the whole of this book gravitates towards achieving excellence in those aims. Excellent teachers need good subject knowledge and have to exhibit an enthusiasm for the curriculum but, as noted earlier, they must also understand how to relate to children and convey ideas and expectations clearly to them. In addition to connecting with each pupil as an individual, promoting class unity and being approachable, you must become expert in pedagogy in eight areas of your work.

1. Building an atmosphere of mutual tolerance and integrity

There are two ways to develop a positive and tolerant climate. The first way is indirectly, by modelling appropriate behaviour for pupils; by using such an approach, the impact is gradual, but pervasive. The second way is directly, through stating unequivocally what is acceptable and unacceptable, and firmly reminding children of these rules when they are infringed. At the heart of a positive working environment is the oft-used but essential notion of 'respect'.

You set an example of high integrity by being a person of your word, consistent in your actions and faithful in your commitment to the children – easily said, but requiring determination and perseverance. Integrity grows from the existence of a moral framework influencing conduct; teachers with colourful, vibrant personalities must also be people who not only know the difference between right and wrong but also behave in a way that reflects those stated beliefs at all times. Excellent teachers are those who, while recognising that children don't always do the right thing, keep matters in perspective and resist the temptation to over-react at the slightest provocation.

Top tip

'Have the courage to say no. Have the courage to face the truth. Do the right thing because it is right. These are the magic keys to living your life with integrity.' Quotation attributed to W. Clement Stone, best-selling author (1902–2002).

Activate your thinking!

Teaching is an amalgam of many elements: interpersonal, intellectual, physical, spiritual, even aesthetic ... It involves notions such as respect, concern, care and intellectual integrity that are impossible to define but which are deeply influential in determining the nature of life in class-rooms ... It is a moral enterprise as well as a practical activity.

(Richards 2010, p. 13)

Reference

Richards, C. (2010) 'Primary teaching: a personal perspective', in J. Arthur, T. Grainger and D. Wray (eds) *Learning to Teach in the Primary School*, second edn, Abingdon: Routledge.

2. Promoting a belief that learning is necessary, enjoyable and worthwhile

Sometimes children cannot be bothered to try hard in their work. Sometimes they are confused by adult expectations. Sometimes, especially in the final primary years, a small number grow cynical and distracted by interests that lie beyond the school curriculum, such as hobbies, electronic games, sport and a growing interest in the opposite sex. Some teachers offer rewards for effort and success in the hope that incentives will encourage pupils to make extra effort; other teachers become animated in a rather contrived way to enthuse reluctant learners; yet others try to persuade children to work hard as it safeguards their future. While all these approaches are useful and achieve a limited amount of success, the best way to promote enthusiasm for learning is to make it a challenge and an adventure. Boys, in particular, tend to respond well to teachers who are upbeat, wholehearted in approach and celebrate success in style. Girls, especially, normally enjoy the stimulation provided by curriculum work in which emotions and feelings are aroused. (See also Chapter 2, Teaching and learning issue 32.) Ultimately, children will learn for one or both of two reasons: either they are fearful of the consequences if they do not or they want to experience the thrill of achievement if they do. The latter form of motivation is clearly preferable, though if the threat of unpleasant repercussions is necessary to make children buckle down to work, you should not hesitate to employ a firm discipline strategy.

Top tip

Never accept shabby or incomplete work. Make it clear from the outset that you expect only the best that children can achieve. As part of the process, encourage pupils to evaluate their own work regularly.

Activate your thinking!

In every class there are a small proportion of pupils who are unwilling to make a wholehearted effort. There might also be one or two pupils who make an active attempt either to sabotage the lesson or, at least, to be as awkward as possible in order to avoid answering questions, applying themselves to the task or co-operating with classmates. The vast majority of children will, however, do their best to respond to your teaching and try their very best to complete tasks. While the troublesome pupils tend to occupy your thoughts and can often grab your attention, it should not be at the expense of the other children.

3. Setting appropriate learning goals

There has been considerable discussion in recent years about establishing learning objectives/aims and designing lessons to try and ensure that pupils achieve them. While such intentions are commendable and have spawned a large number of publications based on this premise, the reality is that, other than in narrowly defined areas of knowledge, the process of learning is rarely so straightforward. Even when a learning objective has apparently been achieved, children forget things, struggle to use the knowledge they have gained in other contexts and fail to grasp how one piece of knowledge connects with other, related forms of knowledge. It would be a strange teacher who did not have a clear idea about what she or he was attempting to achieve with children and permitted such an undirected approach to learning that it became random and unpredictable. On the other hand, excellent teachers are constantly aware of allied learning opportunities. They pick up on critical opportunities that present themselves during the lesson. They follow their plans, but not slavishly. They are acutely aware of children's reactions and what these signify. They probe understanding gently through the use of appropriate questions. They reinforce knowledge through examples and accompanying tasks that help children engage with concepts and develop skills. Such expertise is a real challenge for even the best teachers, but it is well worth striving for.

Top tip

Never assume that children understand something. Always check carefully before proceeding with the 'next step'. Failure to do so can lead to problems at a later stage.

Activate your thinking!

What do you mean when you claim that a pupil has 'met' a learning goal? What evidence do you use?

4. *Teaching in imaginative ways and allowing pupils different types of learning opportunities*

Teachers who use their imaginations and encourage children to do the same might or might not be excellent teachers, but all excellent teachers exploit imagination in their teaching. Imaginative teaching is not to be confused with gimmickry or the occasional 'being daft' that helps to create a bond between teacher and pupils through humorous episodes and laughter. Rather, teachers engage their own and their pupils' imaginations through story, creative use of visual aids, kinaesthetic experiences and dramatic interludes. The difference between good and excellent teachers is that the former group use their imaginations to 'boost' learning when it seems to be dragging, whereas the latter are constantly seeking ways to introduce flair into their teaching. Pupils benefit in many ways from being taught imaginatively, not least from the high interest level that such teaching produces, but also from the combination of spoken word (auditory), visual and hands-on experiences that combine to create a rich learning environment. (See Being imaginative and creative, Chapter 1, Learning skill 10, for further details.)

Top tip

Writing tasks, such as recording results and putting ideas down on paper/screen, are important and sometimes beneficial, but don't feel that you must invariably follow an exciting introductory phase of the lesson with it. Try to vary your practice, for example, by having a question-and-answer 'quiz' time; miming the story; drawing 'before' and 'after' pictures; or chanting in unison. In fact, any way of reinforcing learning that avoids the need to record on paper.

5. Encouraging pupils to think for themselves

The pressure on teachers to get results in formal tests for literacy and mathematics has tended to increase the amount of didactic ('directly telling') method used in teaching and reduce the time given to pupils for what is loosely referred to as 'discovery learning'; that is, time to reflect, probe, examine and enquire rather than being given facts or taken through a highly structured procedure to improve knowledge and competence in a given subject area. (See also Chapter 4, Challenge 5.) It is undeniable that some programmes to 'boost' standards have been successful and have been a worthwhile investment of resources; every teacher wishing to be exceptional must engage with such initiatives wholeheartedly, regardless of nagging doubts that children are being 'force-fed'. After all, if a pupil is falling behind in reading or numbers, it makes sense to exploit every possible means to remedy the position and give the child the chance to gain confidence and competence in that area. On the other hand, the use of structured teaching approaches should not mean the end of opportunities for children to think deeply, engage with issues and explore knowledge more widely. Excellent teachers use whatever methods will assist pupils in becoming competent in basic skills like reading and spelling yet *also* alert children to how their knowledge can be utilised in everyday life. They encourage children to ask questions, meditate on complex matters, discuss ways of resolving dilemmas and contribute to decisions that affect their lives. The teacher needs to provide information for pupils; questions to elicit pupils' knowledge and understanding; and opportunities for children to clarify points of uncertainty. In other words, if pupils are to be encouraged to think for themselves, there should be an emphasis on dialogue (adult–child and child–child) rather than constant teacher monologue.

Top tip

Encourage children to try and sort out issues by thinking carefully and searching for answers *before* seeking help from an adult.

Activate your thinking!

Children who delve into knowledge instead of passively receiving it from a teacher will learn to speculate, reach conclusions and articulate their claims and discoveries. Such an enquiry-based approach to learning, though more time-consuming than using a more didactic approach, results in a more thorough understanding and facilitates long-term memorising.

6. Identifying obstacles to learning and overcoming them

Learning is never smooth and uneventful. There are ups and downs, times of rapid progress, periods of calm and occasional retrogression. One of the teacher's many roles is to take careful note of pupils' uncertainties and confusion, which are sometimes classified under 'misunderstandings' and 'misconceptions'. Broadly speaking, *misunderstandings* result from children failing to grasp what a teacher is saying, confusing instructions, muddling the sequence or not listening carefully enough to what is said, all of which can usually be resolved through explanation, advice and repetition. By contrast, *misconceptions* are more deeply rooted problems where pupils have failed to master fundamental principles that are necessary to progress in that particular area of learning. Excellent teachers spend time in rehearsing key points, revising uncertain areas and, if necessary, providing additional support for children struggling in specific aspects of a subject by allocating some of the teaching assistant's time or providing additional resources (e.g. computer software); they then monitor the individual's subsequent progress closely until the child is able to work independently. These sorts of procedures are simple to list but extremely difficult in practice and very time-consuming, especially if several pupils are struggling. It takes a special kind of courage for you to acknowledge that pupils have failed to grasp ideas and, as a result, allocate time to return to the specific area of learning and revise it in depth. It is much easier to convince yourself that it is the pupils' fault and that they will somehow muddle through – instead of grasping the nettle and returning to the theme with fresh determination to clarify matters by using a different teaching and learning approach. The decision to press on grimly and pretending that all is well is unprofessional, unfair to children and, ultimately, counterproductive.

Top tip

Whenever a pupil gives a baffling response to a question, pause to clarify the reason. Do so gently. Clarify matters immediately if the response is due to a misunderstanding; make a mental note to return to the issue shortly if the answer seems to be due to a misconception.

Activate your thinking!

Teachers have to recognise that children's errors can be due to misunderstanding about what is *required* rather than the inability to grasp the concept. Consequently, clarity of explanation about the task or activity (resources, time allowed, extent of freedom to collaborate, etc.) and explicitness about expectations (ways of working, completion rate, setting out results, etc.) should be essential components of every lesson.

7. Assessing work and offering feedback

The results of formal tests are fed into a computer program to produce graphs and displays, which are intended to demonstrate pupil progress in different year groups and core subject areas. This regimented and closely monitored approach is necessary for the purpose of ensuring that the school's success profile remains high, principally because inspectors, parents and governors must be provided with sufficient data to be satisfied that the quality of teaching is being maintained and, hopefully, enhanced. Whatever your views on testing, the reality is that poor results can have serious consequences for a school; in the worst-case scenario, the head teacher can be removed, the staff reorganised and the school placed in special measures – a prospect that causes everyone associated with schools to shiver.

Factors creating the conditions that result in this sort of dismal school failure are numerous and complex. It is fair to say, however, that the problem begins when teachers have low expectations of pupils, tolerate mediocre work and miss opportunities to guide and direct learning through helpful interventions and feedback each session. In particular, evaluation of work that is variously known as 'formative assessment' or 'assessment for learning' (AFL) is crucially important in building in pupils an awareness of (a) where they are succeeding; (b) where they can improve and amend their work; and (c) what they might aim to achieve beyond the immediate work. (See also Chapter 2, Teaching and learning issue 28.) Providing this level of quality feedback is hugely demanding and cannot easily be learned from a textbook (including this one).

The route to excellence in this area of work is considerably assisted by applying five principles. First, to observe carefully what children are doing and ask them about the work before deciding whether to intervene further. Second, to focus on achievements as much, if not more, than shortcomings. Third, to be uncompromising in addressing unsatisfactory standards of work. Fourth, to foster corporate endeavour throughout the whole group or whole class, such that pupils are learning from each other. Finally, to do everything with good grace and a light but purposeful touch whenever and wherever possible. An excellent teacher remembers how devastated it felt to be criticised when you have done your best. Having high expectations of children should not be equated with a situation where pupils conclude that it is impossible to please the teacher (see also below).

Top tip

Avoid giving the impression that the only reason the children must do well in their work is to please *you*.

Activate your thinking!

The best formative assessments are also *diagnostic*; that is, not merely descriptive, but providing evidence to assist in the formulation of appropriate teaching and learning strategies.

8. Promoting positive attitudes

It is a sobering fact that children who receive constant criticism for getting something wrong will soon learn that it is better not to try than to risk failure. Excellent teachers impress upon the pupils that the only true failure is a failure to make the effort to succeed. At one level there is a need to explain to the child how work can be improved; at another level there is a pressing need, especially with children who have experienced limited academic success in the past, to encourage, praise and celebrate achievement, however modest it may be. Top teachers want to offer the pupils a full education in which perseverance, moral virtue, thoughtfulness and being a positive influence in the lives of their class-mates and friends are deeply embedded. Thus, learning to care, to be com-passionate, to sympathise and to show a deep appreciation of the beauty in the world around are as much part of the educative process as the formal curriculum. Excellent teachers realise that well-educated children exude a positive attitude, not only to themselves and their own learning, but also to those around them, through building effective relationships, behaving with integrity and demon-strating kindness to others.

Top tip

Since approval by touch has become more problematic in school, affirmation through the use of the eyes has assumed even greater significance and must be fully exploited if you want to communicate effectively with the class. A twinkling eye, a bright smile and a simple nod of approval can transform a child's attitude and enthusiasm for learning by conveying approval, amuse-ment and affirmation.

Activate your thinking!

Successful lessons do not happen by chance; they result from a combination of careful planning, sensible organisation, skilful lesson management and enthusiastic teaching that also allows for spontaneous opportunities, creativity and the needs of pupils of all abilities.

1

Key learning skills

Introduction

Learning comes naturally to children, providing that the subject content is interesting and the situation offers sufficient motivation to stimulate curiosity, encourage perseverance and make the goal of task completion worthwhile. Any adult who has worked with a group of enthusiastic children or young people will confirm that, once the 'fire of desire' to learn has been lit, it creates an almost inextinguishable blaze.

Sometimes, however, children's learning is superficial, tentative and easily dissolved. Surface learning of this kind is often associated with memorising unrelated fragments of knowledge; an inability to separate principles from specific examples; and completing a task without fully engaging the mind. By contrast, permanent learning, in which knowledge is transferred from the short-term to the long-term memory (see Chapter 2, Teaching and learning issue 19), takes place when the learner relates previous knowledge to new knowledge, roots ideas in everyday experiences, reflects on the content area, discusses points with others and thereby synthesises existing and new knowledge into a manageable form.

Children can be enthused about an area of knowledge but lack the necessary skills to make best use of their opportunities to learn in depth. They can fall short in their grasp of basic principles and correct use of terminology; fail to make connections between areas of knowledge; lack the ability to co-operate with others; neglect the need for planning; overlook the effects of their decisions and actions; resist making modifications based on changing conditions; communicate poorly; lack creativity and inquisitiveness; and reach unwarranted conclusions.

The list of key learning skills described and explored in this chapter is far from being universally agreed. Indeed, the use of the descriptor 'key' and the concept of 'skills' can be debated at length. When *skill* is used in this book, it is defined as an ability or capacity that is acquired by means of a deliberate, systematic and sustained effort to carry out activities or other functions involving ideas (cognitive), manipulation of things (technical) or dealing with people (interpersonal).

The following twelve learning skills encapsulate many of the attributes that top teachers should hope to inspire and develop in every pupil. A 'Top tip' and

'Activate your thinking!' and 'Requirements for teaching' comments are provided after each learning skill section to link the discussion with classroom practice and help you to reflect on your teaching. The learning skills considered in this chapter are arranged as follows:

1. Understanding key concepts
2. Learning across subject boundaries
3. Developing social skills
4. Working collaboratively
5. Sorting and classifying
6. Planning and sequencing
7. Recognising cause and effect
8. Adapting to different circumstances
9. Speaking confidently
10. Being imaginative and creative
11. Making valid judgements
12. Developing an enquiring mind.

Learning skill 1: Understanding key concepts

Pupils are sometimes intellectually capable of performing a task or solving a problem but their failure to grasp an elementary *concept* acts as a barrier to progress. In its simplest form, a concept can be defined as an idea or notion; thus, a pupil has an elementary understanding of what is going on by listening to explanations, asking questions and engaging with a task or activity to reinforce the principle that has been presented by the teacher. This form of concept development is *deductive*: that is, working from the general principle to the particular instance. For example, the teacher might tell the class that different poles of a magnet attract, whereas others repel. To confirm the truth of the statement, children carry out some simple experiments with magnets to show that the principle always applies, regardless of the shape and size of the magnet or the context in which the event occurs.

Concept development can also be *inductive*; that is, reasoning from detailed facts to general principles, rather as a detective pieces together pieces of evidence to reveal the truth of the case. For example, the teacher might give pupils two sets of numbers that are related through an algorithm and the children have to work out the relationship by manipulating the figures until they discover (say) that the second set of numbers can be derived from the first set by finding the square root. Thus, 16 relates to 4; 25 relates to 5, 36 relates to 6, and so on.

The use of deductive or inductive reasoning has important implications for the teaching method or style employed. *Deductive* reasoning depends on 'front-loading' a lesson with information, followed by tasks and activities, which are subsequently assessed/marked. *Inductive* reasoning usually has a short direct teaching element, followed by a lengthy 'discovery' period and a teacher-led lesson summary during which time the findings from children's enquiries are collated and described, and the principles elicited. In practice, most lessons contain elements of both types of concept formation, but one will always predominate. To summarise:

Deductive: lengthy didactic phase to identify principle, followed by tasks, followed by assessment of the tasks.

Inductive: short introduction to describe the activity, followed by lengthy exploratory phase, followed by elicitation of principle.

Concept development is crucially important if children are to develop understanding. To take a simple yet common example: if children do not realise that an apostrophe in a word indicates the absence of a letter (e.g. they're = they are; it's = it is) they will be mystified about the correct usage. Thus, the child writes: *There trying to win the race* instead of: *They're trying to win the race.* Similarly: *The rabbit ate it's carrot* instead of: *The rabbit ate its carrot.* Such confusion is avoidable once the principle of an apostrophe representing a missing letter is explained and examples are provided to illustrate the implications of correct and incorrect usage.

Again, in science, there is little chance that pupils will understand the factors impacting on the flight patterns of different substances if they are unaware of the existence and effects of gravity and air pressure. The children will notice and describe the variations in flight and faithfully record them but, without grasping the key concepts that relate to aerodynamics, their understanding will never progress beyond the level of basic description. Thus, children can enjoy performing experiments, observing outcomes, commenting on what takes place and writing down findings, yet fail to grasp the underlying scientific principles. Your role is crucial in this regard, so make sure that you know what you're talking about!

We have all had the experience of being cautious about contributing to a discussion for fear of exposing our ignorance through the inappropriate use of a word or expression. The reason for this reluctance is that concept development is highly dependent on possessing an appropriate vocabulary and understanding the significance of the words we employ. Most adults need to be immersed in a particular culture, activity or subject area for a period of time before they gain the confidence to open their mouths. The same is true of pupils in school. If children do not fully understand the meaning of words, especially subject-specific terms, it is almost impossible for them to reflect on issues, contribute to collaborative exercises, employ skills appropriately or express opinions. Instead, they tend to rely on elementary speech and substitute a rudimentary expression for the subject-specific word; for instance, a child might say 'all the way around the edge' instead of using the term 'circumference'.

There are also examples of possible confusion over terminology in the use of multiple terms to express the same function in subjects like mathematics. Thus, dividing is also referred to as 'sharing'; subtraction is called 'take away'; multiplication is known by the vernacular 'times-ing'. A child not only needs to understand that two or more terms are synonymous, but also that (for instance) multiplication is a short form of multiple adding. Without being able to handle key vocabulary and understand its meaning, children will struggle to make sense of ideas and explore them in depth. Too often, they 'muddle through', unaware of the significance of terms and how to employ them in discussion. Bear in mind that establishing clear links between concepts and vocabulary is most effective when rooted in adult–pupil conversations that take place during practical, 'hands-on' experiences. In other words, explanations about the meaning and significance of words and phrases should be taking place constantly during the task or activity being undertaken, such that they are used naturally and contextually.

Top tip

Explain everything carefully – not just at the start of the lesson but also at regular intervals. Do not assume that children understand what you are saying; instead, check that they do so by the use of direct (single-answer) questions and, if necessary, more probing ones. Revise and reinforce ideas by employing different perspectives and examples if the children only have a tentative grasp of things. Always use correct subject vocabulary, but also use the elementary meaning alongside it until the accurate term has taken root.

Activate your thinking!

When a teacher asks the children whether they have understood what they have been told, why do they invariably answer affirmatively? How can you better discover the depth of their understanding?

Requirements for teaching

- To find ways to cater for slow learners and still accelerate the learning of their highly competent classmates.
- To rehearse and reinforce understanding at every opportunity, taking nothing for granted.

Learning skill 2: Learning across subject boundaries

There has been considerable discussion recently about the extent to which the primary curriculum should be organised on the basis of traditional subject areas or on the basis of themes and topics, which encompass several areas of knowledge. Whichever approach is favoured, it is undoubtedly true that the ability to 'make connections' is essential for effective learning. Pupils might show understanding or gain good grades in specific areas of work but fail to grasp that knowledge is bound together in a multitude of direct and subtle ways. To assist this process of interconnecting, teachers need to use every opportunity to alert children to ways in which one area of knowledge links with another.

For instance, reference to the Plague and Great Fire of London in 1665 and 1666 provides a plethora of opportunities to mention issues concerned with healthy living (PSHE – Personal Social Health and Economic education), building materials (Design and Technology – D&T), water pressure (science), population density (geography) and numerous other related areas. Thus, healthy living can be grounded in pupils' experiences of washing their hands and cleaning their teeth. The appropriate use of building materials can be linked with building 'play' shelters, either in the home/classroom or school grounds/garden. The significance of water pressure can easily be illustrated with reference to turning on the tap too quickly or using a hosepipe. Issues surrounding population density can be related to crowds in the local market or style of local housing. In other words, high-quality teachers use every possible occasion that presents itself to feed off and connect with other curriculum areas. While it is important to be focused on the principal learning objectives for the session or sessions, and not to stray unduly from the planned lesson, the process of relating ideas and rooting them in experiences not only helps to cement understanding and stimulate interest, but also brings lessons alive for children.

The use of cross-curricular approaches through thematic teaching or project work, in which a variety of subject areas are woven together, helps reinforce these connections. A curriculum structure in which there is an emphasis upon relationships and patterns in knowledge and systems has been referred to as a 'curriculum flow' (see, for example, Cremin *et al.* 2006), whereby pupils draw upon a range of skills from across the curriculum (e.g. map-reading skills from geography; weighing of evidence sources from history) and other experiences to induce deeper learning as they use their knowledge in a variety of situations.

Teachers have a central role in pointing out related areas of knowledge and helping to weave a comprehensive understanding, rather than one limited by arbitrary subject boundaries. In particular, the use of collaborative problem-solving and investigations allows children to discuss options, select from a range of possibilities and try out their ideas, guided by adults, as appropriate. Encouraging pupils to gain from one another's expertise and insights – sometimes referred to as dialogic learning – is harder to manage than a situation that is wholly controlled by the teacher, but often provides a more powerful incentive to learn (Fisher 2009).

References

Cremin, T., Burnard, P. and Craft, A. (2006) 'Pedagogy and possibility thinking in the early years', *Thinking Skills and Creativity*, 1 (2), pp. 108–19.

Fisher, R. (2009) *Creative Dialogue: Talk for Thinking in the Classroom*, London: David Fulton.

Top tip

Use every opportunity throughout a session to alert pupils to links with other areas of learning, but notably during the summary phase of the lesson. Use topic 'webs' and other visual representations (e.g. Venn diagrams) to illustrate the relationship between related areas of knowledge.

Activate your thinking!

Fox and Surtees (2010) argue that the best teachers use a range of methods, including narrowly focused subject teaching *and* cross-curricular approaches for problem solving and investigations.

Reference

Fox, S. and Surtees, L. (2010) *Problem-Solving, Reasoning and Numeracy in Primary Schools*, London: Continuum.

Requirements for teaching

■ To be alert to cross-curricular links and refer to them at regular intervals.
■ To have the courage to permit and encourage periods of time for enquiry-based ('discovery') learning.

Learning skill 3: Developing social skills

Initially, the development of social skills might appear to be out of place in a chapter devoted to learning skills; it is, however, an essential component if learners are to benefit from others and contribute to the corporate body of knowledge. School offers pupils a unique opportunity to meet a wide range of children and adults in a carefully controlled and safe environment where they can learn, socialise and discover their true worth. When children begin school or change class, the teacher's assessment not only contains an evaluation of children's academic ability but also of their social skills. Teachers of new entrants soon become aware of the widely differing ways in which children have been prepared for life in school or, in the case of teachers of older pupils, how they have matured socially during their time in school. One yardstick used by teachers to identify socially competent children is that they view rejection by peers (e.g. exclusion from a playground game) as temporary or as a situation that they can improve by changing their own behaviour; by contrast, socially deprived children quickly become hurt, defensive and, in a few cases, aggressive, if they feel slighted or criticised.

Well-honed social skills necessitate competence in working with others, collaborating in tasks and communicating ideas. (See Learning skill 4 below.) Those who argue that the academic and social elements of learning are discrete entities and should be kept apart fail to appreciate that effective learning is more likely when: (a) motivation is high; (b) the aim of the task is clear; (c) the situation is relaxed, but purposeful; and (d) there is good communication between learners. The numerous interactions that take place daily between children and adults, and between different children, impact upon the quality of learning in three ways: first, because they learn from one another;

second, because energy is generated through human interaction; and third, because a joint endeavour can develop a sense of team work and mutual respect.

All children go through stages of social development. An infant or very young child will normally play alone happily. If another child wanders onto the scene, the newcomer may be viewed as an intruder. Over time, the same child develops the confidence and maturity to play with another child, gradually learning to share and taking turns. Eventually the number sharing the play experience expands to three or four children. By the time a child enters the formal school system, he or she is usually able to join in and enjoy group experiences, though the induction period can be difficult for a few notable exceptions. Part of the problem might be the presence or emergence of autism, which is basically a communication disorder that can lead to isolation and (in some cases) behaviour problems. (See also Learning skill 9 later in this chapter.)

Children normally prefer to work with their friends and may be reluctant to move outside their preferred social group, but opportunities to interact with a wider range of classmates are an important element of their development. In addition, it is essential for you to establish a learning environment in which children feel free to express opinions, speculate and offer different perspectives without fear of being ridiculed or 'shouted down'. Timid children are usually reluctant to contribute to discussions for fear of being mocked or revealing their own lack of knowledge. Even capable pupils are often in awe of their self-confident classmates, who appear immune to criticism and shoot their hands in the air at every opportunity. There are, of course, times when children fall out with one another, disagree and get upset. You have an essential role on such occasions to provide a calm and reassuring presence and encourage reconciliation.

Social skills are best learned and practised in real situations, so one of the best ways to foster the skills is through projects that entail contributions from the whole group or class. For example, a presentation of ideas in assembly; collecting items from the school grounds for a display; collating photographs and artefacts for a history montage; arranging a 'mock' ceremony (e.g. of a wedding); creating PE games or short dramatic presentations in groups; or designing a representation of a character from a story. The development of a team spirit in co-operating takes time and perseverance but, if successful, it offers the chance for shaping tolerance and acceptance of others' weaknesses, as well as their strengths. Such a unifying process rarely proceeds smoothly and requires that you establish clear guidelines for behaviour; provide a good role model; and offer close guidance for pupils about their conduct in relating to others, regardless of emotional conflicts.

Progress in school is not solely dependent on having the knowledge, practical skills and understanding to complete set tasks to a satisfactory standard or even to achieve high marks. It involves being able to work as part of a team; co-operate with others; listen and learn; respond appropriately; tell the truth sensitively; be a friend to those in need; encourage the downhearted; and enjoy life to the full. Teachers are not the only adults to play a part in helping children to develop these and other related skills and attitudes, but they are certainly among the key ones.

Top tip

Foster a climate of 'all for one and one for all', in which friendliness and helping each other becomes an integral element. Concentrate your efforts on helping children to learn how to listen, encouraging attributes such as maintaining soft eye contact (i.e. looking at the person directly without staring, while smiling encouragingly); waiting until someone has finished speaking before reacting non-verbally or making comments; and summarising what has been said in their own words.

Activate your thinking!

Susan Jindrich in her online article, 'How to develop your children's social skills' (2005) suggests that there are thirteen developmental steps involved, a modified version of which is listed below:

- develop a sense of self and belonging
- develop trust
- learn to separate from their parents
- watch other children play from a distance
- play near other children but not with them
- play with other children
- share and take turns
- state opinions and desires
- use words to solve conflicts and develop control of emotions
- engage in situational or dramatic play
- learn that it is okay to make a mistake
- develop confidence and self-respect
- develop respect for others and feelings of empathy.

Reference

Jindrich, S. (revised 2007) 'How to develop your children's social skills'. Available at: www.meddybemps.com/7.027.html (accessed October 2011).

Requirements for teaching

- To blend children with varying social skills and sensitivities into a coherent whole.
- To assist pupils who struggle to establish friendships and relate to others.

Learning skill 4: Working collaboratively

Collaboration in learning normally involves pupils working in groups on investigative, enquiry-based tasks. Pupil collaboration is intended to facilitate a blending of minds and intellects, as children grapple with problems; discuss alternatives; and search for outcomes by harnessing the contributions of each member. Ideally, the active involvement of every child is necessary to achieve the desired learning outcome, as the group can usually offer a range of learning skills between them, including an ability to speculate, predict, justify, evaluate and generalise. In practice, it requires leadership, consensus about trying new approaches, willingness to countenance failure, pragmatism and determination to succeed. The joint activities do not detract from the principle that each child has a personal responsibility for learning, as no one can learn for somebody else; however, in collaborating a child can assist others to extend and shape their understanding while at the same time reinforcing their own. This process of engagement is sometimes referred to as a miniature 'learning community' (for example, Watkins 2005). In similar manner, Brophy *et al.* (2010) encourage teachers to establish the classroom as a collaborative learning community and to plan the curriculum and provide instruction that incorporates ideas and their applications to life outside school. The authors argue that such an approach motivates pupils to learn with a sense of purpose and thoughtful self-regulation.

Collaboration occurs when pupils are set tasks to complete in small groups of no more than four members, sometimes reporting back their findings to others in the class later in the lesson. It is rooted in the theory of *social constructivism* in learning, defined as the process by which pupils work together to reach a specified and predetermined learning objective. Wray (2006) explains that social constructivism is an approach in which the importance of collaboration is emphasised, whereby pupils are required to 'develop teamwork skills and to see individual learning as essentially related to the success of group learning. This should be seen as a process of peer interaction that is mediated and structured by the teacher' (p. 55). Whereas co-operation involves children working independently or in pairs, but being supportive to others while they do so, collaboration is typically associated with activities in which pupils are interdependent. Investigative tasks that involve collaborative grouping result in *jointly determined* outcomes; by contrast, tasks that involve co-operative grouping often result in *individual outcomes*.

To promote collaborative learning, teachers might establish practical problem-solving opportunities that relate to the existing curriculum work; for example, children might be asked to develop strategies to improve the tidiness of the playground as part of the citizenship programme. Alternatively, pupils can raise an issue about which they feel strongly; the teacher then helps them to shape their ideas into a proposition, which each group discusses independently before recommending possible solutions. Again, children might wish to discuss issues about friendship patterns, school rules, homework, children's TV programmes, playground behaviour or hobbies, all of which provide fertile ground for exploring important principles, such as the importance of sharing, time management, staying healthy, and so forth. Teachers also need to consider ways to include children with special educational needs by insisting that they are allowed a voice in the proceedings and taking serious account of their comments, however whimsical or unconventional they might be (Jelly 2000).

One of the most difficult attitudes for children to develop is having an open mind to consider different points of view and to resist pouring scorn on unusual suggestions or marginalising other children in the group because they are slow to react, lack the intellectual capacity to engage at a deep level with the issues, or struggle with reading and writing. Teachers have to stress with children the need for careful and respectful listening when working with others or listening to a child reporting back from a different group. Such universal accommodation is only valid if the individual concerned is behaving sensibly; unco-operative children need to be dealt with firmly but also given a useful task that helps them to be included in the endeavour, howbeit at a relatively trivial level. An interesting piece of research by Corriveau *et al.* (2009) found that pre-school children as young as three or four years were able to hold opinions and recognise and trust a consensus. However, it is interesting to note that, even at this tender age, the children preferred to work with those of their classmates who conformed rather than those who dissented.

Facilitating children's participation needs to be done in such a way that every child's genuine contribution is valued; it is essential, of course, that frivolous comments and suggestions are given short shrift. In the process of helping children to work together effectively, pupils can be helped to recognise that: (a) 'failure' is part of the learning process; (b) others possess different perspectives from their own; (c) there might be more than one acceptable 'right' answer; (d) compromise is often necessary; and (e) not every solution is linear, smooth and seamless. Ultimately, you have to decide the extent to which you accommodate all findings (however inaccurate) and how much you emphasise the correct or most correct solution to a problem. If the purpose of the exercise is principally to promote collaborative working, the outcome is of less significance than if children are delving into an area of essential knowledge, such as a set of number relationships in mathematics.

To gain optimum benefit from collaborative enterprises, you need to teach children how to summarise their own ideas, evaluate what classmates say and ask sensible questions. This *dialogic* style of learning – a dialogue in which different people provide arguments based on validity claims and not on the power of the individual – allows children opportunities to talk to others about ideas and possibilities; move outside their immediate world; recognise life's complexities; gain self-confidence; learn from sharing ideas; evaluate opinions; and offer support to their peers. It is important to remember, however, that, to make effective contributions, pupils must have some existing knowledge and insights that have been inculcated during previous learning. Collaborative work is therefore not about 'making it up as you go along' but rather about deepening what is already tentatively understood.

References

Brophy, J., Allerman, J. and Knighton, B. (2010) *A Learning Community in the Primary Classroom*, Abingdon: Routledge.

Corriveau, K.H., Fusaro, M. and Harris, P.L. (2009) 'Going with the flow: preschoolers prefer nondissenters as informants', *Psychological Science*, 20 (3), pp. 372–77.

Jelly, M. (2000) *Involving Pupils in Practice*, London: David Fulton.

Watkins, C. (2005) *Classrooms as Learning Communities*, Abingdon: Routledge.

Wray, D. (2006) 'Looking at learning', in J. Arthur, T. Grainger and D. Wray (eds) *Learning to Teach in the Primary School*, Abingdon: Routledge.

Top tip

Monitor the groups to check if any children are being marginalised and whether there are those who are being too dominant. Don't intervene initially; instead, make a general announcement to the effect: 'Please make sure that everyone in your group has a chance to speak'. If necessary, allocate roles to members of the group (scribe, reader, resource provider, leader, or similar), possibly on a rotation basis, so that each child who wishes to accept that role has opportunity to do so; timid children need to be gently coaxed and encouraged to participate.

Activate your thinking!

Fisher (2005) argues that collaborative work helps children to learn from each other, deepen their understanding through engagement in exploratory talk, develop problem-solving skills, learn to take turns and negotiate, see other points of view and present their own opinions. While it might be tempting to set children to work in groups and stand back, having minimal interaction with them until the work is finished, your role in stimulating children's verbal contributions is significant as you guide their thinking, suggest alternatives and raise searching questions.

Reference

Fisher, R. (2005) *Teaching Children to Learn*, second edn, Cheltenham: Stanley Thornes.

Requirements for teaching

- To ensure that children in groups spend most of their time grappling with the work, not chatting informally.
- To draw the threads of the lesson together into a coherent whole.

Learning skill 5: Sorting and classifying

Our eyes and ears have to absorb so many different sights and sounds in various areas of life that, if we did not have a system for classifying and sorting, the world would be intolerably confusing. We therefore train our brains to automatically classify and process the things around us to make better sense of what we experience. If people did not sort the information that their senses throw at them, it would be akin to the postal service piling the millions of letters and parcels they receive into a heap and attempting to deliver them to the correct addresses without bothering to examine the labels. Most adults become adept at organising their lives into identifiable and accessible sets of objects, items and tasks; thus, the cutlery drawer is divided into knives, forks and spoons; computer files are grouped under titled folders; finances are allocated according to their purpose, and so on. Children take time to reach such proficiency and need to be taught how to use criteria to make appropriate selections that bring coherence and order to a random situation, not only in subject knowledge but also in practical areas of school life.

Owing to the importance of sorting, classifying and organising, younger children have to spend a lot of time in activities concerned with sorting objects into 'sets' and identifying items on the basis of shared characteristics; for example, a child might learn to separate objects into different colours or shapes. Similarly, children might classify by using scent, texture, utility (e.g. items for use in the kitchen, bathroom, living room and garden); response to a stimulus (such as magnetism); or behaviour under 'fair test' conditions (such as observing flight patterns using different thicknesses of paper and card to construct the flying object). Again, common objects such as buttons can be sorted according to a variety of characteristics: size, colour, number of holes and texture. The leaves of plants can be similarly sorted according to structure and, perhaps, recategorised using different criteria to emphasise the point that classifying is not always a precise process but can vary according to the criteria used and circumstances; in this instance, classification of leaves will be influenced by the season of the year.

The use of worksheets is a useful and common way to help develop and reinforce the concept of classifying, especially for younger pupils. For instance, pupils have to colour in outline shapes on a sheet by category (e.g. depicting different kinds of creature) – numbers of legs, land or sea habitat, domesticated or wild – and then count and record the items in each category. Again, names of objects can be listed down one side of the page with pictures in random order down the other side. Yet again, children might have to identify and link items from a series of pictures across the page spelt with the same initial letter. Older children might classify a series of words into nouns, verbs and adjectives; or classify tunes that are in 4/4 time and 3/4 time; or separate prime numbers from numbers that are multiples of three and those that are multiples of four. The possibilities are endless. Importantly, however, the best teachers recognise that deep learning occurs when the results from such activities are shared, discussed and, perhaps, recategorised. Completing tasks is good; talking about tasks during and after completion is even better.

As classification depends upon possessing a shared vocabulary, such that ideas can be communicated and discussed within a group, you might wish to create opportunities to introduce targeted vocabulary as a means of assisting children to more accurately describe the shared properties of items. For instance, whereas a child might refer to a substance as being 'smelly' or 'stinky', you can suggest alternatives such as 'pungent' or 'sour' or 'sharp'. Although it is necessary to begin from pupils' existing vocabulary, the chance must be seized to extend and deepen the children's word bank as they make decisions about distinctive properties and features, remembering that the full meaning of a word or phrase is only cemented by using it in a range of different sentences. For instance, *Lucy told her mummy that she couldn't drink the milk because it had gone sour and tasted funny*; or *John's nose twitched and his head jerked backwards as he sniffed the pungent odour from the disinfectant*. It is not difficult to see how, in these examples, the use of body language and, perhaps, a touch of melodrama, can help to cement learning.

An ability to classify is particularly relevant to number work in mathematics but it has considerable significance in many other areas of the curriculum. Pupils need to apply sophisticated methods in areas such as language work (e.g. recognising word types); science (classifying natural objects); geography (identifying climatic regions); music (designating types of composition); design and technology (distinguishing styles of construction); physical education (performing types of gymnastic movements); history (recognising clothes of the period); art (putting into genres); and so on. There are also classification issues concerned with beliefs (in RE); forms of behaviour (in citizenship); and even ideologies (e.g. voting preferences). In other words, the use of classification systems permeates most areas of the curriculum and can lead to discussions about ethical and moral themes in topics as wide-ranging as hygiene, streaming of pupils and making appropriate life choices.

Classified objects can be recorded using pie charts for simple division into component parts; Venn diagrams with overlapping circles to indicate distinctive and shared characteristics; trees (similar to a family tree); and geometric tabulations of various kinds. Importantly, the results and their implications need to be discussed and explored; the mere existence of attractively recorded findings is not, as popularly supposed, the end product, but rather a starting point for dialogue and extended learning.

Top tip

With younger children, suggest less obvious criteria for classifying objects (e.g. utility rather than colour; ability for an object to roll rather than its 3D-shape). With older children, use a range of advertising images as a basis for classifying into categories such as convincing/ confusing/ conniving. Where appropriate, get the children to organise items into sets in two or more ways.

Activate your thinking!

Krnel *et al*. (2003) asked eighty-four children between the ages of three and thirteen to classify four sets of objects and 'matter' and to explain their classifications. The sets of objects and matter were made up of different substances of various shapes and particle size, and of different compositions. The researchers found that younger children tended to classify using both 'extensive properties' (what was observable) *and* 'intensive properties' (properties of matter – its composition), whereas older children (above nine years old) tended to use only intensive properties most of the time. The research raised issues concerning the way in which children of different ages perceive objects and categorise them.

Reference

Krnel, D., Glazar, S.S. and Watson, R. (2003) 'The development of the concept of matter: a cross-age study of how children classify materials', *Science Education*, 87 (5), pp. 621–39.

Requirements for teaching

- To encourage pupils to use a variety of criteria for sorting, classifying and organising.
- To employ classification systems as a means of understanding the interconnections between areas of knowledge.

Learning skill 6: Planning and sequencing

Many inexperienced cooks have encountered a situation in which they are attempting to create a meal, only to find that the vegetables are ready before the pasta, while the sauce goes cold waiting for the steam cooker to finish its cycle. Experienced cooks know when to commence each part of the meal and co-ordinate the preparation to perfection. The need for planning and correct sequencing belongs not only to the kitchen, of course, but also applies to almost every other area of life, including holidays, home repairs and shopping.

Children often have plenty of ideas about what they want to do but sometimes struggle to assemble them into a useful, manageable order; instead, they rely on a random, spontaneous assault on the task, which, though enjoyable initially, results in confusion and disappointing outcomes. Sequencing is a skill that can be incorporated into any subject area, but it is often associated with teaching early readers and contributes significantly towards pupils' ability to comprehend what they read. For instance, children need to identify the components of a story, such as the beginning, middle and end; similarly, they benefit from gaining the ability to retell events based on a text in the order in which they occurred.

In investigative science – where groups of pupils are encouraged to think about solutions to problems and use their imaginations to find innovative ways of testing – suggestions from them about the best option will inevitably include simplistic and sophisticated ones. One test for the validity of an idea is for children to sequence the steps required to bring about a result. For instance, a popular activity is for children to build a free-standing tower using newspaper and sticky tape, which often results in a flurry of unco-ordinated activity and numerous failed attempts. Although trial-and-error is an important aspect of learning, pupils fare better if they are encouraged to plan and sequence their actions before launching into the task.

There have been concerns expressed that pupils spend an undue amount of time in planning and committing predictions and results to paper at the expense of active engagement with the task in hand, the result being that enquiry-based sessions are dominated by too much writing and insufficient scientific or mathematical thinking. A balance needs to be struck between the supporting processes of planning and sequencing ideas, discussion prior to and after the activity, the enquiry itself, and the formulation of results in tabulated, diagrammatic or written form.

Top tip

Insist that children spend a short time thinking about and discussing options before engaging with the task – but allow plenty of time for the practical work and make allowance for false starts and reformulated ideas. Make it clear that the investigation is not a race; that there are several possible lines of enquiry; and that thoroughness is more important than speed. You will probably want to give some provisional guidance about ways to approach the task, especially with less able children.

Activate your thinking!

Robson (2006) argues that young children are usually so eager to solve a problem and find a solution that they fail to think through which strategy is likely to be most effective; instead, they launch into an immediate attempt to find a solution. They also tend to be over-optimistic about what is achievable despite repeated failures. By contrast, older children tend to plan better and be more realistic about what can be achieved. Importantly, however, Robson claims that young children can make use of planning strategies as successfully as older children and adults if taught to do so.

Reference

Robson, S. (2006) *Developing Thinking and Understanding in Young Children*, Abingdon: Routledge.

Requirements for teaching

- To ensure that children possess the skills and insights to plan successfully.
- To help children discern the most effective route to finding a solution.

Learning skill 7: Recognising cause and effect

Cause and effect is threaded throughout life's experiences. We all learn a lot about the world by trial-and-error, repetition and random tests, as well as through systematic experimentation. Babies drop toys out of their prams and discover that they don't come back. Infants run fast across the grass because they find out that their legs cannot move quickly enough, so they lose balance and topple over. Great fun! A child beneath a bridge will shout again and again to hear the echo. Children find delight in repeating actions to see if it has the same effect or, if not, how variations in the action bring about different outcomes. The expression 'fair test' is often used to denote the fact that definite conclusions cannot be reached unless the enquiry takes place under consistent conditions. Children enjoy seeing that something 'works' and, while applauded for being entrepreneurial, have to be guided by an adult to understand the constraints and limitations of one-off experiments.

Children can be taught to use a Cause and Effect (CE) diagram, also referred to as a 'fishbone' representation, which is a tool for discovering all the possible causes for a particular effect. Quite simply, a horizontal arrow is drawn with the 'cause' written on the left hand side and the 'effect' on the right. For instance, the cause and effect terms might be: 'A few children work noisily' (cause) and 'It is hard to concentrate' (effect). The fishbone effect is created by considering all the factors that contribute to the cause and drawing them as oblique lines coming from the horizontal spine like ribs, some pointing up and back; others down and back. Thus, in the example being described, the contributing factors might include: loud voices; busy teacher; excitement; echoing room; objects dropped; moving around; squeaking chairs; and calling out. A further step is to link supplementary factors to each of the 'ribs'. For example, the 'loud voices' rib might be embellished with expressions such as 'shouting to be heard' and 'forgetting the rule' and 'speaking too fast' and 'getting angry' and 'being confused'. There are two ways of organising the lesson:

1. The teacher can lead the whole group or class through the whole procedure and act as scribe (using the whiteboard or computer).
2. The teacher can provide a fishbone 'skeleton' (i.e. a basic shape without words) on a sheet of paper for each group, who separately generate their own key words and phrases.

The results are recorded on the sheets and shared with other groups during a plenary to produce a comprehensive range of terms for all the class to see. Subsequently, the completed fishbone product forms the basis for a class discussion about cause and effect.

Cause and effect is not confined to practical situations, as every word, attitude and decision has consequences. Children may find it difficult to empathise with others and have to realise that things they say and the way they behave have an impact upon people for their benefit or to their detriment. Teachers therefore have an important role in helping pupils to think carefully about the impact of their words before expressing them and their actions before carrying them out. Pupils have to be made aware of their responsibilities to others; to be alert to the emotional impact of their words; to appreciate that everyone can and should contribute to making the class and school a happy place. Older primary children can be taught how to discuss and debate issues rather than expressing their opinions brazenly; to realise the consequences of antisocial behaviour; and to recognise their responsibilities to the community. Teachers who aspire to be highly effective practitioners ensure that children reflect on spiritual, moral, social and cultural issues that impinge on the way they behave and the effect it has on those around.

Top tip

The best teachers emphasise regularly to the children that every decision has a consequence. Illustrate this point by reference to behaviour and discipline using four options:

1. A pupil might behave in a commendable way that has positive consequences, which increases the likelihood of the behaviour recurring under similar circumstances. For instance, a child's spontaneous offer to befriend a lonely classmate results in a 'Well done!' from the teacher.
2. A pupil might behave in a way that simply avoids negative consequences that would otherwise have happened, which increases the likelihood of the good behaviour occurring under the same circumstances in the future. For instance, a child remaining still and quiet in assembly after being told off for talking avoids a punishment that would otherwise have been administered.
3. A pupil might behave in an unsatisfactory way that results in negative consequences, which deters the child from behaving that way again. For instance, a child who constantly calls out answers when not invited to do so loses one minute of playtime for each incident.
4. A pupil might regularly behave in a sensible fashion, such that no negative consequences result, which increases the likelihood of the good behaviour occurring under the same circumstances in the future. For instance, children who line up sensibly not only avoid being admonished but probably receive praise from an adult.

Activate your thinking!

Pre-school children will sometimes behave in what appears to be an irresponsible way to 'see what happens if', rather than being a wilful act of naughtiness. However, a similar type of behaviour in school-age pupils might indicate a deep-rooted psychological problem requiring specialist attention.

Requirements for teaching

- To persuade pupils that it is unwise to jump to conclusions, and to extol the virtues of fairness and patience, while allowing space for their imaginations and creativity to flourish.
- To emphasise that selflessness is a prerequisite if we are going to live happily in our community.

Learning skill 8: Adapting to different circumstances

Very young children tend to be ushered through life. They are told what to do and when and how to do it. They might complain or resist but, for the most part, will comply. Gradually, children ask for reasons why they should or should not do something and demand explanations about the ideas that underpin adult decisions. Some children hanker for more freedom and their behaviour can become a source of concern. Other children baulk at the prospect of deviating from a familiar pathway or routine and become fixated about the way things are meant to happen; suggestions by well-meaning adults about doing things differently are met with stubborn resistance. This kind of reaction is normally due to a lack of confidence or previous unhappy experiences and requires a lot of adult patience and gentle persuasion. You have the tricky task of allowing bolder pupils to express and explore their preferences within safe boundaries while encouraging timid children to move outside the regular procedures, while taking account of context, available resources and time factors. Adaptable children are likely to be happier and more successful than those who struggle to respond to the varying demands and opportunities afforded by changes in circumstance.

In the academic sphere, it is commonly the case that children who appear to master a skill or body of knowledge in one context struggle in a different one. For instance, a pupil might learn the alphabet forwards and backwards yet flounder when using a dictionary. Again, a pupil might learn a song in one key and be unable to transpose it to another. Yet again, a pupil might recite a spelling rule and get full marks in a test, yet make elementary errors in free writing. Some knowledge is superficially learned through repetition and regular use. The ability to apply knowledge in different situations is a hallmark of what is sometimes referred to as 'deep learning' and is the true test of children's understanding.

All new pupils take time to adjust to the school situation, but it is particularly challenging for a child who has recently arrived from a school elsewhere in the world and with a culture that differs from the host nation's culture in respect of conventions, rules and ways of relating. The adjustments are not only located in the mastery of new knowledge and interpreting the intricacies of the school system, but also in understanding the nuances attached to a different language and social behaviour. For example, a new pupil might have arrived from a country in which silence during lessons is the norm and transgressors are dealt with harshly; as a result, it will take a great deal of persuasion to convince the child that talk during collaboration activities is not only permitted but actively desired. Again, a new pupil might be used to a lot of recitation and uniform responses to a teacher's questions; the idea of raising questions with the teacher or offering suggestions will seem alien to the child's experiences and instincts.

Regardless of the pupil's background, assessing his or her competence in English, as disclosed through an ability to comprehend by listening, speaking, reading and writing, is commonly applied to all children. Thus, you need to distinguish between children who can respond to regular instructions or questions (e.g. 'What is your name?'); those who can understand what is said but do not respond (elective mutes); and those children who respond in a way that demonstrates understanding. You can soon tell whether the child is able to say a few words, sustain a conversation, or modify speech according to context and circumstances. Some children will be capable of grasping basic written conventions; others will be able to read with support; yet others will be able to read competently. Finally, you can distinguish between children who are able to write English letters and their names; those who can use letter patterns; and those who can write recognisable letters, words and phrases. It is worth bearing in mind that children from a number of countries will be used to reading and writing from right to left. New children might appear to be slow academically when in fact they are very capable but lacking the necessary language skills and confidence to demonstrate their abilities. The use of peer support and, where possible, a sympathetic and patient assistant will facilitate gradual progress, but it is likely that initial progress will be slow.

Top tip

Gently ease children away from a dependence upon adult approval towards greater self-confidence by adopting a 'yes, you can' and 'I will support you' philosophy.

Activate your thinking!

Close liaison between you and parents of younger children is essential if extreme forms of anxiety are to be dealt with satisfactorily, thereby avoiding the possible onset of school phobia and, in extreme cases, the disillusionment that might follow later in the child's schooling.

Requirements for teaching

- To encourage children to face new situations as a challenge rather than a threat.
- To assess the capability and learning deficiencies of new children as quickly as possible, taking particular account of their language needs.

Learning skill 9: Speaking confidently

It is estimated that fear of public speaking, also known as glossophobia, affects an estimated three-quarters of the adult population, so it is unsurprising if many children hesitate to speak out in front of others. However, good communication is not only beneficial for those listening but also for the one speaking, as a child wrestles to clarify and organise his or her thinking before and during the verbal contribution. Many children are reluctant to offer a comment publicly for fear of their ideas being ridiculed or their ignorance exposed; the problem is compounded if children also have problems of poor articulation or suffer from a speech defect. Teachers can encourage children to organise their thoughts beforehand, such that they are able speak with greater confidence. Furthermore, the use of simple whole-class 'loosening' techniques (such as gentle humming to bring the words 'forward' in the mouth) and practising choral-speaking a poem or a piece of text in unison will offset the tendency for children to mumble or speak too quietly when they speak individually.

Although a problem in speaking confidently is usually rooted in shyness and a natural fear of being humiliated, it can also be due to the presence of autism, which is a developmental disability affecting the way a person relates to and interacts with others. The most striking feature of autism is when a child has difficulty with social communication, such as maintaining eye contact, conducting a normal conversation and seeing things from another person's perspective. In addition to having persistent difficulty with language and communication, children with autism can be seen to struggle when they are interacting with their peers; with flexibility of thought; and with exercising imagination – the so-called 'triad of impairment'. Autism comes in varying degrees of seriousness, hence the concept of 'autistic spectrum disorder' (ASD) to describe the varying degrees of difficulty experienced (Wing 2003). To accommodate this range of behaviours, some educators promote the use of creative means to stimulate children with autism through using art, movement and music. As with many strategies to assist pupils with special needs, it is the case that all children who can be described as 'unconventional' (whether autistic or not) benefit from a programme of work that provides a wide variety of enjoyable exercises, activities and games that impact upon their bodies, minds and spirits (Tubbs 2007).

Public performance (e.g. during assembly) can be nerve-wracking for children but it builds confidence if preparation is thorough and the outcome successful. It is not obvious to every child that speaking is principally for the benefit of listeners, not for themselves, so you need to reinforce this point constantly. You can assist the process by emphasising the importance of correct breathing, bearing in mind that good breath control depends upon approaching the task in a positive frame of mind to minimise tension and anxiety. An upright posture together with careful control of the flow of air from the lungs to the mouth are also important in supporting clear speech.

In promoting the techniques described above, it is important to be sensitive to the impact of dialect and the numerous instances of children struggling with English as an additional language. It is not a case of depreciating children's existing speech, but rather enhancing the clarity with which they use it. There is a fine line between covert criticism of children's natural way of speaking and the affirmative practice of teaching them to communicate more effectively; the latter approach leads to greater confidence and self-belief; the former approach can lead to anxiety and, if handled badly, complaints from parents about your clumsy attempts to make pupils all speak 'the Queen's English'. (See also Chapter 3, Professional theme 27 for more information about public speaking.)

References

Tubbs, J. (2007) *Creative Therapy for Children With Autism, ADD and Asperger's*, New York: Square One Publishers.

Wing, L. (2003) *The Autistic Spectrum: A Guide for Parents and Professionals*, London: Robinson Publishing.

Top tip

Emphasise with pupils the 'four Ps' in speaking: pace, pitch, power and pausing.

Pace: children tend to speak too quickly (often due to nerves), so encouraging 'half-speed' talking and reading aloud is beneficial. Children will not literally speak at half the normal speed, but it will help to curb rapid talking and aid articulation.

Pitch: when children get anxious and excited, the pitch of their voices rises and becomes strident. Such speech is unpleasant to listen to, which reduces its attractiveness for the listener and leads to people 'switching off'. One of the symptoms of anxiety is shallow breathing, which results in a lack of air for speaking clearly and makes the voice 'squeak'. Teaching children to relax, breathe naturally and take pauses will counteract the worst excesses.

Power: being confident about what they want to say allows pupils to speak with greater power and authority. Spending time beforehand in discussing the issues covered by what they will say, and summarising the key points, helps to provide for clarity of thought. Children also need to be taught how to emphasise key words and elevate certain phrases above others to provide 'colour' and variety to their speech.

Pausing: good public speaking is as much about silences (i.e. inserting appropriate pauses) as it is about saying the words out loud. If a child is reading aloud from a sheet, a useful tip is to write the words *pause* and *take a breath* at key points in the text to remind him/her of when to breath, a technique assisted by the instruction to count silently to three at such times.

Activate your thinking!

Choral speaking, with the whole class speaking in unison, allows less confident pupils to be involved without undue pressure. With longer and more complex pieces (e.g. the poem 'The Highwayman' by Alfred Noyes) it is possible to divide up the speaking into extracts for smaller groups of children to say together, with the rest of the class providing gentle background sounds. Pupils can be encouraged to emphasise key words and use tonal shading for greater impact.

Requirements for teaching

- To gradually introduce opportunities for every child to experience speaking out loud.
- To value the 'pupil voice' in learning, including questions, complaints and concerns.

Learning skill 10: Being imaginative and creative

Kieran Egan, a noted education thinker, claims that imagination is not a desirable-but-dispensable frill, but should form the heart of any truly educational experience (see, for example, Egan 1992). Consequently, imagination should be integral, not marginal, to basic training or disciplined thought or rational enquiry, as it gives them meaning; it is not the sole province of the arts in education or a leisure activity, but central to all areas of learning. Egan goes so far as to say that imagination is the hard pragmatic centre of all effective human thought, which contrasts markedly with the objectives-driven agenda that currently dominates work in school.

Another criticism of a formal, test-driven education system is that it suppresses pupil instinct and spontaneity by undue reliance on procedures and predetermined ways of doing things. By contrast, creativity releases pupils from the rigid constraints of a regulated curriculum to explore and investigate ideas by active participation in genuine events and enterprises that interest them. The old adage that children should be seen and not heard might be appropriate in certain classroom situations but can also result in an unhelpful passivity that does not awaken curiosity or excite eager young minds to explore ideas. Bowkett (2005) argues that creativity 'is as much an attitude as it is a set of mental processes. It incorporates playfulness, curiosity, sensitivity, self-awareness and independence' (p. 3). Inspection reports about creativity in schools seem to agree that best practice is more likely to be found in teaching situations where teachers are not bound by orthodox teaching methods, but make use of cross-curricular themes and spend time developing a stimulating learning environment.

On the assumption that every child has a vivid imagination nestling close to the surface, the response to external stimuli such as stories, puppets, television, electronic games and films is likely to be enthusiastic. Teachers can stimulate children's imaginations and elicit a sense of awe and wonder by strategies such as reading or relating an exciting short story; using fictional characters and placing them in today's world; asking children to think of what they would do if placed in a difficult or, perhaps, dangerous situation (e.g. on a desert island);

using puppets to describe an event; dressing up in different sorts of costumes, and so forth.

Being imaginative and creative therefore depends on engaging children's interest, stirring their curiosity and promoting a desire in them to explore and discover new things. Such an approach leads to more active pupil involvement, responsibility and independence, and assists them in developing the ability to work collaboratively on a topic to solve problems or find solutions (see Newton 2012). However, topic-centred (as opposed to strictly subject-specific) learning of this kind has three potential disadvantages:

1. Cognitive overload – that is, too much to think about at one time.
2. Pupils developing misconceptions ('wrong ideas') that are left unchecked for too long and become embedded in their minds.
3. Too much time spent on superficial activities that require minimum thought. Pupils also need to possess basic skills and understanding relevant to the enterprise before being given the freedom to experiment with ideas.

For instance, there is little point in asking children to design plans without having a grasp of ratios and perspective; experimenting with different shades of colour requires a knowledge of how to correctly mix paints; children will struggle to write a musical ditty for use in assembly if they have no concept of rhythm and pitch, and so forth. The extent of adult guidance is therefore an important consideration for, whereas excessive intervention might reduce children's self-sufficiency, too much freedom can lead to haphazard and aimless meandering in a search for meaning.

The challenge for teachers is to translate the children's energy of lively minds into creative forms of learning. There are at least five ways to achieve such an outcome: (1) Use phrases such as 'Just imagine if ... ' and 'Suppose that ... ' and 'What might happen if ... ' to steer children into less predictable ways of thinking; (2) invite and welcome speculative notions; (3) give pupils more control over decisions affecting their work; (4) encourage them to use a full range of expressing ideas and recording results – written; diagrammatic; pictorial; spoken; dramatised; (5) provide ample opportunity for children to explore ideas through practical activities, including tactile art and craft.

Finally, it probably goes without saying that one of the best ways to encourage creativity in your pupils is to adopt an imaginative teaching approach yourself. It would be highly contradictory to encourage pupil creativity while teaching unimaginatively. (See also Chapter 3, Professional theme 28.)

References

Bowkett, S. (2005) *100 Ideas for Teaching Creativity*, London: Continuum.

Egan, K. (1992) *Imagination in Teaching and Learning: The Middle School Years*, Chicago: University of Chicago Press.

Newton, L.D. (2012) *Creative Thinking and Problem Solving in the Primary Curriculum*, Abingdon: Routledge.

Top tip

Dressing-up, playing, inviting local celebrities to meet the children, drama days and attending live theatre all help to promote lively imaginations.

Activate your thinking!

Authentic imagination that prompts positive action is different from *hopeful* imagination that is characterised by a passivity that leaves the active work to others (i.e. daydreaming or fantasising). Jeffrey and Woods (2009) reveal how pupils act as a powerful resource for creative learning for each other and for their teachers. Good teaching, together with opportunities for children to explore and exploit their creative potential, facilitates higher levels of accomplishment.

Reference

Jeffrey, B. and Woods, P. (2009) *Creative Learning in the Primary School*, Abingdon: Routledge.

Requirements for teaching

■ To encourage children's use of their imaginations without lapsing into unproductive wool-gathering.
■ To teach creatively in such a way that children are inspired to learn.

Learning skill 11: Making valid judgements

A key skill that children must develop is the ability to be discerning, evaluate propositions and make sound judgements based on evidence rather than instinct or popular opinion. Such sophisticated ability is not easily acquired and even adults can struggle to view situations rationally. Using evidence and reasoning is not to suggest that intuition and common sense should be dismissed, for they are often based on life experience and a deep-seated sense of 'knowing' that sometimes supersedes rational approaches.

In evaluating the validity of a claim, it should be acknowledged that reasoning alone is unable to explain certain phenomena. For instance, children will observe a bumblebee flying and flitting from flower to flower in a search for pollen. They might also have seen a heavily laden bee walking along the ground unable to get lift-off. In fact, according to the law of physics, a bumblebee should not be able to fly at all, as it is aerodynamically impossible owing to the weight of the bee and the small size of its wings. Evidence, therefore, is not invariably based on observable or scientifically verifiable factors but comes in a variety of forms, both *rational* ('it can be shown that') and *non-rational* ('it cannot be demonstrated directly but is a reasonable proposition'). The teacher's role is to steer pupils away from *irrational* conclusion based on fantasy, wishful thinking or confused logic. For example, consider the statement: 'Whales are mammals; humans are mammals; therefore all humans are whales', which is obviously incorrect. On the other hand, if a stick of celery remains its original colour when placed in water but changes colour after the addition of a dye, it is reasonable to conclude a cause-and-effect link; that is, the addition of the dye has caused the change in colour. In experiments of this sort, it is usual to have a 'control' version against which to compare the experimental version and ensure a 'fair test'. In this particular instance, the control version would be a stick of celery placed in plain water alongside the experimental one.

Making valid judgements about *ethical* matters is even more challenging for children than making them about scientific ones. Primary-age children normally accept their parents' version of events and adopt their stance on moral issues, so you have the tricky task of opening pupils' eyes to other possibilities whilst being careful to take account of home influences. A frequently used example of a conflict between values promoted at home and in school is the child who insists that 'my dad told me to stand up for myself' after being admonished by the teacher for hitting another pupil. The use of Biblical parables (e.g. the Good Samaritan as an example of true friendship), Aesop's fables (e.g. the greedy dog with a bone who saw his reflection in the water and dropped the bone to seize the apparently larger one) and nonsense poems (especially humorous ones) can be useful starting points to evoke a critical engagement about life issues and help pupils to make valid judgements about right, wrong and the need to consider others. (See also Chapter 2, Teaching and learning issue 9.)

Top tip

Set an ethical question to which there are (say) three possible answers or responses. Discuss the issues relating to the topic and ask pupils to vote immediately, then after further reflection, and again the following day after they have consulted with others and reflected on the arguments. Find out whether any children changed their minds and, if so, on what basis.

Activate your thinking!

Younger children tend to speak more plainly and honestly than older ones. One explanation for the increasing reluctance to 'say it like it is' as they grow older is that children gradually learn through social interactions that it is not always to their advantage to tell the truth. For example, a public comment such as, 'Mummy, that man smells' usually brings a reprimand. Again, admitting guilt over breaking a school rule is more likely to result in punishment than approval for being honest. Children also come to realise that words can be used as a weapon to get their own way, offend others and manipulate adults (e.g. through embarrassment). The adage that 'sticks and stones may break my bones but names will never hurt me' is, of course, total nonsense.

Requirements for teaching

- To help children understand the distinctive characteristics of lying, being tactful and behaving politely.
- To discuss issues with pupils such as: Why should you tell the truth? What is right and wrong? When is something a lie? Is it ever right to tell a lie? What does it mean to be true to yourself? (See Maymin (2010) for further examples.)

Reference

Maymin, Z. (2010) *Truth: Ethics for Your Child*, North Charleston, SC: Create Space Publishing.

Learning skill 12: Developing an enquiring mind

The old saying goes that 'curiosity killed the cat'. As far as learning is concerned, however, the opposite is true: curiosity generates enthusiasm in children and brings them alive. Teachers who are capable of motivating and inspiring their pupils not only help them to gain academic success but also have better behaved and contented classes. Although the expression, 'enquiry-based learning' has replaced the somewhat discredited concept of discovery learning that was associated with superficial project work in the past, children's school experiences should be one continuous enquiry/discovery, as they are introduced to new ideas, explore their implications and talk about their relevance. It is unfortunate that education has, in some people's minds, been reduced to a rather bland 'mastery' of reading, writing and arithmetic. Although it is vitally important that children learn to read, write and do sums, the way in which it is taught makes a considerable impact on a pupil's keenness and urgency about delving deeper and discovering more about that area of knowledge. Two pupils in different classes can gain the same formal test score, yet the one taught by a teacher with charisma, who 'lights a fire' in the child and encourages further exploration of the subject will become self-motivated and eager to ask questions, find out more and make an extra effort to succeed; such a child has much better long-term academic prospects than the one taught mechanically.

Curious children ask searching questions. They are not easily distracted. They are sometimes a little reckless in their determination to find out how things work and why things happen. Their parents sigh with dismay when asked yet another question by their inquisitive offspring. The child's favourite response is 'yes, but' and he or she will spend lengthy periods of time captivated by the latest idea or gadget or phenomenon. Sometimes, the child becomes extremely well informed about a topic and is constantly referring to aspects of it and sharing the latest fascinating fact with anyone who is willing to stop and listen. The best teachers make good use of such eagerness by giving the children opportunities to share their ideas and knowledge with classmates.

As noted in Learning skill 11 above, children gradually become aware that their words and actions can have consequences for themselves and others. This fact is particularly relevant in their use of questions. Parents are sometimes embarrassed by a child's candour and lack of subtlety; pre-school children point out other people's physical characteristics and ask direct questions about events that adults note and think about but rarely refer to, other than in private. Thus, the child who asks why a person walks with a pronounced limp is told to be quiet; the child who laughs at a disabled person's strange speech is told not to be rude. It takes time for children to learn how to conform to societal expectations and norms, but as far as most young children are concerned, they are simply being candid and trying to understand more about the world.

Teachers can all too easily give the impression that children should accept what they are told and not question statements too closely or express their doubts. Of course, children must realise that offence and hurt can be caused by inappropriate comments or intrusive questions, but harsh adult disapproval can undermine children's willingness to offer opinions and seek explanations. Once children enter the formal education system with its many rules and constraints, they can easily become withdrawn; thus, the lively, eager and occasionally fun-loving character can all too easily become subdued and docile, though some children have a seemingly untameable personality that defies all attempts to shape it, as hard-pressed teachers will wearily affirm! It requires a great deal of hard work to harness the inborn enthusiasm and energy such children bring to school while ensuring that they understand and conform to acceptable boundaries of behaviour and conduct. Other pupils are exactly the opposite; they lack self-confidence and are initially intimidated by being in school but benefit from the stimulation of the new environment and opportunities to learn and have fun with other children. Slowly, and with gentle persuasion from caring adults, they realise that it is not only acceptable to have an enquiring mind but the route to fulfilment in learning.

While high-quality teachers encourage pupils to ask questions and devote a lot of time to stimulating a desire to learn, they also have to inculcate awareness that questions have a moral dimension and should not be used as a verbal weapon. For instance, it is one thing for children to ask questions of their peers because they wish to know more about a subject, but quite another to ask questions that convey a subtle form of mockery. The age and maturity of the child are major factors in determining whether the enquiry is serious or flippant; whereas a four-year-old might genuinely want to know why a classmate has stick-out ears, the same question from a ten-year-old would have to be viewed as unkind, not inquisitive.

To be an excellent teacher, you need to become adept at finding ways to motivate and engage pupils by use of enchanting stories, dressing up, humorous poems, colourful pictures, mimicry, theatre and practical activities. Thus, you can:

- bring in unusual objects to stimulate interest and elicit comments and questions;
- ask speculative questions and encourage children to think widely ('lateral thinking');
- show obvious pleasure when children say something funny and especially when shy, reserved pupils contribute, however tentatively;
- make learning an adventure rather than being predictable;
- avoid telling children in advance what they are 'supposed' to learn by the use of predetermined learning outcomes/objectives and instead foster a culture in which knowledge is like buried treasure to be discovered and enjoyed.

Aspire to be such a teacher.

Top tip

Include a talking-time session for a few minutes each day based on a 'mystery item'. Use some of your own objects initially and gradually encourage children to bring in simple items from home that can fit inside a 'mystery box' – ensuring they have parental permission, of course. Allow children to use their imaginations in speculating as to the object's origin and purpose. If appropriate, use these experiences as the basis for writing, art and drama. You will be amazed at the richness and diversity of outcome.

Activate your thinking!

Thomas Alva Edison (1847–1931) asked his teacher so many questions that the teacher became exasperated. Thomas was eventually branded as 'impossible' and his mother was obliged to teach him at home. In doing so, she exposed him to books at a far higher conceptual level than anyone of his age, so that Edison's curriculum included subjects such as philosophy, English and history. By the time he was eleven, he had established his own laboratory in a basement, where he acquired and honed yet more skills. Edison subsequently became one of the greatest American inventors with over one thousand US patents and many more in the United Kingdom, France and Germany. He is credited with a variety of inventions relating to mass communication, especially telecommunications. Not bad going for a so-called 'school failure'!

Requirements for teaching

- To introduce a hint of mystery into teaching as a means of stimulating pupil interest and curiosity.
- To be constantly asking rhetorical and speculative questions 'out loud', not directed towards any child, to set an example as an interrogator of ideas rather than a passive recipient of knowledge.

2

Teaching and learning issues

Introduction

A characteristic of teachers who aspire to move from 'ordinary' to 'advanced' status is a desire to interrogate closely issues that relate to teaching and learning, and to gain a more thorough understanding of their implications for classroom practice. The following forty examples, taken from a spectrum of education positions, offer a wide selection of such issues to sharpen your knowledge, shape your philosophy of education and implement some of the ideas into your classroom practice. Key publications are used for the core of the explanatory text in each issue, followed by Questions to consider and discuss as a means of extending your thinking and providing a platform for personal reflection, discussion with tutors and sharing more widely with colleagues. The teaching and learning issues are divided into four sections, each of which contains ten units:

Section A: Child development and education
Section B: Pupil learning
Section C: Classroom practice
Section D: The teacher.

Section A: Child development and education

Teaching and learning issue 1: The nature–nurture debate

There has been a great deal written and spoken about the relative influences of 'nature', which is broadly defined as what is passed down as a result of heredity; and 'nurture', which refers to the environmental influences on children during their formative years. Scientists know that specific genes encoded in each human cell determine physical characteristics such as eye and hair colour. There is considerably more intense debate about whether abstract traits such as intelligence, personality, aggression and sexual orientation are also encoded in an individual's DNA. Some educators express concern that if we accept the premise that children's actions result from their genes and have little or nothing to do with the way that they are reared, it can be used to excuse poor behaviour on the grounds of 'it is just the way that I was made'. Consequently, the key issue is not whether it is nature or nurture but rather the extent to which the way in which we behave was engrained in us before we were born, and the extent to which it develops after birth in response to our experiences. There is also evidence to support the view that the quality of the stimuli received by the unborn baby plays a key role in determining his or her life chances. Despite these areas of uncertainty, there is general agreement that while a gene might increase the likelihood that a child behaves in a particular way, it does not *make* him or her do things. In other words, children (and adults) can exercise choice over the way that they act, regardless of their natural tendencies.

Despite the fact that brain development normally continues throughout childhood and beyond, it is nevertheless true that growth in the womb and during the first few years of life are the most critical periods in terms of development, though in most children it appears that the main phase is more or less complete by the age of about twelve. Studies suggest that a child's brain is particularly receptive between the ages of about four and twelve years, which means that parents and primary educators bear a significant responsibility to ensure that children are given the best possible chance to reach their potential through a variety of stimulating and motivating learning opportunities.

Children are acquiring language before and during the whole of primary school; they benefit from hearing adults talk, sing and read to them during their formative years and affirm their attempts to use and create different language forms (notably, speaking and writing; see Eke and Lee 2008). *Spatial-temporal* reasoning is the expression used in referring to the brain function controlling difficult, complicated tasks like mathematics or playing chess. In schoolwork, such reasoning helps younger children to understand that vessels of different proportions but with the same volume hold the same amount of water.

Silcock (2008) argues that both nature and nurture have a bearing upon learner success in and out of school, but claims that the particular ways in which gene-determined inheritance systems ('nature') interact with circumstances ('nurture') to affect learning are not easily interpreted. He proposes that genes not only make experience possible by scaffolding the biological mechanisms by which we learn, think and perceive, but that they also affect the moment-to-moment experiences themselves. He insists that the ability to read, write, solve mathematical puzzles, pose scientific hypotheses, use computers or play musical instruments each has to be taught and learned, so cannot be ascribed purely to innate ability (i.e. hereditary factors). Equally, however, cultural customs can inhibit as well as aid progress: for instance, adults can underestimate children's potentialities on the basis of low expectation and hinder children from achieving their full capabilities.

Silcock goes on to object to the tendency for some curricular initiatives in England to be based so completely on environmental input that they totally ignore biological evidence and predetermined competence. He adds that much educational debate assumes that all pupils can reach high standards in key studies if they and their teachers work hard enough, regardless of 'nature' factors. As a result, politicians and education advisers make wholesale recommendations of ways that *all* pupils should learn and become independent problem-solvers, creative, empathetic, enterprising, and so forth. In an educational setting, it is of considerable importance for educators to know what can be changed with relative ease because it comes naturally to the child concerned; and what can only be altered with dedicated effort because it does *not* come naturally. See also Music (2010) for perspectives on the nature–nurture debate with reference to key developmental stages from life in the womb to the pre-school years and on to adolescence.

Questions to consider and discuss

- How much does a child's home background influence a teacher's expectations?
- What evidence should educators draw on to construct an appropriate curriculum?
- What do you understand by the phrase 'comes naturally'?

References

Eke, R. and Lee, J. (2008) *Using Talk Effectively in the Primary Classroom*, Abingdon: Routledge.

Music, G. (2010) *Nurturing Natures*, Abingdon: Routledge.

Silcock, P. (2008) 'Towards a biologically informed primary school practice', *Education 3–13*, 36 (2), pp. 161–69.

Teaching and learning issue 2: The impact of pre-school education

The Effective Pre-School and Primary Education (EPPE 3–11) project in the UK, which ran from 2003–08, was a major longitudinal investigation into the effects of pre-school education on children's developmental outcomes at the start of primary school (Sammons *et al.* 2006, Sammons *et al.* 2008, Siraj-Blatchford *et al.* 2008). EPPE 3–11 was managed by the Institute of Education, University of London and tracked 3,000 children from the time they started pre-school until they reached eleven years of age. The project developed to explore four themes:

1. Do the effects of pre-school continue into the upper stages of primary education?
2. What are the characteristics of 'effective' primary classrooms and schools?
3. Who are the resilient and the vulnerable children in the EPPE sample?
4. What is the contribution of 'out-of-school learning' (homes, communities, internet) to children's development?

The EPPE research provided evidence about the combined effects of pre-school and primary school in shaping children's later development. One unsurprising result was that, the better the *home learning* environment, for pre-school and primary school, the better academic results children achieve. The concept of 'better home environment' was defined in terms of ratings for how often parents participated in seven activities with their children: (1) being read to; (2) going to the library; (3) playing with numbers; (4) painting and drawing; (5) being taught letters; (6) being taught numbers; and (7) singing songs. Notably, the study found that boys were more than twice as likely to have a poor home learning environment than girls. The research also indicated that, as children got older, the home learning environment became less significant.

At age five, girls were more advanced in reading than boys, but the majority of boys had caught up with the girls by the age of ten. Factors other than gender – in particular, the home environment and type of school – appear to have had a powerful influence on children's academic attainment.

Questions to consider and discuss

- In what ways might the home learning environment impact on children's academic performance in (a) reading (b) speaking (c) mathematics?
- In addition to the seven 'better home environment' factors cited above, what other forms of home learning might be influential?
- According to the EPPE survey, what significance might gender have on children's attainment and how should teachers respond?

References

Sammons, P., Taggart, B., Siraj-Blatchford, I., Sylva, K., Melhuish, E., Barreau, S. and Manni, L. (2006) *Effective Pre-school and Primary Education 3–11 (EPPE 3–11) Summary Report: Variations in Teacher and Pupil Behaviours in Year 5 Classes*, Research Report No. 817, Nottingham: DfES Publications.

Sammons, P., Sylva, K., Melhuish, E., Siraj-Blatchford, I. and Taggart, B. (2008) *The Effective Pre-school and Primary Education 3–11 Project (EPPE 3–11) – Influences on Children's Development and Progress in Key Stage 2: Social/Behavioural Outcomes in Year 6*, London: DCSF / Institute of Education, University of London.

Siraj-Blatchford, I., Taggart, B., Sylva, K., Sammons, P. and Melhuish, E. (2008) 'Towards the transformation of practice in early childhood education: the effective provision of pre-school education (EPPE) project', *Cambridge Journal of Education*, 38 (1), pp. 23–36.

Teaching and learning issue 3: Motivation and pupil background

Children are not born with a particular view of themselves or their level of self-worth; rather, it is something that they develop over the years, shaped through their relationships with family and friends and their wider social experiences. Studies of pupils' educational experiences suggest that the extent of satisfaction with their education experience decreases with age and drops quite sharply when they reach secondary school (e.g. Cullingford 2002). Thus, a large majority of primary pupils think that school is a positive experience; this contrasts with about one-quarter in secondary schools who feel similarly enthusiastic. When measuring pupils' views about the relevance of what they learn and retain while in school, the motivation gap between the primary and secondary phases is even more pronounced.

Day and Burns (2011) examined achievement motivation in pre-school-age children from low- and middle-income families. During problem-solving tasks (using challenging puzzles) the authors found that children from low-income families made more negative self-evaluations about their ability and more statements that indicated concern about being able to complete the task satisfactorily than their middle-income peers. Using the children's private speech (i.e. words spoken to self rather than to another) as a guide, the comments made by children from low-income families reflected their concerns with their *performance* more than with the *learning processes* associated with mastering the task. In other words, the low-income group appeared to have more of a performance orientation than their middle-income peers. On the other hand, pupils from higher-income families might simply have had more confidence that they would eventually complete the task and were focusing their minds on understanding the process.

If, as argued by educators such as Vygotsky, children's private speech is indicative of their current and future cognitive processes (ability to reason and understand), negative private speech could have a damaging impact on motivation. It might also be the case that the differences in private speech shown by the two groups of pre-school children noted above is a predictor of even larger differences in motivation levels between pupils from low- and middle-income families in the future. Because children from low-income families revealed such negative thoughts about their ability to solve the puzzles, it might lead them to establish maladaptive (i.e. related to problematic thinking and behaviour), performance-oriented motivation patterns in their future work. Whatever the truth of these claims, it is undeniable that children from poorer families seem to lack confidence and self-belief. You have an essential role in correcting such a negative image by (a) being specific and clear in your instructions; (b) setting manageable short-term targets; and (c) praising minor achievements.

Questions to consider and discuss

- What factors might have contributed to the 'complete the task' attitude of the children from low-income families as opposed to 'learn from the task' attitude of children from high-income families? What steps might you take to correct this tendency?
- What other learning traits and orientation are commonly discernable at pre-school age?
- What strategies might you employ to combat the educational disadvantages rooted in poor self-image that appears to typify a sizeable percentage of pupils from poorer homes?

References

Cullingford, C. (2002) *The Best Years of their Lives? Pupils' Experiences of School*, London: Kogan Page.

Day, C.D. and Burns, B.M. (2011) 'Characterising the achievement motivation orientation of children from low- and middle-income families', *Early Education and Development*, 22 (1), pp. 105–27.

Teaching and learning issue 4: Developing parental involvement

There is general agreement among educators that parental involvement in learning is crucially important, such that the family makes vital contributions to pupils' academic and social achievements, not only in the pre-school period but throughout the whole of formal schooling. A home environment in which learning is encouraged and fostered is more important to education success than factors such as household income, parents' education attainment or cultural background. See Rodriguez-Brown 2008 for research about parental involvement in culturally and linguistically diverse communities.

Parents help their children by talking to them regularly about things that happen during school; actively organising and monitoring their time; assisting with homework; and discussing their concerns calmly and non-judgementally. Such positive parental involvement is likely to improve pupil achievement, reduce unauthorised absenteeism and improve behaviour. It is also of interest that parental involvement is liable to increase the confidence of parents about their children's experiences at school, with a concomitant growth in their positive affirmations of teachers.

Studies suggest that, when parents are involved in their children's education *at home*, pupils do better in school. Furthermore, when parents are involved *in school* in some capacity, their children make stronger progress still, possibly due to the fact that those parents are education-oriented in the first place. Reading achievement is particularly dependent on learning activities taking place in the home; the more that children share books with parents, the greater the likelihood that they become competent readers. It is also claimed that reading aloud to children, as well as talking about the books and stories that are read to them, is the best way that parents can increase their child's chance of reading success.

Jeynes (2011) argues that, contrary to popular belief, parental involvement is not a recent phenomenon. He claims that some of America's earliest European settlers were strong believers in the primacy of parents contributing to their children's education through regular practices such as evening joint-reading sessions. The author explains that the early curriculum focused on reading, writing, arithmetic and religious instruction and quotes from a law passed by the Massachusetts legislature of 1642 requiring that the head of every household must actively help to teach all the children in the home – girls as well as boys – to read and understand the principles of religion and the country's laws. The settlers believed that children could reach their highest potential in school if the family, church and school all worked together in what became known as the 'holy triad'.

The father had a particularly important role in raising boys, in the belief that the more time a boy spent with his father, the better equipped he would be for life. In the same way, a girl would follow her mother and learn cooking and sewing skills and any trade in which the mother participated. Parental involvement also had a pragmatic dimension in that children were given responsibilities at an early stage and therefore had to 'mature' more quickly than most of their modern counterparts. In addition to children learning survival skills and contributing to the family income, parents and schoolteachers were expected to foster both academic development and upright citizens. An effective partnership between home and school was seen as having a powerful and positive effect

on morality and behaviour. Despite the passage of years, most of these fundamental principles remain intact and form the bedrock for a child's complete
education. (See also Chapter 3, Professional theme 19.)

As a new teacher, you will undoubtedly encounter a small number of parents
who seem determined to complain about anything that involves their children
and are quick to let you know what they think. Although few in number, such
parents can be a source of anxiety, as they imply by their comments that you
are failing to do your job properly. There are four points to note. First, parents
represent a cross-section of society and there are bound to be some who, for a
variety of reasons outside your control, adopt a negative attitude towards
almost anything that impinges upon them and their families. It is highly likely
that the parents who challenge you also complain about other aspects of their
lives outside school that fail to meet their expectations. Second, despite your
reservations about the critical parents' motives and your dislike of their personalities, listen carefully to what they say, as it may be that they are making
valid points. If so, thank them sincerely and be silently glad that someone has
drawn your attention to the issue, however insensitively it might have been
done. Third, avoid arguing, but also explain firmly why you have decided to
take the course of action that lies at the heart of the complaint. It might not
satisfy the parent, but you have then fulfilled your professional responsibility in
the matter. Finally, try not to agonise over the situation or allow it to undermine your confidence. If the circumstances become unpalatable, seek advice
urgently from a senior colleague. Remember that, for every dissatisfied parent,
there are dozens of satisfied ones.

Questions to consider and discuss

- What strategies might classroom practitioners use to help parents understand the crucial importance of their role?
- How might a teacher respond to parents who argue that they: (a) do not
  have time to spend much time with their children and (b) are not trained
  teachers, so might do more harm than good?
- How should you respond when faced with a parent who is constantly complaining about minor issues?

References

Jeynes, W. (2011) *Parental Involvement and Academic Success*, Abingdon: Routledge (see
    especially Chapters 1 and 3).
Rodriguez-Brown, F.V. (2008) *The Home-School Connection*, Abingdon: Routledge.

Teaching and learning issue 5: Adults as effective role models

A simple definition of role model is someone whom others wish to imitate and
whose example they are determined to follow. There are, of course, many different kinds of role model, some desirable, others much less so. All teachers
provide a role model for children, whether they like it or not, so the notion of
choosing *not* to be one is untenable.

We all like to think that we are providing a positive role model for pupils, characterised by the respect we show for others, the choices we make and the confidence we show by our actions. In school, adults who are willing to explain things patiently, to 'think aloud' about their decisions and, where necessary, admit their mistakes, are providing a solid moral framework for children. Good role models are self-disciplined, keep their word and follow through a commitment to its conclusion. They enjoy learning, get excited about fresh knowledge and insights, speculate about possibilities, celebrate the success of others and shrug off disappointments.

Children tend to model themselves on adults they respect and admire, which places a heavy responsibility on teachers and assistants to act, respond and speak appropriately. Pascal and Bertram (1997) identified three attributes in adults that promote good-quality thinking, learning and development in children: (1) *sensitivity*, such that the adult is aware of the children's feelings and emotional wellbeing; can empathise and acknowledge children's feelings of insecurity; and offers support and encouragement; (2) s*timulation*, reflected in the way an activity or resource is introduced in a positive, exciting and stimulating manner; the advice and guidance that is provided for the children; and how well the adult joins in with children's activities to extend their thinking and develop their communication skills; and (3) *autonomy*, in which an adult gives children the freedom to experiment; supports their decisions and judgements; encourages expression of ideas; and involves children in rule-making for the benefit of everyone's safety and wellbeing.

Johnston (2002) suggests that adults influence children's learning through interacting with them in two principal ways. First, as noted above, by providing a role model for the children and demonstrating these qualities through example. Second, by using skilful teaching techniques to focus the children's attention on essential facts and interrogating issues by asking open-ended questions. Johnston underlines the point that, by interacting with pupils in these ways, adults show a willingness to learn alongside the pupils. As a result, children do not see adults as having a complete set of knowledge, understanding and skill, or as the fount of all wisdom, but rather as being fellow seekers after truth.

Questions to consider and discuss

- Why should children fashion themselves on teachers when there are so many other adults to act as models?
- How valid are Pascal and Bertram's three attributes (above)? What other attributes would you add to the list?
- In what ways might adults in school inadvertently model unacceptable behaviour to children?

References

Johnston, J. (2002) 'Teaching and learning in the early years', in J. Johnston, D. Chater and D. Bell (eds) *Teaching the Primary Curriculum*, Maidenhead: Open University.

Pascal, C. and Bertram, A. (1997) *Effective Early Learning: Case Studies for Improvement*, London: Hodder & Stoughton.

Teaching and learning issue 6: Emotional development

From a careful review of the relevant literature, Salovey and Mayer (1990) concluded that there might exist a human ability that could be described as emotional intelligence, whereby some people reasoned with emotions better than others. Emotional intelligence can be measured as a *Quotient*, which describes an ability, capacity or skill to perceive, assess and manage the emotions of one's self, of others and of groups. The phrase 'emotional literacy' is used to describe programmes to increase emotional intelligence. Goleman (2005) popularised emotional intelligence in the business realm by describing its importance as an ingredient for successful business careers and as a crucial component for effective group performance.

Hyson (2003) suggests that there are six goals in achieving what she describes as an 'emotion-centred curriculum': (1) creating a secure emotional environment; (2) helping children understand emotions; (3) modelling genuine, appropriate emotional responses; (4) supporting children's regulation of emotions; (5) recognising and honouring children's expressive styles; and (6) uniting children's learning with positive emotions. Hyson goes on to offer evidence of the damage to a child's emotional development when appropriate teaching is lacking. For example, when the curriculum does not adequately address emotional issues, stress and anxiety increases in children, notably among boys and low-income Black children.

Macklem (2007) refers to 'emotion regulation' and argues that, with targeted training in the classroom, at home and among peers, children can better attain the vital skills they need for a lifetime of social interactions. One important consideration was to ensure that children possessed an appropriate vocabulary to express their feelings; emotionally vulnerable pupils, who are liable to vent their frustrations by shouting, complaining or physical acts of violence, benefit particularly from such verbal expertise.

Tense and frustrated teachers might themselves resort to harsh control methods, both to enforce pupil discipline and to relieve their own suppressed emotions. Insecurity about being able to cope produces an emotionally draining cocktail of fatigue and anger. By contrast, teachers whose lives are calm and orderly will carry those emotions into the classroom for their own benefit and for the children they teach.

Questions to consider and discuss

- Evaluate the validity of Hyson's six goals as described above.
- What 'vital skills' do children need to acquire for successful social interactions?
- What 'vital skills' do teachers need to acquire to remain calm and orderly under duress?

References

Goleman, D. (2005) *Working With Emotional Intelligence*, New York: Bantam Books.
Hyson, M. (2003) *The Emotional Development of Young Children*, New York: Teachers College Press.

Macklem, G.L. (2007) *Practitioner's Guide to Emotion Regulation in School-aged Children*, New York: Springer.

Salovey, P. and Mayer, J.D. (1990) 'Emotional intelligence', *Imagination, Cognition, and Personality*, 9, pp. 185–211.

Teaching and learning issue 7: Emotional intelligence, children and learning

As noted in Teaching and learning issue 6, above, Salovey and Mayer are credited with originally coining the term 'emotional intelligence'. In the first article (Salovey and Mayer 1990) they reviewed literature throughout the disciplines of psychology and psychiatry, artificial intelligence and other areas, and concluded that there might exist a human ability by which some people were better able to reason by using their emotions than others. In a companion article (Mayer, DiPaolo and Salovey 1990) the authors presented a model of emotional intelligence in which they suggested that it could be measured as a genuine form of intelligence through an *Emotional Intelligence Quotient*.

Colverd and Hodgkin (2011) examine ways to develop emotional intelligence in the primary school setting. They argue that teachers are being asked to facilitate the emotional life of the children in their care, regulate their behaviour and control and analyse their emotions. The school environment is of great significance because it is a child's other home and should be a safe, caring environment 'in which the child can experience the good home, with positive, nurturing adult role models, and can access not only an academic experience but [also] a social and emotional life-enhancing one' (p. 5). The authors link their analysis to the work of Abraham Maslow's hierarchy of needs. (See Teaching and learning issue 13 later in this chapter.)

Our emotions have an impact on our readiness and ability to learn, and feeling safe is vital within the school environment. A child who does not feel emotionally safe, valued or listened to can come to school feeling frustrated, angry, distracted or withdrawn, especially when faced with trying to learn something new or difficult. Some pupils have learnt that the classroom can be an exposed place such that, if they risk answering a question incorrectly, they might open themselves to criticism, derisive comments and, perhaps, mockery from their peers or negative comments from the teacher. The emotions are significant, therefore, with respect to children's willingness to explore, clarify and interrogate ideas and concepts, as well as to working collaboratively with peers. Teachers have a key role in creating a culture of mutual tolerance, encouragement and group cohesion, where questions are treated seriously, opinions respected and genuine errors used to enhance learning rather than confine it.

Questions to consider and discuss

- What evidence from regular classroom practice could you use in evaluating the claim that some pupils are better able to reason by using their emotions?
- What attitudes and behaviour might characterise a pupil with a high emotional intelligence quotient?
- In what ways might we place too much/too little emphasis on children's emotions and their impact on learning?

References

Colverd, S. and Hodgkin, B. (2011) *Developing Emotional Intelligence in the Primary School*, Abingdon: Routledge.

Mayer, J., DiPaolo, M. and Salovey, P. (1990) 'Perceiving affective content in ambiguous visual stimuli: a component of emotional intelligence', *Journal of Personality Assessment*, 54, pp. 772–81.

Salovey, P. and Mayer, J.D. (1990) 'Emotional intelligence', *Imagination, Cognition and Personality*, 9, pp. 185–211.

Teaching and learning issue 8: Children's happiness

The deep-seated need to be happy is common to all of us. Parents worry that their children might be unhappy at school. Teachers worry that their pupils are not enjoying school. Some children worry because they fear being unhappy through loss of friends, insecurity at home, being asked to tackle work that is too difficult, social pressures from peers, or even bullying. An increase in mental health problems, drug abuse and antisocial behaviour among young people has caused some educators to suggest that, in addition to happiness emerging naturally from creating pleasant and caring learning conditions in school, teaching happiness should form part of the curriculum. Other educators dismiss the notion of *teaching* happiness, preferring to emphasise the need for all adults to *encourage* happiness by establishing a positive environment and fostering the right attitudes among children to facilitate it.

As a practical example of placing happiness at the centre of school life, MacConville (2008) piloted what she termed 'the happiness curriculum' in West London schools during the autumn of 2007 with classes of ten–thirteen-year-old pupils to help them to negotiate the transition from primary to secondary school. (See Chapter 3, Professional theme 44.) The programme was designed to build resilience, increase optimism, promote adaptive coping skills and teach children effective problem-solving skills. Children were given strategies to resist negative and unhelpful thinking and replace them with positive emotions. In all the activities, there was an emphasis on developing thinking and participatory skills. The need to be optimistic about situations, other people and their own abilities was promoted as an integral part of the programme. In a word, the programme reflected a 'yes, I can' attitude.

Research by Holder *et al.* (2008) shows that children who feel their lives have meaning and value, and who develop deep, quality relationships, are happier than those who lack these things. In particular, the personal (i.e. in one's own life) and communal (i.e. reflecting the quality and depth of interpersonal relationships) aspects of spirituality were strong predictors of children's happiness. Findings also suggested that strategies aimed at increasing personal meaning in children, such as expressing kindness towards others and recording these acts of kindness, as well as acts of altruism and volunteering for tasks, can help to make children happier. The authors claimed that children who possessed deep spiritual awareness were happier than those who lacked it.

Evidence from a variety of other studies strongly indicates that happy teachers produce happy pupils. In other words, regardless of their competence in teaching, ability to design interesting programmes of work and aptitude for hard work, teachers experiencing unhappiness in their lives were likely to transmit the unease to pupils, with negative consequences. One conclusion to be drawn from these studies is that time spent in nurturing teachers' wellbeing benefits children as well as adults. Schools in which teachers are encouraged to look after their own and colleagues' welfare, and where senior members of staff are available for advice and counselling, advantage both children and adults.

Questions to consider and discuss

- What sort of indicators can be used to gauge children's happiness?
- What are the advantages and potential hazards of focusing directly on ways to be happy rather than achieving happiness indirectly through actions such as showing kindness to others?
- What credence do you give to the belief that success breeds contentment, which results in happiness? What are the implications for teachers?

References

Holder, M.D., Coleman, B. and Wallace, J.M. (2008) 'Spirituality, religiousness and happiness in children aged 8–12 years', *Journal of Happiness Studies*, 11 (2), pp. 131–50.
MacConville, R. (2008) *Teaching Happiness: A Ten-step Curriculum for Creating Positive Classrooms*, Milton Keynes: Speechmark Publishing.

Teaching and learning issue 9: Children's moral development

The claim that a moral development programme in school (e.g. through citizenship or religious education) will succeed in creating 'morally upright' people has been the subject of intense debate, not least because people who are capable of pontificating about standards of morality do not always behave accordingly. There is general agreement that valuing the self, others, society and the environment provides a helpful framework within which issues of morality can be presented and discussed. In fact, every time a child is praised or admonished by a teacher, told how to behave, presented with choices or guided into a course of action, an ethical position is being established and a moral statement is being made. Thus, whether deliberately or passively, teachers influence the development of children's characters and exercise moral authority in school.

Day (2004) argues that: 'Moral purposes are at the heart of every teacher's work. They underpin their sense of commitment to their pupils, which includes but goes beyond the instrumental policy agendas of governments' (p. 24). Chater (2002) poses a variety of possibilities about the process by which young people develop morally: by being told what is right and wrong; by discovering pleasure, meaning and intellectual and emotional satisfaction in doing right; or through being encouraged to discover right and wrong for themselves. He also poses a blunt question for all parents and educators as to whether moral development would happen anyway, regardless of adult intervention (p. 44).

Sigmund Freud claimed that the quality of relationship between a child and his or her parents is the key factor influencing moral development. By contrast with Freud's ideas, *social learning theories* are based on the premise that children initially learn how to behave morally through modelling or imitating appropriate adult behaviour – not necessarily that of parents. A different perspective is propounded through *cognitive developmental theories*, which claim that a child's ability to reason morally depends on his or her general thinking abilities (i.e. through the intellect).

American psychologist Lawrence Kohlberg was interested in children's reasons for making moral choices and established a theory based on six stages (Kohlberg 1981):

1. Obedience and punishment. The earliest stage of moral development is especially common in young children, who see rules as fixed and absolute. Obeying the rules is important because it is a means to avoid punishment.
2. Individualism and exchange. At this stage of moral development, children account for individual points of view and judge actions based on how they serve individual needs.
3. Interpersonal relationships. This stage of moral development is focused on living up to social expectations and roles with an emphasis on conformity, being nice and how choices influence relationships.
4. Maintaining social order. The focus is on maintaining law and order by following the rules, doing one's duty, and respecting authority.
5. Social contract and individual rights. People begin to account for the differing values, opinions, and beliefs of other people.
6. Universal principles. People follow their own principles of justice, even if they conflict with laws and rules.

Virtually all teachers care deeply for pupils they consider to be 'their' children and want them to do well in their studies, to prosper in their relationships and to be contented without being complacent. They want to reveal something profound to children about life and its meaning, encourage them to persevere and discover something about their own worth and the value of others. (See also Chapter 3, Professional theme 8.)

Questions to consider and discuss

- What influence do teachers have on children's moral development? How might the effect be reflected in classroom behaviour and discipline?
- Evaluate the validity of the oft-stated premise that children must learn to make their own decisions about what is right and wrong.
- What are the merits and limitations of the Kohlberg development theory?

References

Chater, M. (2002) 'The child as spiritual citizen', in J. Johnston, M. Chater and D. Bell (eds) *Teaching the Primary Curriculum*, Maidenhead: Open University Press.

Day, C. (2004) *A Passion for Teaching*, Abingdon: Routledge.

Kohlberg, L. (1981) *Essays on Moral Development 1*, San Francisco: Harper & Row.

Teaching and learning issue 10: Alternative forms of education

Children do not have to attend school in order to receive an education. Indeed, parents and family are not only the first educators, but continue to play a vital role in furthering children's knowledge and understanding. The concept of formal schooling with an established curriculum and a set pattern of routines is a relatively new phenomenon. Historically, State-funded education is less than one hundred and fifty years old. The Church established the earliest schools for the *general* population during the mid-1800s. It was only at the start of the twentieth century that the State became the major funding provider and gradually assumed control over the curriculum and education policy. During the late 1900s, conformity across schools was promoted as necessary for continuity of provision and maintenance of standards; today, the emphasis is upon retaining a 'core' through the National Curriculum and testing, while encouraging diversity of practice.

Despite the Government's attempts to introduce greater flexibility into education provision, there is a percentage of parents who are dissatisfied with the school situation and prefer to educate their children at home. It appears that many parents who home-school do so because: (a) they think children are required to start formal school too early; (b) they are worried about bullying and poor discipline; or (c) they feel dissatisfied with the overall quality of education (York Consulting 2007). There appears to be a prevailing view among such parents that the education system is too bureaucratic, inflexible and assessment-driven, all of which acts against the best needs of the children. In addition, some parents considered that their children's special learning needs, including dyslexia, autism and the needs of those identified as gifted and talented, were not being adequately met in school.

One feature of home-schooling is that it is often a short-term expedient rather than a continuous process. Parents withdraw their children for a period of time and allow them to return to the maintained sector after they perceive that the crisis is past or a phase of education is ended. When a child returns to the regular school system after being home educated, it is almost inevitable that he or she will take some time to adjust to the new circumstances, in much the same way as any 'new entrant' might do. Teachers have not only to find out how much the new pupil knows and understands but also to make allowance for the fact that the child has probably followed a more random curriculum and taken fuller advantage of spontaneous learning opportunities than is possible in a school setting. Time spent at home with, perhaps, one or more siblings may have inculcated greater independence than is typically present in the majority of classmates; the child might also be unused to working collaboratively. Furthermore, unless the new pupil has friends from the class outside school, establishing secure friendships might also be an issue.

Questions to consider and discuss

- What lessons can teachers learn from parents who home-school about every parent's aspirations for their children?

- What substance is there in the accusation that schools are too bureaucratic, inflexible and assessment-driven?
- What strategies can teachers use to ensure that any home-schooled child new to the school is made to feel welcome and secure?

Reference

York Consulting (2007) *The Prevalence of Home Education in England: A Feasibility Study*, Research Report 827, Annesley: DfES Publications.

Section B: Pupil learning

Teaching and learning issue 11: Learning and concept-mapping

Joseph Novak of Cornell University, New York was among the first educators to give serious attention to concept-mapping, building on the theories of David Ausubel, who stressed the importance of prior knowledge in being able to learn about new concepts (Ausubel 1963). Concept-mapping is a process to aid memory and understanding by visually representing ideas, such that children can see that knowledge traverses subject boundaries and, as a result, help them to develop a more complete understanding of their world. Novak, working largely in the field of science (e.g. Novak 1991) concluded that meaningful learning involves the assimilation of new concepts and propositions into existing cognitive structures, resulting in a concept map, consisting of a graphical representation where nodes (points or vertices) represent concepts, and links (arcs or lines) represent the relationships between concepts. The links between the concepts can be one-way, two-way or non-directional. The concepts and the links may be categorised, and the concept map may show temporal ('time-related') or causal relationships ('cause and effect') between concepts.

Fisher (2005) advises that this type of cognitive-mapping is also known as concept-mapping, semantic-mapping, knowledge-mapping, word-webbing, networking, clustering, think-links, idea branches, structured overviews and graphic organisers, which include: (a) sequences of key words or pictures; (b) Venn diagrams; (c) sets of words or pictures; and (d) rank ordering with respect to size, significance or frequency.

Concept-mapping became popular in school through the process originally referred to as 'brainstorming', in which ideas about a theme are shown diagrammatically with arrows between them, producing an effect resembling a cluttered spider's web. A concept map will typically focus on a designated theme. For instance, the theme might be a broad ranging one such as 'Healthy eating', which would probably consist of numerous key words (e.g. diet), specific vocabulary (e.g. nutrition), some technical terms (e.g. proteins) and links to show relationships between them. On the other hand, the map could have a narrower focus such as 'Victorian homes', and cover familiar examples of design (e.g. 'one-up, one-down'), some key features (e.g. tin bath) and some comparisons with modern homes (e.g. lack of technology).

One way of approaching concept-mapping involves giving pupils a list of 'prompt' words derived from a whole-class session or through another initial stimulus such as a graphic image, television programme or a first-hand account to use in creating relational links. For example, a theme based around the experiences of children during the Second World War might include words such as: air raid, rations, gas mask, Blitz, blackout and bombing. Importantly, the maps produced by pupils act as a starting point for discussion, clarification and further research (perhaps using technology or inviting someone who can provide a first-hand account) to deepen understanding of the emotions attached to wartime experiences, expand knowledge and open up moral issues.

Some teachers encourage children to become 'expert' in a particular field, using concept-mapping as a basis. For example, a study of 'classifying mammals' can commence with whole-class involvement, the development of concept maps by pairs of children and further research by each child about the animal of choice. Subsequently, pupils present their findings individually to their classmates, aided by teacher questions.

Teachers can use the insights from the way that each pupil addresses the topic for assessment purposes; for instance, using the child's ability to: link key words; create a map; use the map as a basis for further research; employ books and technology; work collaboratively; produce findings; present findings; answer questions; show awareness of what still needs to be discovered; and make lateral links with other areas of knowledge.

Questions to consider and discuss

- What benefits might accrue from visually mapping concepts?
- How would you define 'meaningful learning' in the above context?
- How might the technique of concept-mapping be extended beyond the introductory phase to promote deeper learning?

References

Ausubel, D.P. (1963) *The Psychology of Meaningful Verbal Learning*, New York: Grune and Stratton.

Fisher, R. (2005) *Teaching Children to Learn*, second edn, Cheltenham: Stanley Thornes.

Novak, J.D. (1991) 'Clarify with concept maps', *The Science Teacher*, 58 (7), pp. 45–49.

Teaching and learning issue 12: Cognition and Bloom's Taxonomy

Bloom's Taxonomy is a classification that was developed in the 1950s (Bloom 1956) but experienced a revival at the start of the twenty-first century. It was originally written as a classification of different types of educational objectives but is now seen as a means of considering forms and hierarchies of learning. The stated aim of the original study was to provide a classification of the goals of the education system on which teachers could build a curriculum. As well as a framework for testing pupils, one other suggested use for the taxonomy was as a tool for analysing a teacher's success in teaching. The taxonomy contains three domains: cognitive, affective and psychomotor. Thus:

1. The *cognitive* domain is that of knowledge and intellectual abilities and skills. It also includes the 'behaviours', such as remembering, reasoning, problem-solving, concept formation and creative thinking.
2. The *affective* domain includes objectives that describe changes in interest, attitudes, emotions and values, and the development of appreciation. In the affective domain, the hierarchy is less clear but there is a broad continuum from an awareness of value issues → responding → valuing → organising and conceptualising values.
3. The *psychomotor* domain was weakly developed by Bloom's team but ranges from imitation and reflex movements → manipulation → skilled, articulated and precise movements.

The taxonomy in the cognitive domain is of principal interest to educators and became a hierarchy of six major classes, supposedly moving from simple to complex, as follows: (1) knowledge; (2) comprehension; (3) application; (4) analysis; (5) synthesis; and (6) evaluation.

Atherton (2011) refers to each class as follows:

1. *Knowledge* is mainly about remembering and factual recall: specific terms and facts; ways and means of dealing with specifics through organising, judging, and criticising ideas and phenomena; conventions; processes and changes over time; causes and effects; classifications such as genres of literature; criteria for testing or judging; enquiry techniques; and principles, laws, explanations and theories.
2. *Comprehension* includes summarising ideas; simplifying a problem; expressing things in straightforward language; giving an example or illustration of an abstract idea; interpreting data; distinguishing warranted from unwarranted conclusions from a body of data or evidence; drawing conclusions; making inferences; and predicting trends and consequences.
3. *Application* involves applying laws, theories, rules or principles to particular, often practical, situations, and solving problems by using acquired skills and knowledge.
4. *Analysis* involves activities such as seeing patterns, identifying key components and dissecting arguments; distinguishing facts from hypotheses; analysing relationships between interconnecting ideas; distinguishing cause and effect from other types of relationship; detecting logical fallacies in an argument; detailed examination of organisational principles (e.g. form and pattern in literary or artistic work); and recognising a writer's bias in a historical account or rhetoric in a persuasive account such as an advertisement or political speech.
5. *Synthesis* involves integrating ideas, creating novel ideas from old ones, connecting and relating knowledge from different areas, and producing conclusions and generalisations.
6. *Evaluation* involves assessing, judging, appraising, weighing up, criticising and defending a hypothesis, theory or argument. It is placed at the top of the hierarchy since it is said to involve all the other 'behaviours' outlined above.

Anderson and Krathwohl (2001) suggest a modified version of the taxonomy from 'remembering' (at the base of the pyramid) to 'creating' at the top. Thus:

Remembering → understanding → applying → analysing → evaluating → creating.

Bloom's Taxonomy is useful in areas such as lesson-planning or assessing pupils' work to indicate the broad level at which children are working, though it does not provide a statistically valid method. It is also important to note that the taxonomy is only a model of learning, and individual progress can fluctuate considerably; thus, even quite young children are sometimes capable of engaging with the supposed 'higher' elements of the taxonomy if helped and encouraged to do so. By contrast, adults cannot always manage what the taxonomy claims to be quite elementary concepts, such as memorising basic facts.

Questions to consider and discuss

- What are the principal strengths and limitations of the hierarchy?
- How might the six classes be used in assessing pupil achievement?
- Which of the six classes in the cognitive domain do you regularly employ in your teaching? How might you broaden the range?

References

Atherton, J.S. (2011) *Learning and Teaching; Bloom's Taxonomy*, online: UK, retrieved 11th October 2011 from www.learningandteaching.info/learning/bloomtax.htm.

Anderson, L.W. and Krathwohl, D.R. (eds) (2001) *A Taxonomy for Learning, Teaching, and Assessing: A Revision of Bloom's Taxonomy of Educational Objectives*, New York: Longman.

Bloom, B.S. (ed.) (1956) *Taxonomy of Educational Objectives: The Classification of Educational Goals – Handbook I: Cognitive Domain*, New York: McKay.

Teaching and learning issue 13: Motivation and Maslow's Hierarchy

Despite the fact that some parts of the curriculum are less appealing to children than others, top teachers always strive to create a learning environment full of diverse experiences, where pupils' interest is maintained through a combination of lively personality, varied activities and links with other areas of knowledge. Learning becomes more worthwhile when the lesson content is perceived by pupils as challenging but achievable, and teachers design the lesson imaginatively by using a combination of clear instruction, interactive questioning and discussion, manageable tasks, co-operative activities and well-defined end points that leave pupils feeling that they have gained something worthwhile. In reality, no teacher, however committed and talented, can maintain a dynamic and stimulating ambience throughout every day, regardless of how hard she or he tries. Even so, the percentage of good or excellent lessons can and should outweigh below-average or poor ones.

Teachers also know that restless children, who are uncomfortable due to factors such as a cold or stuffy classroom, thirst, hunger, hard seats and the like, cannot concentrate and engage with the lesson wholeheartedly. Pupils who are anxious about what is happening at home, in school or in the wider community will inevitably be influenced adversely by these negative factors; similarly, children who are happy, contented and feel secure will prosper. Experienced teachers instinctively recognise when a child is lacking motivation due to extraneous influences rather than the effects of the lesson, but responding appropriately is far less straightforward. In truth, the sound relationships that adults build with children from day to day pay dividends when a pupil is distressed because (a) the child is more likely to confide in the teacher, and (b) the teacher is able to explain to the child why a sanction is being applied for unacceptable behaviour without provoking undue rancour. Similarly, a good relationship between teacher and parent allows for a more rational discussion of the issues concerning the child's behaviour and unhappiness.

One reference point that you can use in evaluating the quality of the learning environment for pupils is to make use of Maslow's Hierarchy. Abraham Maslow was a psychologist who, during the 1940s, developed a theory based on human needs, which was subsequently extended to include observations about humans' innate curiosity (Maslow 1954). The basis of Maslow's *Theory of Motivation* is that human beings are motivated by unsatisfied needs, and that so-called 'lower needs' need to be satisfied before 'higher needs' can be addressed. Maslow's hierarchy of needs is often portrayed in the shape of a pyramid (or a triangle), with the largest and most fundamental levels of need at the bottom of the pyramid (or triangle) and different horizontal layers representing increasingly complex conditions, such that the conditions necessary to optimise achievement are at the pyramid's apex.

Maslow argued that the fundamental layers of the pyramid consist of 'deficiency needs' or, simply, 'D-needs'. Thus, *physiological* needs (health, food, sleep, etc.) are fundamental to everything that follows. *Security and safety* (stability, freedom from fear) are concerned with a child's need for a predictable and orderly world in which unfairness and inconsistency are minimised. *Belonging* (social connections, friendship, love) involves the strong desire to feel accepted, which at times can even surpass physiological needs and security needs. *Self-esteem* (achievement, mastery, knowledge, understanding, etc.) is the need to be respected and also to possess high self-esteem and self-respect. *Self-actualisation* describes the point that is reached when an individual's basic and emotional needs are fulfilled and the person's full potential can then be realised. These needs, from bottom (1) to top (5) of the triangle, can be summarised thus:

1. physiological needs (health, food, sleep and drink)
2. safety needs
3. belonging and emotional needs
4. esteem needs
5. self-actualisation.

Maslow also coined the term *metamotivation* to describe the drive of people who go beyond the scope of the basic needs and strive for constant improvement. Metamotivated people are driven by 'B-needs' (Being needs), as opposed to deficiency needs. Naturally, the best teachers do their best to create the conditions whereby pupils gain the security and motivation to become B-needs people and press forward with confidence in learning.

Among the various criticisms of Maslow's Hierarchy is a concern that he places too much emphasis on the needs of individuals and takes insufficient account of social and societal factors. Teachers work hard to develop a sense of community and oneness in the classroom, so, while individuality is important and deficiency needs must be addressed as far as possible, these considerations always have to be weighed against lesson content and structure that facilitate broader educational and social aims. For example, it is sometimes unpleasant to do sporting activities when cold and damp, but personal comfort has to be subordinated to the overarching aim of achieving fitness and, perhaps, learning to confront and overcome challenges.

Whatever view we take of Maslow's attempt to describe the factors that influence pupil learning, teachers realise that motivating a child to do well does not, of itself, produce a sudden transformation from uncertainty to optimism. However, your positive approach, coupled with appropriate support and direction, allows a child to persevere in the certain knowledge that there is an adult 'safety net' beneath.

Questions to consider and discuss

- What strategies can teachers use to motivate pupils who are finding the work dull?
- Over which of the D-needs do adults in school have greatest and least control? How might that control be exercised?
- How can teachers achieve a balance between the needs of individual pupils ('individualised' curriculum) and the needs of the class community? (See also Chapter 3, Professional theme 16.)

Reference

Maslow, A.H. (1954) *Motivation and Personality*, New York: Harper.

Teaching and learning issue 14: Pupil learning styles

Initially, the statement that everyone learns differently is so obvious as to invite derision. More difficult to pinpoint, however, are the variety of ways that pupils differ from one another in their learning and the implications for teaching. Learning becomes more enjoyable and challenging if teachers show awareness in their teaching techniques and strategies of the fact that some pupils learn more effectively through use of visual stimuli, some by practical 'hands-on/ kinaesthetic' means and others through more traditional auditory means (see Teaching and learning issue 15, below). The most familiar model for describing learning styles identifies learners as conforming most readily to one or more of three types: visual (designated V), auditory (designated A) and kinaesthetic (designated K). The acronym for this model is, therefore, VAK. Other educators include R, which stands for 'reading', as some pupils seem to readily absorb facts from written sources. The inclusion of this extra category results in the acronym VARK.

Researchers such as Sharp *et al.* (2008) claim that, although developments in neuroscientific knowledge have the potential to enhance our understanding of the learning process, they are presently of little practical use for teaching. The authors note that many enthusiasts of VAK are uncritical about the evidence on which they base their claims and that proposed models of learning styles have weak validity. Other educationists accept the existence of preferred learning styles but point to the fact that tests have shown that a supposed auditory learner might or might not learn something presented in an auditory form better than someone who has a different learning style. The same is true for people who prefer visual information and those who favour a kinaesthetic approach. The explanation for this paradox is that learners are first and foremost looking to extract meaning. The different learning styles contribute to that aim but are not individually able to achieve it. Virtually all learning consists of an amalgam of understanding that is brought about through the use of every possible means; the fact that a pupil enjoys and responds to one stimulus more than another does not mean that teachers have to artificially adjust their teaching – but simply be aware of the need for variety.

The second limitation of the theory is that not all learning lends itself to the full VAK range. For instance, many children learn that Italy is in the shape of a boot and might have been taught the rhyme, 'Big old Italy kicked little Sicily into the middle of the Mediterranean Sea'. For recognising Italy on a map, then, a visual learning style is undoubtedly the most suitable strategy to use. However, to extend this example, most countries have far less memorable shapes than Italy and a visually accurate picture of the other countries' outlines relies to a large extent on verbal description, such as explaining the juxtaposition of neighbouring countries; or perhaps to a mixture of visual and kinaesthetic means, such as physically tracing the outline onto a transparency.

In summary, while it is true that pupils might express a preference from the VARK 'menu', it is simplistic to suggest that they necessarily learn any better from their preferred approach. In fact, some studies indicate that pupils actually learn *less* from their preferred style, despite enjoying the work more. You should therefore exercise caution when making decisions about learning styles and their implications for teaching.

Questions to consider and discuss

- How useful is VAK as a theoretical model to guide teaching and learning?
- How might you adjust your teaching to take account of pupils' different learning styles?
- What percentage of your teaching is (a) verbal (b) visual (c) kinaesthetic (d) based on reading? What are the implications of these figures?

Reference

Sharp, J.G., Bowker, R. and Byrne, J. (2008) 'VAK or VAK-uous? Towards the trivialisation of learning and the death of scholarship', *Research Papers in Education*, 23 (3), pp. 293–314.

Teaching and learning issue 15: Learning through auditory means

We noted in Teaching and learning issue 14 that one way of explaining learning styles is by use of the acronym VARK (visual, auditory, reading, kinaesthetic), of which the most significant element is auditory (literally, 'by sound'). In school, a lot of emphasis is placed on conveying information by auditory means, especially towards the top of the primary school. Children who learn easily by listening, without the need for visual stimuli or hands-on experience, prefer to receive information, guidance and explanation through the ear, as opposed to receiving it through the eye (visual learners) or fingers (kinaesthetic/tactile learners) or via investigation or problem solving. They particularly benefit when directions and instructions are read aloud, feedback is required or information is orally presented and requested.

Auditory learners are often characterised by being confident to speak and read out loud in front of peers and competent at explaining things. They are normally good at remembering details (such as telephone numbers and names). Typically, an auditory learner has a firm grasp of grammar and picks up a foreign language with relative ease. In the classroom, such children will follow the teacher's spoken directions and contribute well to group activities, but they are also likely to be garrulous and liable to interrupt their classmates and the teacher. Owing to their outgoing personalities and self-confidence, many auditory learners enjoy drama, acting and performing in front of an audience.

Auditory learning is associated with a teaching approach in which the teacher conveys knowledge and explains concepts directly to pupils by using a lecture-style of teaching (adult speaks; children listen), a method often referred to as 'didactic'. This form of teaching and learning contrasts sharply with a 'constructivist' approach, in which children work collaboratively to discuss, debate and investigate issues; that is, they construct meaning for themselves rather than receive it through a teacher's verbal explanation. Didactic teaching particularly suits children who, owing to maturity or inclination, have the capacity to concentrate on what is being said and absorb the spoken word without the benefit of visual aids or supporting practical ('hands-on') activities. In this respect, the use of auditory means is often more appropriate for educating older or more able pupils, who have a greater capacity to concentrate and to retain and memorise information. In this regard, it is helpful to note the rule of thumb that children can concentrate continuously on what is being said for approximately the number of minutes equivalent to their ages; for example, a six-year-old can concentrate for about six minutes, though this figure varies depending on the interest value of the subject.

To impart meaning to their words, teachers have to not only consider the vocabulary and expressions they use but also pay particular attention to the tone, speed and pitch of voice. For example, the simple question, 'What are you doing?' can indicate fascination or threat, depending on the way in which the word 'what' is emphasised. Teachers sometimes get frustrated that pupils do not grasp the meaning of things they say when, in fact, the children are more intrigued by the tone of the teacher's voice than by the content of the words. In addition, the rapidity of speech, frequency and length of pauses and number of hesitations can enhance or detract from the central message that the words convey. As noted under Teaching and learning issue 29 later in this chapter, while speaking and listening play a vital role in learning, it is worth pondering the fact that numerous studies have shown that a combination of methods is more effective in conveying meaning than submerging pupils in a cascade of words.

Questions to consider and discuss

- What do teachers need to consider when addressing a group or class in which there is a wide range of auditory capabilities and preferences?
- What practical techniques can teachers use to improve their auditory communication in class?
- How might a teacher's voice tone and body language affect the way in which pupils receive what is said?

Teaching and learning issue 16: Questions and higher-level thinking

Wragg and Brown (2001) claim that teachers ask between 200 and 400 questions every day, so the ability to ask intelligent and searching questions, to use questioning for different purposes and to know what to do with the answers is crucial for teaching all subjects and age groups.

Questions are commonly categorised into 'lower-' and 'higher-' order questions, the former requiring little active thinking; the latter demanding thoughtful responses from the pupils. Another form of categorisation divides questions into 'open' (multi-answer) types and 'closed' (single-answer) types. A further division is into 'spontaneous' questions ('say the first sensible thing that comes into your mind') and 'speculative' questions ('imagine if this were the case').

Teachers sometimes 'shoot' a question from pupil to pupil until someone answers correctly, which suits able children and fast thinkers but disadvantages those who need time to ponder their responses. It is often preferable to start with more straightforward questions as a means of involving all pupils – perhaps including a 'hands-up if you agree with what I say' technique to promote a unified response – and to increase the level of difficulty gradually, rather than beginning with conceptually challenging questions that immediately place a limit on the number of children who can participate.

A study by Gillies (2011) observed teachers' use of questions during interactive sessions and noted that they used a range of questioning strategies. Some questions probed for information and challenged children's perspectives; other questions demanded that pupils provide reasons for their responses, make connections between facts or think about the mental process by which they arrived at their answer. Gillies found that, while the different types of questions all encouraged informative and detailed replies from children, it was the higher-level questions that challenged children to consider alternative ideas and perspectives, or to connect information and ideas that elicited explanations, reasons and justifications. Only the higher-level questions generated dialogue and reciprocal interactions that were sustained and cognitively demanding, often requiring three or four 'turns' (specific verbal contributions) before arriving at a final response that combined the different pupil comments and perspectives to construct new understanding. In short, the combined knowledge and insights from different pupils as they responded to questions helped to construct meaning and reinforce understanding, all of which the teacher drew together and summarised.

Furthermore, Gillies suggests that children probably learn new ways of thinking and talking by listening to teachers model these behaviours. Pupils utilise many of the questioning strategies used by the teacher in their small group discussions to challenge each other's understanding, build connections and develop new learning. If you want to encourage children to engage in higher-level thinking and talking, you need to explicitly guide and scaffold this type of discourse pattern in your interactions with pupils.

As a means of encouraging pupils to think deeply, top teachers stimulate pupil interest by bringing into school unusual items and fascinating books that foster a sense of mystery and wonder; they then encourage children to do the same. To promote higher self-esteem and recognition, some teachers urge children with knowledge about a hobby or pastime to act as experts among their peers by being in the 'hot-seat' and talking to the class about their interest and handling questions that are put to them by their classmates.

Questions to consider and discuss

- What characterises higher-order and lower-order questions? How might questions be otherwise graded in terms of the intellectual demands they place on children?
- What sorts of cognitively demanding questions might be used with (a) reception-age children; (b) seven-year olds; (c) eleven-year-olds?
- What techniques might teachers employ to guide and scaffold discourse patterns for pupils?

References

Gillies, R.M. (2011) 'Promoting thinking, problem solving and reasoning during small group discussions', *Teachers and Teaching*, 17 (1), pp. 73–89.
Wragg, E.C. and Brown, G. (2001) *Questioning in the Primary School*, Abingdon: Routledge.

Teaching and learning issue 17: Pupil ability and capability

The use of phrases allegedly describing the capacity of pupils to learn and achieve are replete in education vocabulary. Teachers speak of 'clever children'. Parents compare their children by distinguishing intellectual ability from practical expertise; thus: 'Chloe's the bright one; Adam's good with his hands'. Publications about differentiating lessons to accommodate 'brighter' pupils and 'slow learners', and about assessment strategies to measure pupil competence and address their shortcomings have saturated education debate in recent years. In school, older children are divided into 'sets' for mathematics and English. A sizeable minority of primary schools stream children from the age of seven into separate classes for pupils deemed very able, able and less able. (See Teaching and learning issue 21 later in this chapter.)

There has also been an explosion of interest in the existence of 'intelligences' (plural) rather than a single, measurable intelligence (singular). (See Chapter 3, Professional theme 11.) Children who struggle in core subjects are sometimes acknowledged as having great potential in other areas of the curriculum or perhaps in relational areas; thus: 'Brendan is poor at reading but is popular with his classmates'. Owing to the emphasis placed on achieving good test results in literacy and mathematics, it is inevitable that phrases like 'able child' are appended to pupils who do well in reading, in writing and in arithmetic. Poorly performing pupils in these areas are usually offered additional help to 'reach the required standard'.

In addition, phrases such as 'gifted artist', 'natural talent' and 'innate intelligence' have entered the education discourse in recent years. (See also Teaching and learning issue 18, below.) However, Shenk (2010) argues that it is wrong to claim that exceptional ability is a genetic inheritance that some people are fortunate enough to have and others do not, and cannot possess. The author insists that everything we do contributes to the developmental process, part of which depends on our genes and part of which is due to the environment in which we grow up. In reality, our genes interact with their surroundings, resulting in different outcomes. As explained in Teaching and learning issue 1 earlier in this chapter, genetic factors cannot be studied independently, as account must always be taken of context. There are also children who work hard and achieve more than might have been anticipated; and others who are basically unmotivated, so underachieve. The important point is to be aware of the demise of the long-standing belief that there is a single 'fixed' intelligence, which cannot be altered through good teaching, steadfast learning or any other means.

Based on the premise that both genes and environment are significant in creating the people we are, it is valid to conclude that personality, intelligence (in its different forms) and range of abilities are shaped by the lives we lead, and are not just inherited characteristics. Consequently, the notion of 'innate ability' as the sole factor in determining or predicting the extent of a child's success in life is highly suspect. In reality, the child's direction in life is affected principally by (a) the influence of home; (b) the attitudes of those around; (c) teachers' teaching styles; and (d) the amount and nature of physical exercise and other lifestyle choices. No child is therefore 'doomed' to be incapable or incompetent unless there is a chronic fault in the child's brain that is impossible to rectify, though it is amazing what can be achieved with the right level of support, resources and dedication.

Furthermore, children's brains adapt in response to the weight of demands that are placed on them. Thus, high academic achievers are not necessarily born with greater intelligence than their contemporaries; they might simply work harder and develop more self-discipline in completing tasks; or their teachers might have had higher expectations of them, urged and motivated them to try harder and given them excellent support in achieving elevated goals. Teachers who believe that intelligence is not fixed but can increase under the right conditions are likely to be more purposeful and determined than those who have resigned their pupils to low standards in the belief that some children are hopeless cases.

While the above arguments are valid, it would be foolish to suggest that any child can literally achieve or become anything if provided with ideal circumstances and appropriate guidance. On the other hand, it is equally wrong to assume that a proportion of pupils are unable to achieve anything of worth and that no form of intervention can or will change the situation. Ability is not set in genetic stone. The best teachers are level-headed optimists.

Questions to consider and discuss

- How do the above arguments about the limitations of innate ability accord with your own experience as a learner?
- How do the arguments match your experience of the way that children learn?
- What are the implications for classroom practice of a belief that hard work and self-discipline invariably lead to higher academic achievement?

Reference

Shenk, D. (2010) *The Genius in All of Us*, New York: Doubleday.

Teaching and learning issue 18: Gifted and talented pupils and accelerated learning

The terms 'gifted' and 'talented' are often used interchangeably. Even so, a commonly held view is that *gifted* is when pupils show exceptional ability in the curriculum areas of literacy, mathematics and science; more rarely, it is attributed to success in the non-core areas. The word *talented* tends to be reserved for children who display exceptional ability in subjects where there is more of a performance element, notably, art and design, music, physical education, dance and drama. By contrast, Knowles (2006) claims that giftedness is the potential a child may possess in any particular subject or area of human activity, characterised by the child's ability to learn in that area faster than children of similar age. Talent is seen by Knowles as the *realisation* of giftedness, identified through performance.

Talented/gifted children are usually creative and imaginative, possess keen insight and intuition and can work independently. They often have a good, though unconventional, sense of humour and are highly motivated (particularly in self-selected tasks), demonstrating exceptional critical thinking skills during investigations and solving problems. Pupils will normally have a wide spread of interests, strong powers of reasoning, intellectual curiosity, a long attention span and a superior vocabulary to their classmates.

Very able pupils enjoy active dialogue with the teacher and like to be challenged *within* the regular curriculum rather than by special provision outside it (Dickinson 1996). In other words, pupils do not want to be isolated from the normal tasks and activities of the class, but rather to be given opportunity to extend their thinking and be innovative in the way they approach their work. Another characteristic of gifted pupils is that they tend to be motivated by teachers' comments more than grades; they also appreciate being given focused and challenging feedback as a means of improving further.

It is a paradox that some pupils who are identified as talented (as defined by exceptional ability in arts or sport), who might be unexceptional at mathematics and literacy, are expected to spend additional time on the core subject work, thereby reducing the opportunity for them to concentrate on the subject areas where their natural abilities lie. Some studies also suggest that teachers are (understandably) tempted to leave more capable pupils to work independently or give them additional work to keep them busy, while they direct most of their attention towards slower learners. Top teachers know that the highest levels of academic performance by children of all abilities are achieved when teachers interact with pupils in a way that encourages them to grapple with concepts and issues of appropriate difficulty in the sure knowledge that failure is defined as 'not trying' rather than 'trying but not succeeding'.

Accelerated learning (AL) is sometimes referred to as a brain-friendly learning technique. It employs an approach to teaching that actively uses music, colour, emotion, play and creativity in order to speed and enhance the learning process. It is viewed as a strategy to promote learning for pupils deemed gifted or talented, but can be used for children of any ability. The concepts behind accelerated learning were developed in the USA during the 1980s and 1990s by pioneers such as Colin Rose (e.g. Rose 1998) and later developed by enthusiasts like David Meier (Meier 2000). However, it wasn't until the late 1990s that the concept was developed for teachers in the United Kingdom.

The AL approach takes close account of Gardner's theory of multiple intelligences (Gardner 1983, 1999). Gardner questions the idea that intelligence is a single entity that results from a single factor and can be measured solely through the use of Intelligence Quotient (IQ) tests. Instead, he argues that everyone has a unique blend of intelligences and teachers need to attend to all their forms. (See also Chapter 3, Professional theme 11 and Teaching and learning issue 14, earlier.) It is helpful if pupils understand what they are likely to learn in any particular lesson and the process for achieving this aim, as an objectives-based approach of this kind provides a predefined goal for the pupil to work towards and a higher sense of achievement when it is attained. On the other hand, teachers who inject a hint of mystery into the proceedings rather than blandly stating the 'learning objectives' (and writing them on a whiteboard) are more likely to engage the interest of every child, not least those with creative minds who see learning as a panorama, not a single peak.

It is always worth having an interesting extension activity in mind for faster workers. For example: (a) to create a more elaborate version of whatever they have just completed; (b) to design some problems for a friend to solve; (c) to create a 'cloze' exercise based on the finished piece of writing; (d) to make a rendering of the key words in code, together with the key – for instance, where a = z, b = y, c = x, d = w, and so on – for another pupil to work out; (e) to design an attractive title for the artwork; (f) to make an activity sheet of problems; (g) to draw a cartoon strip to show the progression or stages of the investigation.

Questions to consider and discuss

- To what extent are terms like giftedness and talent helpful/ unhelpful to the child and to the teacher? How might exceptional ability be otherwise described?

■ How can teachers ensure that they spend an appropriate amount of time and effort on and with pupils of every ability level?

■ What are the benefits and pitfalls of accelerated learning? What learning climate, techniques and strategies might a teacher create to foster AL in a mixed-ability class?

References

Dickinson, C. (1996) *Effective Learning Activities*, Stafford: Network Educational Press.

Gardner, H. (1983) *Frames of Mind: The Theory of Multiple Intelligences*, New York: Basic Books.

——(1999) *Intelligence Reframed*, New York: Basic Books.

Knowles, G. (2006) 'Gifted and talented', in G. Knowles (ed.) *Supporting Inclusive Practice*, Exeter: Learning Matters.

Meier, D. (2000) *The Accelerated Learning Handbook*, New York: McGraw-Hill Professional.

Rose, C. (1998) *Accelerated Learning for the 21st Century*, New York: Dell.

Teaching and learning issue 19: Memory and learning difficulties

Children with memory strengths are easy to identify because they can accommodate large amounts of information and retain it effortlessly from a variety of sources. By contrast, children who struggle with memory weaknesses can initially appear to understand a concept, yet need a considerable amount of repetition, careful explanation and opportunities to explore ideas through problem-solving and investigations before they grasp it thoroughly. The majority of children with poor working memory are slow to learn in the areas of reading, mathematics and science, across both primary and secondary school years (Gathercole and Alloway 2008).

Memorising is a complex phenomenon, the most familiar aspect being an *active working memory* that pupils use immediately after they see or hear something. The active working memory provides a mental 'jotting pad' for them to store information necessary for everyday activities, such as following directions and instructions, and keeping track of items on lists. A working memory of this kind allows children to hold information in their heads and manipulate it mentally; for example, adding up numbers without using pen and paper or a calculator. A common way in which teachers are alerted to a weak memory is when the child's written work is characterised by poor sequencing, missing words and inadequate grammar, despite the fact that they can probably express their ideas verbally.

Some psychologists refer to the active working memory as a temporary storage facility where information is kept until the brain can process the information into what is commonly referred to as *short-term memory*, which is effective for brief periods of time but does not accommodate complete retention. Thus, children may appear to learn something one day but forget it by the next and have difficulty transferring the information to the third type of memory, known as *long-term memory* (permanently stored). In extreme cases a child will have difficulty grasping information for long enough in the active working memory to transfer it to the short-term memory. However, when memory works well, knowledge will be transferred from the active to the short-term and eventually to the long-term memory with minimum intellectual effort. Both episodic memory (memory for events) and semantic memory (memory for facts) are significant for pupils in class.

A poor working memory, rather than low intelligence, appears to be the principal reason for underperformance in school. Alloway *et al.* (2008) found that a tenth of more than 3,000 school children in Britain across all ages suffer from poor working memory, which had a more detrimental effect on their learning abilities than intelligence measures. The authors developed the Working Memory Rating Scale (WMRS) on the basis of interviews with teachers to provide a quick way for early identification of working memory problems that could impair learning.

Burden (2005) found that children with attention deficit and hyperactivity disorder (ADHD) and non-ADHD groups performed similarly on tests of *explicit* memory (recall and recognition) and on *perceptual* aspects of implicit memory (word stem completion and picture fragment identification) as a function of age, retention interval and the stimulus used (i.e. showing a picture or word). However, boys diagnosed with ADHD seemed to struggle with a *unique* kind of memory deficit associated purely with the condition. In other words, there are both similarities and crucial differences in the memory functions of children with and without the disorder. DuPaul *et al.* (2011) stress the importance of forming partnerships among school professionals, such as between teachers and psychologists, to work collaboratively on providing interventions for children with the condition.

It is self-evident that pupils are more likely to remember facts and understand information when the topic is interesting and relevant to them, so the best teachers are constantly seeking ways to enliven repetitive lessons through creative and interactive means, such as role play, stories and use of visual images. Using multiple and entertaining ways to study enhances learning for all children, but especially for those with poor recall, as the combination of different and captivating approaches makes the work quite literally 'memorable'. Highly motivated children are also more likely to share what they have done in school with family and friends, thereby further reinforcing learning through discussion and having to order their thinking to communicate their ideas.

Questions to consider and discuss

- In what ways might a memory weakness impact adversely upon children's learning? What strategies can you use to make learning memorable?
- What strategies might you use to ensure that a child's short-term memory is translated into long-term memory?
- How much credence do you attach to the claim that a poor working memory, rather than low intelligence, is the reason for underperformance in school?

References

Alloway, T.P., Gathercole, S.E. and Kirkwood, H. (2008) *The Working Memory Rating Scale*, London: Pearson Assessment.

Burden, M.J. (2005) 'Implicit memory development in school-age children with ADHD', *Developmental Neuropsychology*, 28 (3), pp. 779–807.

DuPaul, G.J., Weyandt, L.L. and Janusis, G.M. (2011) 'ADHD in the classroom: effective intervention strategies', *Theory into Practice*, 50 (1), pp. 35–42.

Gathercole, S.E. and Alloway, T.P. (2008) *Working Memory and Learning: A Practical Guide for Teachers*, London: Sage.

Teaching and learning issue 20: Television as a learning tool

As the number of families without a television set in the UK can probably be numbered in just a few thousand, it is clear that this medium has a powerful influence on children. Considering that most children spend more time watching TV than any other daily activity, it is hardly surprising that it has a marked impact on their perceptions of the world, attitudes and behaviour. The idea that television can educate effectively is a subject that has generated considerable debate, though nearly all schools take advantage of programmes that are specifically designed for education purposes.

Television can be a powerful entertainment and education tool for children given the right programming, but numerous studies indicate that TV and other popular media can also have a damaging effect. Some studies indicate that, if exposure is unmonitored and unlimited, viewing has the potential to shorten attention span, distort body image, work in conjunction with other factors to escalate obesity, create fear and increase aggressive and antisocial behaviour. Casey *et al.* (2002) advance five reasons to support a negative view of television's educational influence:

1. TV is perceived by most children to be recreational, not educational.
2. Viewing is largely passive, requiring minimal intellectual engagement.
3. Most programmes consist of a one-way flow of information in which the child has little or no control over its pace and delivery.
4. TV depends largely on oral and visual modes and neglects the printed word.
5. Productions edit and reorganise material and, in doing so, deprive children of the skills attached to making decisions about extracting, prioritising and organising complex information so as to be manageable.

Hannaford (2005) goes further and argues that children should not watch television until the age of eight years owing to the fact that the images move too rapidly for the developing child's brain to absorb. In addition, the author insists that the well-documented fact that TV features thousands of acts of violence has a detrimental effect upon the younger child's attitude to life and physiology. By contrast to these negative points, others argue that children quickly learn to distinguish between fact and fantasy, and so are able to enjoy the delights of viewing without appropriating its less desirable facets. Programmes in which there is an active and sometimes interactive element have also increased in number over recent years, such that children are less passive than was previously the case.

Television viewing can deprive children of essential sleep. Heins *et al.* (2007) found that 28 per cent of nine- and ten-year-old German children reported going to bed after 9 pm on week nights; 16 per cent reported watching television for more than three hours daily; and 11 per cent played computer or video games for more than three hours daily. Assuming that primary schoolchildren need to be awake at 7 am on weekdays, only one in four of the children surveyed enjoyed the required nine–ten hours' sleep on weekdays that they ideally require to function efficiently. The children's apparent obsession with visual imagery also appears to have an adverse effect on their concentration levels in school.

Finally, Chudacoff (2007) notes that the toy industry has become closely allied with the television and film industry, based on licensing deals with toy manufacturers, which have raised concerns that media-generated toys limit children's imaginations owing to the familiar storylines that are attached to them that children absorb from regularly viewing the programmes. The tempting sights and sounds from advertising may be stimulating a desire for possessions and instant gratification that blunts the self-discipline attached to waiting for something pleasurable. Such attitudes might be impinging upon pupils' willingness to persevere with tasks and their expectations of tangible rewards for achievements rather than completing a task for its own sake.

Questions to consider and discuss

- What specific educational benefits does television offer?
- How might teachers counteract the negative influences of television, reflected in 'tired minds' and the need for instant gratification?
- In what ways might children's home television viewing be positively utilised in school?

References

Casey, B., Casey, N., Calvert, B., French, L. and Lewis, J. (2002) *Television Studies: Key Concepts*, Abingdon: Routledge.

Chudacoff, H.P. (2007) *Children at Play: An American History*, New York: NYU Press.

Hannaford, C. (2005) *Smart Moves: Why Learning is Not All in Your Head*, Marshall, NC: Great Ocean Publishers.

Heins, E., Seitz, C., Schüz, J., Toschke, A.M., Harth, K., Letzel, S. and Böhler, E. (2007) 'Bedtime, television and computer habits of primary children in Germany', *Gesundheitswesen*, 69 (3), pp. 151–57.

Section C: Classroom practice

Teaching and learning issue 21: Ability grouping

Every teacher groups children for learning, sometimes to make the groups homogeneous with children of similar academic ability in that subject; sometimes to make the groups heterogeneous with a mixture of abilities. Groups based on similar academic ability tend to be more prevalent in mathematics and literacy, whereas the mixed ability groups tend to be used for other curriculum subjects, including physical education and enquiry-based activities. See Chapter 3,

Professional theme 11 and Teaching and learning issue 17 (above) for a discussion about the concept of ability.

Within schools, there are two common ways of organising pupils on the basis of their ability: (1) *streaming*, in which pupils are separated into groups according to their all-round ability – they remain in these groups for all or almost all of their curriculum work; (2) *setting*, in which children are separated into different groups by ability for particular subjects – for example, a child might be in the top set for mathematics and the second set for English. Thus, streaming defines a situation in which all pupils are permanently allocated to a class during the school year on the basis of their overall academic ability: Class 'A' contains the most academic children; Class 'B' contains pupils of average ability; Class 'C' contains children who are least able, and so on. Many teachers of older primary children enjoy teaching pupils who are ability-grouped for mathematics and English because it allows them to focus their planning and teaching more narrowly than if they are faced with widely diverse abilities. On the other hand, pupils who struggle academically need to be taught in smaller groups; as a result, the middle group and upper group sometimes contain larger numbers of pupils.

Studies about children's views have found, unsurprisingly, that the majority of pupils want to be in the top group, especially for reading, because it confers status and feelings of satisfaction. However, children in the middle and lower academic bands seem to prefer all-ability, whole-class lessons so that they don't feel stigmatised by their lesser status, while pupils in the top group enjoy their privileged position. Children in classes where there is no ability grouping seem to be more socially adjusted; what is more, clever pupils have a more positive attitude towards their less able classmates in mixed groups. By contrast, where there is an emphasis on setting, attitudes about, and towards, those in the lower streams by the pupils in the top group tend to be patronising. Additionally, there is some evidence to suggest that pupils of below-average ability in non-streaming schools who are taught by teachers who strongly believe in streaming are disadvantaged, owing to the teacher's subconscious antipathy towards them. By contrast, Condron (2008) found that there is little evidence that ability grouping exacerbates inequality in achievement any more than instruction in situations without ability groups. The situation is therefore far from straightforward but certainly depends to an extent on teachers' attitudes and the way in which less capable children are viewed and treated. In other words, it is the impact of social factors as well as academic organising that affects pupils' attitudes and learning outcomes.

According to research by the Institute of Education (*Millennium Cohort Study*, Hallam and Parsons 2011) about one in six children in the UK is streamed on the basis of ability by the time they are seven years old, with boys more likely to be placed in the bottom stream than girls, who were over-represented in middle streams. The highest incidence of streaming (one in five pupils) from the research was found to be in Wales; the figure was slightly lower in England and Scotland; in Northern Ireland the figure was roughly one child in every ten. The study found no apparent link between stream placement and ethnicity.

Another important finding of Hallam and Parsons's study was that children born in the autumn were statistically more likely to be in the top classes than those with birthdays later in the academic year. The research indicated that children in larger, mixed-sex, non-faith, non-fee-paying schools were more likely to be in streams than pupils in small, independent, single-sex or faith schools. Children at schools with mixed-year groups and those attending larger primary schools were more likely to be streamed than their peers in smaller primary schools, where numbers per year group and staff resources did not permit much flexibility. (See Chapter 4, Challenge 6 for insights into teaching multi-age classes.)

Questions to consider and discuss

- Does the organising of pupils on ability basis benefit teachers or pupils more?
- In what specific ways might a teacher's attitude: (a) lift or (b) further damage struggling pupils' morale?
- Why is there a reluctance to put pupils into ability sets for non-core subjects? What does this decision tell us about our subject priorities and view of learning?

References

Condron, D.J. (2008) 'An early start: skill grouping and unequal reading gains in the elementary years', *The Sociological Quarterly*, 49 (2), pp. 363–94.

Hallam, S. and Parsons, S. (2011) *Millennium Cohort Study*, London: Centre for Longitudinal Studies, Institute of Education.

Teaching and learning issue 22: Alternative education and Steiner-Waldorf

In the United Kingdom, it is a requirement that all children between the ages of five and sixteen years must receive an education appropriate to their maturity and intellectual potential. The vast majority of children attend a school funded through taxation, though independent (fee-paying) schools still flourish, and the growth of many different types of school in recent years, so-called 'free' schools, means that an increasing number of pupils attend schools with a distinctive ethos and curriculum. One of the more celebrated types of schooling defers to a concept of education traceable to principles established by Rudolf Steiner (1861–1925).

Steiner was an innovative academic born in Austria, who fervently believed that education should be designed to meet the changing needs of children as they develop physically, mentally, emotionally and spiritually. He founded Steiner-Waldorf schools that are now commonly referred to more simply as *Steiner Schools*. The name Waldorf is derived from the school that Steiner was asked to open in 1919 for the children of workers at the Waldorf-Astoria cigarette factory in Stuttgart, Germany. Steiner education is posited on the basis that learning should be interdisciplinary and integrate practical and artistic, as well as overtly academic, elements.

The curriculum of the early Steiner schools emphasised the relation of human beings to nature and natural rhythms, including festivals, myths, ancient cultures and celebrations. Today, as then, practical skills – playing a musical instrument, weaving and woodcarving, and knitting and painting – are defended as being an essential part of a child's education, rather than viewed as a fringe activity. The Steiner philosophy rejects the premise commonly associated with mainstream schooling that children and young people should only aim to achieve goals set for them by adults or society in general; rather, they should be closely involved in setting their own agendas. Modern-day Steiner schools are co-educational and fully comprehensive, accepting pupils from between three and eighteen years of age. See Nicol and Taplin (2012) for details relating to early years' Steiner education.

Steiner schools' published aims are to provide an unhurried and creative environment where children can find joy in learning and experience the richness of childhood rather than being directed towards early subject specialisation or placed under intense academic pressures. The curriculum itself is a flexible set of pedagogical guidelines, founded on Steiner's principles that take account of the 'whole child', designed to work in harmony with the different phases of the child's development. The strengths of a Steiner education are claimed to include the following:

- it is appropriate for all children, irrespective of their academic ability, class, ethnicity or religion;
- it takes account of the needs of the whole child;
- it is based on an understanding of the relevance of the different phases of child development;
- it helps develop a love of learning and an enthusiasm for school;
- it sees artistic activity and the development of the imagination as integral to learning;
- it is tried and tested and part of state-funded, mainstream provision;
- it produces very able young people, who have a strong sense of self and diverse capacities that enable them to become socially and economically responsible citizens.

While the majority of primary teachers in state-funded schools would doubtless applaud many of the above objectives, the pressure from Government to ensure that pupils meet pre-established academic targets has, in many cases, created an underlying unease about deviating too far from conventional pedagogy or the prescribed curriculum. On the other hand, evidence from inspections suggests that schools that commit time and resources to foster a creative environment are successful in achieving high standards using more formal measures of achievement.

Questions to consider and discuss

- Which theories of learning appear to underpin the Steiner philosophy of education?
- To what extent are the priorities of Steiner schools visible in, and different from, mainstream practice?
- What do you understand by the oft-used expression 'educating the whole child'?

Reference

Nicol, J. and Taplin, J. (2012) *Understanding the Steiner Waldorf Approach: Early Years Education in Practice*, Abingdon: Routledge.

Teaching and learning issue 23: Maintaining discipline

Losing control of the class is every new teacher's secret fear and 'behaviour management' has emerged as the favoured strategy for ensuring that pupils do what they are told, when they are told, and in the manner expected by the adult in charge (normally the teacher). Whether, in fact, it is ever possible or desirable for a teacher to 'manage' the way a child behaves is open to question, not least because the word 'behaviour' includes other characteristics such as exhibiting shyness, level of engagement with mainstream activities, idleness, assertiveness, social attitudes and so forth. Nelson (2006) insists that the key to positive discipline is not punishment but mutual respect.

The word 'discipline' is normally reserved for the actions taken by the person in authority (a teacher, parent or helper) to modify the behaviour of the subordinate (the child), especially to teach self-control and conform to accepted norms. Consequently, a working definition of *behaviour* refers to children's actions and decisions, whereas *discipline* refers to the words and actions of adults that are used to guide children in making appropriate decisions about their behaviour and, where necessary, invoking sanctions when the behaviour is inappropriate. (See also Chapter 3, Professional themes 34–37.)

Classroom disruption in primary schools in England appears to be a significant problem for some teachers. Teachers place the blame for unruly behaviour on the apparent inability of parents to control children at home (see Garner 2008). Some pupils appear to lack the social skills required to get on in class owing to highly permissive parents who admit to indulging their children, often for the sake of peace or because they run out of alternative incentives and effective sanctions.

Results of a longitudinal study by Sammons *et al.* (2008) about the influence of school on three- to eleven-year-old children's cognitive and social/ behavioural development in England – referred to as EPPE 3–11 – showed (amongst many other things) that pupils who most enjoyed primary schools were not necessarily those who achieved highly, but that this depended to a large extent on the prevailing standard of behaviour in school. Thus, the quality of enjoyment seemed to be linked closely to pupils' perceptions that teachers were interested in them as individuals and capable of ensuring good behaviour throughout the class.

Taking appropriate action when faced with poor behaviour is one of the challenges that teachers face as they seek to establish a well controlled yet inspiring classroom environment. Experience shows that teachers who tolerate minor instances of unacceptable behaviour regret doing so, as the minority of pupils that take advantage early will continue to test the boundaries. Some inexperienced teachers reflect sadly that they were 'too soft' early on in their teaching and insufficiently firm in the opening encounters with a new class. By contrast, other teachers employ unnecessarily heavy-handed tactics when a lighter touch would be more appropriate, thereby causing ill feeling and dismay among the children. All teachers have to exercise sound judgement about the forcefulness of their insistence, as being fierce rather than firm sours the atmosphere, creates unease among more timid children and disrupts the smooth flow of a lesson. Unfortunately, some children misinterpret a teacher's reasonableness as a sign of weakness.

Wright (2006) emphasises the concept of passivity, warning that 'the passive teacher is characterised by efforts to be popular that include ingratiating herself. She will have fragile feelings and will take criticism badly' (p. 58). Children like adults who are fair-minded, interested in them as people, transparent in their dealings, clear about their intentions, helpful in their explanations, non-judgemental in their words and unflinching in confronting unsatisfactory situations when necessary. Surveys to determine what type of teacher is most popular nearly always place those with good discipline coupled with good humour near the top.

Canter (1998) claims that an *assertive discipline* approach is based on the idea that pupils and teachers have rights as well as responsibilities, such that pupils need and respond to limits set by teachers, and teachers ensure those limits are established and maintained. Assertive discipline can only succeed in a positive classroom atmosphere in which pupils' needs are met, classroom rules and regulations are planned and implemented consistently, children are taught how to behave appropriately, and teachers engage in productive dialogue with pupils who behave unacceptably. Assertive teachers effectively communicate the type of behaviour they expect and how they intend to achieve this behaviour, notably the sanction attached to a particular type of action. Importantly, teachers must carry through their stated intentions without fear or favour. In addition, however, teachers must respond positively to pupils who display appropriate classroom behaviour, as a means of recognising children's efforts to conform to and achieve the goals set for them. Throughout the process of 'child-action, adult reaction', teachers must act relationally and not in a contrived 'detached' manner reminiscent of a judge in court.

Some teachers believe that 'punishment' is a more appropriate term than sanction because it stresses the fact that misdemeanours result in consequences for the miscreant. Other teachers avoid sanctions altogether unless it is absolutely necessary, preferring to enhance the quality of learning and stress the benefits of behaving well. In truth, both extreme positions are untenable. Punishments do not address the root causes of the behaviour, whereas relying on pupils' willingness to respond positively to a teacher's goodwill is ignoring the fact that some children enjoy being naughty and won't control their actions voluntarily. Nevertheless, it is undoubtedly true that teachers who trust their children and are well disposed towards them nearly always reap dividends.

There are some principles to consider when implementing any form of discipline:

■ Be consistent in applying sanctions.

This principle is not always possible, as a persistent offender might require a different sanction from the occasional transgressor. Nevertheless, make it your aim to treat pupils in broadly the same way to maintain consistency and avoid accusations of favouritism. It is confusing for children and creates a degree of discord if something pupils do on one occasion earns a negative consequence but similar behaviour is overlooked on another occasion. Even this apparently fair rule is not always applicable; during special times of excitement (sporting events, wet playtimes, the final day of term, etc.) it is good to show some flexibility and exercise common sense in approach and not be harshly judgemental.

- Employ short and manageable sanctions.

Sanctions should not be harsh, punitive or borne solely of your desire to exhibit a 'show them who is boss' mentality. Adopting a short and manageable sanction has two benefits. First, you are not caught up in a prolonged monitoring or supervising process. Second, the child is given an opportunity to show a repentant attitude and succeed quickly afterwards, thereby inviting praise and approval. For example, if you withdraw a prized piece of equipment for (say) five minutes because two pupils are at loggerheads over its use, they will have to solve the problem in a different way and, when the equipment is returned, learn to be co-operative rather than selfish if they want to continue with the privilege of using it. The sanction is brief yet effective. By contrast, a sanction that involves (say) a child being kept in each break time for one week involves considerable inconvenience for you and is scarcely worth pursuing other than in extreme circumstances (e.g. to prevent bullying). The essence of effective management is to keep everything in proportion and be decisive without overreacting.

- Clarify the likely consequences of pupils' actions.

When indiscipline invites sanctions, it is often sufficient to resolve the matter immediately rather than delay the consequence. For instance, a garrulous child might be told to remain silent for a period of time (five minutes, say) or face a harsher penalty at a later stage. This two-part strategy should not be confused with threatening a child, which is a poor substitute for firm, fair, instant action; for example, 'If you don't keep quiet I'll be sending you to the headmaster!' is clear but far too punitive and should only be used as a last resort. While clarifying the likely consequences of inappropriate actions is important, the best teachers nevertheless ensure that they focus first and foremost on the positive outcomes that will result from sensible behaviour, and only refer to the sanctions attached to poor behaviour as a way of contrasting them with the good. For example, to praise a pupil and promise him the chance to be 'first in the queue for home time' (which is a much-cherished reward for many younger children) when he tries hard to be obedient is preferable to warning him that he will be last in the queue if he disobeys. Furthermore, teachers who talk regularly to their pupils about the consequences of poor and of good behaviour are less likely to be faced with resentful and angry individuals when the sanctions have to be implemented. Explaining why a sanction is being imposed should not, of course, result in a discussion between you and the pupil about its appropriateness. You have the final word. Even so, always have in the back of your mind how you would justify the sanction to the child's parent, were you to be asked.

■ Give fair warning before you implement the consequence.

Inexperienced or agitated teachers sometimes impose a sanction with minimal warning when it would be far better to slow the tempo and calmly announce their intentions. For example: 'Stop, please, and listen to me. I have asked you to keep your voices low three times. I shan't warn you again. I'll simply put a cross on the board every time the noise gets too high. The number of crosses will equal the number of minutes you miss of your playtime. Now carry on working, please.' Some teachers fall into the trap of giving repeated warnings and not following them through, which makes their task of maintaining order much harder, as the children do not treat them seriously. The exception to imposing a sanction without warning might be where a pupil deliberately disobeys a well-established rule that is known and accepted by everyone (e.g. to walk not run in the classroom), though it is essential to distinguish wilfulness from forgetfulness. A reminder is preferable to imposing a sanction, if the child had a momentary lapse of concentration.

■ Do not impose a sanction when you are feeling very angry.

Anger is the great deceiver; it makes us feel that we are being decisive when in fact our senses are dulled. Decisions made when we are angry are likely to be ill judged, too harsh or simply unjust. It is far better to halt proceedings and say to the children something stern such as, 'I am feeling rather cross at the moment. I want you to carry on with your work in absolute silence until I decide what to do.' The period of silence should be no more than about one minute. If a child breaks the silence, a simple finger on the lips is normally adequate to rectify the situation. Once you have calmed down, announce your decision.

■ Employ peer mediation.

Peer mediation is a conflict resolution tool that schools can use to help pupils sort out some of their problems on their own or with minimal adult involvement. Children and young people are trained in the principles and skills of mediation to help disputants of their own age group or younger find solutions to issues that are causing friction between them. Baginsky (2004) claims that peer mediation has the potential to engender a more relaxed and positive learning climate and reduce staff time in dealing with pupil conflicts. Others view it as adults abrogating their responsibilities.

Questions to consider and discuss

■ What rights and responsibilities do pupils have? Do these vary according to the child's age?
■ How might you ensure that you effectively communicate the behaviour required of your pupils? How will you know if you are successful?

■ What characterises a teacher's 'positive but fair response' from a pupil's perspective? What might they say to their parents when relating the event?

References

Baginsky, W. (2004) *Peer Mediation in the UK: A Guide for Schools*, London: NSPCC.

Canter, L. (1998) 'The assertive discipline approach', in H. Ayers and F. Gray (eds) *Classroom Management*, London: David Fulton.

Garner, R. (2008) 'Parents get the blame for naughty children', *The Independent*, 24th November.

Nelson, J. (2006) *Positive Discipline*, New York: Ballantine Books.

Sammons, P., Sylva, K., Melhuish, E., Siraj-Blatchford, I. and Taggart, B. (2008) *The Effective Pre-school and Primary Education 3–11 Project (EPPE 3–11): Influences on Children's Development and Progress in Key Stage 2*, London: DCSF/ Institute of Education, University of London.

Wright, D. (2006) *Classroom Karma*, London: David Fulton.

Teaching and learning issue 24: The use of rewards and incentives

There is a widespread assumption that rewards encourage children to work harder and persevere to achieve the goals that have been set for them. Most teachers employ stickers, 'smiley' pictures, extra playtime and the like as a means of promoting a positive attitude in pupils. There is also evidence from studies during the mid-twentieth century that, although offering incentives has the desired effect in the short term, it can be detrimental in the long term for two reasons. First, it denies children the opportunity to develop their internal motivation; that is, a desire to learn for its own sake and not based on external inducements. Second, although children respond well initially to tasks that carry rewards, their enthusiasm wanes quite rapidly afterwards. By contrast, involvement in activities that bring an unexpected reward or no reward at all seems to be more deeply meaningful for children as time goes by. In practice, the best teachers utilise a variety of incentives, both verbal and visual, and foster a belief that achievement is rewarding for its own sake.

A study by Harrop and Williams (1992) into rewards and punishments in the primary school found that primary pupils' views about suitable rewards were different from those of teachers in a number of respects. Findings showed that, whereas teachers tended to believe that adult approval *within* school – such as public praise and merit points – constitutes the most powerful reward, children particularly valued adult approval *outside* school (notably, parental satisfaction). The top ten motivational factors for children were as follows:

1. parents informed about good behaviour
2. good written comments made about work
3. good marks awarded
4. work put on display
5. achievement mentioned in assembly
6. private praise from an adult
7. praise given in front of other pupils
8. the whole class praised

9. merit or house points allocated by the teacher
10. praise given from other pupils.

By contrast, teachers placed the above factors in the following order:

1. praise given in front of other pupils
2. merit or house points allocated by the teacher
3. achievement mentioned in assembly
4. good written comments made about work
5. private praise from an adult
6. work put on display
7. the whole class praised
8. parents informed about good behaviour
9. good marks awarded
10. praise from other pupils.

In a major study of eleven- and twelve-year-olds, Shreeve (2002) found that, in schools where the pupils are motivated by an intrinsic desire to learn and achieve, formal systems of rewards and penalties were often unnecessary. Behaviour management was established and maintained by means of a positive relationship between teacher and pupil, good lesson planning and the provision of interesting work. Penalties were rarely used by teachers to signal disapproval.

Questions to consider and discuss

■ What are the implications of the Harrop and Williams survey for teachers and teaching?
■ What factors should be taken into account when deciding the nature of rewards and how to allocate them?
■ What are the advantages and disadvantages of a formal system of rewards and penalties?

References

Harrop, A. and Williams, T. (1992) 'Rewards and punishments in the primary school: pupils' perceptions and teachers' usage', *Educational Psychology*, 7 (4), pp. 211–15.
Shreeve, A. (2002) 'Student perceptions of rewards and sanctions', *Pedagogy, Culture and Society*, 10 (2), pp. 239–56.

Teaching and learning issue 25: Pupil time on task

Time on task is defined as the amount of time that pupils spend directly involved and concentrating on curriculum activities. Studies suggest that an average child's formal attention span (in minutes) is approximately as long as the age of the child; in other words, a five-year-old can normally only manage five minutes of *uninterrupted* concentration, while a ten-year-old can manage twice that amount. Croll (1996) argues that time on task is important to teachers for at least three reasons. First, it is one of the factors that influences academic achievement, though there are, of course, many other factors that have an impact, such as pupil and adult motivation, relevance of the work, behaviour and discipline, and health. The second reason is that children with 'time on their hands' usually find unhelpful distractions that make discipline more challenging to enforce. Third, high levels of time on task are equated with high levels of whole-class interaction; engagement with the work leads to heightened enthusiasm and responsiveness from across the class rather than from isolated pockets of keen children.

When teachers interact with the whole group or class – as opposed to children being an audience with the teacher doing all the talking – through questions, inviting suggestions, offering feedback, summarising conflicting opinions and showing lively interest in children's ideas, not only are high rates of time on task maintained during the interactive phase but also during the individual work that normally follows. In other words, where teachers spend more time in whole-class interaction, children are also more on-task when they work on their own.

In a study of nine-year-old children in numeracy classes, Chalk and Bizo (2004) found that *specific* praise (i.e. praise that highlighted a precise aspect of a child's work) promoted more on-task behaviour (i.e. concentrating on the work in hand) than even positive praise (i.e. general congratulatory praise, such as 'good, well done!') and significantly increased pupils' academic self-concept, the so-called feel-good factor. The major implication of this finding is that children take their work seriously and expect that teachers will do the same, as reflected in giving each child targeted feedback and commendation where appropriate.

Questions to consider and discuss

- How might the claim that a child's undivided attention span (in minutes) is approximately as long as the age of the child impact upon practice?
- How might time on task vary according to the activity being undertaken, for instance, completing a set of sums, investigating a scientific phenomenon, designing a short piece of drama with a partner, writing a fictional story?
- What are the possible explanations for the fact that specific praise has such a liberating effect on children compared with general positive praise? What are the implications for formative assessment? (See Teaching and learning issue 28 later in this chapter.)

References

Chalk, K. and Bizo, L.A. (2004) 'Specific praise improves on-task behaviour and numeracy enjoyment: a study of year four pupils engaged in the numeracy hour', *Educational Psychology in Practice*, 20 (4), pp. 335–51.

Croll, P. (1996) 'Teacher-pupil interaction in the classroom', in P. Croll and N. Hastings (eds) *Effective Primary Teaching*, London: David Fulton.

Teaching and learning issue 26: Boys and girls in school

During the later part of the twentieth century it was popular to declare that there was 'no difference' between boys and girls other than biological ones, with the result that every child should be 'treated the same'. In retrospect, such a faulty diagnosis would almost be amusing were it not for the fact that some people accepted the premise without question, one consequence of which was the spawning of numerous influential writers and educators pursuing the agenda with unremitting zeal. Classroom practitioners, who were well aware of differences in attitude and aptitude, were confused as they attempted to comply with what was clearly a simplistic view of children. Thankfully, since those days we have recovered a more measured and accurate view of the ways in which boys and girls are similar in their learning preferences and responses, and ways in which they differ. Of course, it is also evidently the case that it is foolish and educationally unsound to consider the needs of all boys, and the needs of all girls, as being broadly the same across each sex. Every child has unique strengths, weaknesses and propensity for learning in particular ways. What we can reasonably claim is that specific learning characteristics apply to the majority of boys, just as specific but different learning characteristics apply to the majority of girls.

It is a 'suburban myth' that girls outperform boys in every aspect of schooling at all levels. However, it is certainly the case that the literacy skills of most girls advance more rapidly than those for the majority of boys. On the whole, girls apply themselves to their work conscientiously and enjoy being neat, tidy and correct, in stark contrast to a large proportion of boys. It is also true that the majority of pupils designated as having special educational needs are boys; the same statistic is true for pupils experiencing behavioural difficulties. However, it has been shown that boys tend to cope better than girls with solving problems, especially those requiring an awareness of spatial factors and number. Furthermore, boys often have greater enthusiasm for technology and construction, and being neat, tidy and conscientious is not a priority compared with getting the job done. However, these generalisations do not tell the whole story, as adult expectations and attitudes to boys and girls can influence their confidence and willingness to apply themselves to the subject. For instance, younger girls can be intimidated by boys who behave roughly, and avoid playing with construction toys as a result; similarly, some older boys can be very assertive when dealing with information technology, with the result that girls' interests are subordinated to their own. Teachers not only need to examine the factors affecting children's behaviour but also their own responses and class management strategies to ensure that every child gets a fair chance.

In Northern Ireland, the annual *Kids' Life and Times* survey is an evaluation of all eleven-year-old children in Northern Ireland, conducted by Queen's University Belfast and the University of Ulster, about what they think of school and other issues that are of importance to them. The 2008 survey found that 26 per cent of primary seven boys were completely happy coming to school, compared with 44 per cent of girls. Boys were less happy than girls with writing, reading, spelling, working by themselves and coming to school. The survey also found that just over half of older primary children think pupils in their school have been bullied. In the 2009 survey, girls were reportedly happier than boys at school, with some 84 per cent of girls and 73 per cent of boys saying that they were 'mostly happy' at school. More than one-fifth

(22 per cent) of top primary school children reported at the time that they had been physically bullied at school in the previous two months. Another 36 per cent reported being bullied in other ways at different times. Significantly, children who said they were mostly unhappy at school were seven times more likely to say they had been bullied during the previous two months.

In her study of older primary age pupils, Renold (2005) noted that primary school is a key social arena for exploring sexuality, which in turn shapes children's friendships and peer relations. Results from her research showed that, from a pupil perspective, being a 'proper' girl or boy involves investing in a heterosexual identity; as a consequence, children used gendered or sexual insults to maintain gender and sexual norms. Renold also observed that, while the children subscribed to the dominant versions of gender (reflecting predominant societal views on 'maleness' and 'femaleness'), they also made attempts to resist such stereotyping. The author proposes that educators should construct sex and relationships education in such a way that it provides children with knowledge that is critical, progressive and empowering rather than merely 'utilitarian'. It is also worth noting the sobering fact that children learn a great deal, not only from teachers and other adults, but also but from each other, especially in the playground.

Questions to consider and discuss

- What factors might impact on the contrasting attitudes to school of boys and girls?
- What steps might teachers take to address the relative lack of enthusiasm for learning among some boys?
- How can teachers ensure that all pupils gain the maximum benefit from their schooling, both academically and socially?

Reference

Renold, E. (2005) *Girls, Boys and Junior Sexualities*, Abingdon: Routledge.

Teaching and learning issue 27: Raising boys' achievement

One of the issues occupying the minds of teachers is a concern that boys are underachieving while girls are fulfilling their potential. Not all educators agree about the level and extent of the problem of boys' underachievement or even whether it exists at all; even so, teachers have expressed concern about their perception that the gap between boys' and girls' achievements and positive attitude to school in general is wide and tending to increase. (See also Teaching and learning issue 26 above.) In addressing these challenges, it is often assumed that girls as a group outperform boys across the whole curriculum; in fact, boys broadly match girls in the areas of mathematics and science. The one area of the curriculum where boys seem to underachieve is English; in particular, poor reading and writing scores at primary school are directly linked with low achievement in secondary school. Martino *et al.* (2009) explore issues associated with the theories, politics and realities of boys' education across the world, the role of male teachers and strategies for dealing with boys who are on the margins of the system.

Research by Cawdell (2000), based on twenty-three teachers in three infant/nursery schools and three junior schools, highlighted the importance of raising boys' self-esteem. The research project was established (a) to identify factors that influence boys' learning negatively; and (b) to find ways of overcoming the influences. From observations in the case study schools, good practice in supporting boys' learning incorporated the following seven strategies:

1. Giving pupils more responsibilities, such as training boys with low self-esteem to act as partners assisting less able boys in reading.
2. Implementing behaviour policies to counteract 'boy culture' activities such as bullying, sexual harassment and swearing.
3. Careful grouping of pupils to complement pupils' individual strengths.
4. Developing a strong partnership with home at an early stage in children's reading activities.
5. Monitoring and analysing gender differences in the interactions between teachers and pupils and using it to inform practice.
6. Modifying learning materials to balance gender bias in content or style.
7. Presenting boys with short, achievable tasks.

Other important findings included the need to: (a) provide clear lesson structures, as some boys struggled to stay on-task with more open-ended activities where they had to control and physically organise themselves; and (b) get to know more about boys' expectations and aspirations, fears and concerns. Importantly, however, any interventions designed to address boys' attainment must not act to the detriment of girls.

The *Raising Boys' Achievement* project (see Ford 2009) examined exciting and innovative ways of raising achievement across a range of primary, secondary and special schools. By working with over sixty schools across England, the research team identified and evaluated strategies that are particularly helping in motivating boys. Significant factors included: (a) a clearly articulated ethos with a focus on the individual; (b) a friendly, caring environment; (c) a culture of equality where no one is allowed to dominate; and (d) an emphasis on enhancing self-esteem and confidence.

Many boys thrive in an active environment where they can use their hands as well as heads, so teachers do well to ensure that lessons are not dominated by talk and writing. It is a common experience that boys enjoy stimulating interaction with the teacher, contributing ideas verbally and doing practical tasks, but then lose their enthusiasm for learning during the 'writing-up' phase. (See also Chapter 3, Professional theme 41.) There is also some evidence to suggest that other factors that have the potential to assist achievement include: the use of merit awards, badges, achievement assemblies, 'choosing time' (freedom to select what to do from a range of options), an emphasis on a disciplined environment, and giving rewards and praise, all located within a learning climate in which there are high expectations of each child. Finally, clear routines, carefully explained and reinforced, provide a sense of security and help to reduce conflict that might arise under more lax conditions.

In a world saturated with detailed sources of information, even the most outstanding teacher can introduce children to only a proportion of all the available knowledge. So, in addition to the so-called 'basics' of reading, writing, mathematics and use of ICT, teachers need to concentrate on developing pupils' capacity to work with others, find out information and use their imaginations and creativity to solve problems. To gain the greatest benefit from their schooling, every pupil needs to develop qualities of co-operation, inventiveness, empathy and perseverance. They have to learn to be respectful of the rights of others and show determination to succeed. In addition, however, some pupils require a change of attitude and have to be convinced, encouraged or otherwise persuaded that success demands hard work and determination. A resolute pupil (boy or girl) of average ability with a good attitude will eventually achieve more success than an indifferent, intelligent one.

Questions to consider and discuss

- How can you teach boys in a way appropriate to their needs without disadvantaging the girls?
- To what extent is the list of suggestions to 'assist achievement' exclusive to boys?
- How is it possible to reconcile imaginative teaching and learning with the need for 'clear routines'?

References

Cawdell, S. (2000) 'How can primary schools encourage boys to develop a more positive attitude towards learning?' TTA publication no. 82, pp. 9–99, London: Crown Copyright.

Ford, C. (2009) *Practical Advice on How to Inspire Boys*, London: Optimus Education.

Martino, W., Kehler, M.D. and Weaver-Hightower, M.B. (2009) *The Problem With Boys' Education*, Abingdon: Routledge.

Teaching and learning issue 28: Use of formative assessment

Assessment of pupil learning has become endemic in schools and is seen as a means of identifying and subsequently rectifying or building on existing knowledge and understanding. The argument propounded to support close assessment of pupils relies on a belief that noting achievement in specific curriculum areas provides teachers with the insights about children that allow for appropriate guidance and intervention, and facilitate higher standards of attainment. Top teachers know that, to be of optimum value, the process of assessment must be located in the overall framework of planning, practice and recording, in the following way:

Planning for teaching and learning: based on the school's agreed curriculum programme
↓
Teacher assessment for learning (formative assessment): daily observation and professional judgements based on the quality of work that children are producing
↓
Modified practice: adjustment of work patterns on the basis of the formative assessment
↓
Evaluative assessment (assessment of learning): focused judgements with reference to National Curriculum (NC) documents
↓
Recorded findings: using recording sheets
↓
Reporting findings: to parents and colleagues, in person or in writing.

Bennett (2011) argues that there are six interrelated issues in formative assessment, as follows: (1) reaching an agreed definition of formative assessment; (2) the claims commonly made for its effectiveness; (3) the limited attention given to domain (different areas of learning) considerations; (4) the under-representation of measurement principles in our understanding; (5) the teacher-support demands that formative assessment entails; and (6) the impact of the larger educational system. Bennett concludes that the phrase 'formative assessment' does not yet represent a well-defined set of artefacts or practices, such that it is both conceptually and practically a work in progress. As a result, we need to be more sensible in our claims about it, as well as in our expectations for it.

Briggs *et al.* (2008) claim that assessment is the process of finding out about what children can do and where there may be difficulties. They go on to say:

> At its best, it provides clear information for the planning of teaching and learning, or at least for further targeted areas. At its worst, it is the process of collecting lots of data that are not used to inform individual or group needs.
>
> (p. 7)

In recent years the process of *formative* assessment has been 'rebranded' as 'assessment for learning' (AFL), with an emphasis on the word 'for', and involves the teacher and each pupil being engaged in a continual review of progress. It is more or less assumed that formative assessment (i.e. information given to pupils during times of active learning) supports and enhances pupil learning. In an ideal world, you should conduct assessments with the child present, but in practice you might have to evaluate the work independently and later inform the children of the outcome. Assessment of work in art and design is normally verbal and ungraded; that is to say that, especially in the case of younger pupils, individual efforts are commended, regardless of the quality of the outcome. There is greater emphasis on assessment *of* learning (AOL) among older primary pupils; by contrast, teachers spend more time on the more immediate formative assessment ('assessment for learning', AFL) with younger ones.

Kirton *et al.* (2007) reported from a study about formative assessment in sixteen Scottish primary schools and two junior high schools. They concluded that there was some evidence that use of formative assessment 'led to pupils taking more responsibility for their learning, contributing to improved motivation, confidence and classroom achievement, especially for lower attainers' (p. 605). The authors warned, however, that the tension between constructive formative assessment and summative assessment (assessment of learning) is an uneasy one for the simple reason that formal assessments through testing assume such significance for teachers and pupils. 'Such a tension between summative and formative assessment needs to be resolved so that the dominance of assessment for accountability does not drive out assessment for learning' (p. 624). They quote one pupil who, when asked about formal assessment, replied that, if you got it wrong in a national test, 'to me it would be the end of your life'. It is clear that, from both an academic and personal perspective, the stakes are high.

The manner in which teachers employ formative assessment makes a considerable difference to the way in which pupils respond. A teacher who insists on finding fault with a pupil's work without an accompanying word of encouragement is unlikely to motivate the child. A teacher who is full of praise but rarely shows a pupil where work can be improved can expect mediocrity in quality. A teacher who combines explicit praise with clear guidance about the best way to progress has found the correct balance of commendation and correction, which inevitably leads to an improvement in standards.

Questions to consider and discuss

- How would you rate your assessment practice in the light of the Briggs *et al.* quotation above?
- How much does the practice of formatively assessing pupil progress vary across different subject areas? What message does this variation carry about priorities and evaluating success?
- How would you describe your feedback 'manner'? How might you improve it?

References

Bennett, R.E. (2011) 'Formative assessment: a critical review', *Assessment in Education*, 18 (1), pp. 5–25.

Briggs, M., Woodfield, A., Martin, C. and Swatton, P. (2008) *Assessment for Learning and Teaching in Primary Schools*, Exeter: Learning Matters.

Kirton, A., Hallam, S., Peffers, J., Robertson, P. and Stobart, G. (2007) 'Revolution, evolution or a Trojan horse? Piloting assessment for learning in some Scottish primary schools', *British Educational Research Journal*, 33 (4), pp. 605–27.

Teaching and learning issue 29: The value of speaking and listening

The educational value of speaking and listening (sometimes referred to as 'oracy') rests on a belief that combining children's knowledge, understanding and insights through allowing them opportunity to talk together and hear what others say about a topic of common interest leads to deeper learning than would occur with one pupil working alone. Exploratory talk of this kind is an effective way of using language to think, which forms one of the principal building blocks of literacy.

Although the vast majority of children arrive in school with the capacity to talk, discuss and contribute ideas, there are concerns about a growing number that seem unable to express themselves clearly. Studies suggest that parents are talking less to their children at home due to the need to work long hours and the isolating influence of television and electronic games. (See Teaching and learning issue 20 earlier.) This worrying trend is supported by a study from the USA by Griffin *et al.* (2004) that provided evidence to show that early oral discourse is a predictor of later reading and writing skills. Thirty-two children participated in speaking tasks at the age of five years and reading comprehension and writing assessments at the age of eight years. The research found that children's ability to mark the significance of narrated events (i.e. events told to them) at age five predicted reading comprehension skills at age eight. Children's ability to include content knowledge ('facts') in expository talk at age five also predicted their reading comprehension at age eight.

While it is important that pupils talk freely and develop a good vocabulary, teachers have to ensure that the talk is effective and useful for learning, rather than merely conversational. Children have to be taught how to speak meaningfully to one another and encouraged to listen carefully to what others are saying. Such skills do not always come easily to younger children, who are often over-eager to express their own views and share their own ideas. By posing interesting and speculative questions, inviting children to think aloud, and offering alternative explanations for events and phenomena, teachers can gradually foster a more inquisitive attitude and thirst to discover more. (See Chapter 1, Learning Skill 12.)

To promote listening, teachers encourage pupils to wait their turn while a classmate is speaking and carefully attend to what the other child is saying. However, effective listening involves more than hearing the words and taking them at face value. It also entails observation of the speaker's body language, registering the feelings and perceptions that lie behind the words, being sensitive towards verbal clues and making inferences from the tone of voice. As they develop these skills, children gradually come to acknowledge that views other than their own exist and understand that their own opinions and judgements are open to scrutiny and criticism from others. To make classroom talk purposeful, children must not only understand the rules for taking turns and offering their opinions, but also learn strategies for expressing ideas openly and enabling everyone else to do the same. As many adults struggle to accomplish these things, it is not surprising that some children are similarly challenged.

Questions to consider and discuss

■ What insights do we gain from the Griffin *et al.* study about the importance of speaking and listening?

- What significance should we attach to the phenomenon that some children chatter freely outside the classroom yet they remain largely silent when they are in formal learning situations?
- When do children have opportunities for expository talk (explaining and demonstrating) in your class? How might the position be improved?

Reference

Griffin, T.M., Hemphill, L., Camp, L. and Palmer Wolf, D. (2004) 'Oral discourse in the preschool years and later literacy skills', *First Language*, 24, pp. 123–47.

Teaching and learning issue 30: Learning to read

There are four basic approaches to reading: (1) The 'look and say' method, where children learn to recognise whole words or sentences rather than individual letter sounds; (2) an 'experiential' approach using the child's own words to help him or her read – the child provides a word or sentence for the adult to write down and in due course reads the words aloud; (3) the 'context' method that involves using books selected by children; this approach is based on the belief that they will be more enthusiastic about reading a relevant text that interests them than books that are chosen for them; (4) phonics, that relies on children learning the names of the letters of the alphabet and the sounds they make, then blending two letters together to make simple words, followed by three letters, and so on.

Recently, the Government has emphasised the importance of every primary teacher being an excellent teacher of reading. While the National Literacy Strategy that was introduced in the late 1990s is said to have increased levels of attainment in reading, as measured by national tests, the *PIRLS (Progress in International Reading Literacy Study) Report* by Twist *et al.* (2007) noted a concomitant decrease in reading for pleasure. The report compared the progress of British children with their international counterparts in Europe and elsewhere and suggested that British pupils were losing their love for reading, not least because of the uninspiring manner in which literacy was taught in school.

The report suggested that blame for this loss of motivation for reading is a direct result of national policy during the first years of the twenty-first century that emphasised the teaching of reading in terms of a narrow set of skills. Under government direction, phonics and word recognition, coupled with language comprehension, were focused on at the expense of a wider view of reading – an approach that was formerly referred to as 'barking at print'; that is, reading words correctly but without comprehending their meaning.

In responding to government advice, the tendency of teachers to isolate and closely analyse passages of text that had been lifted from the body of the chapter or story contributed to a situation in which children viewed reading as purely functional (e.g. for information or evaluating an author's opinion) rather than functional *and* pleasurable. Even among some teachers of younger children, the ubiquitous habit of ending a story-time with questions about details contained in the text appears to have damaged the depth of enjoyment that pupils experience from hearing a story read to them.

Mart (2011) declares that her aim is to re-establish the importance of 'becoming a reader' rather than just a child who can read. She argues that readers need nurturing, so the teacher with whom pupils share at least one year of their lives is essential as an excellent role model to feed the children's imaginations and develop their appetite for reading a wide range of material. The author further stresses the importance of teachers as readers and their role as 'lead reader' in their classrooms. In fact, Mart goes so far as to insist that teachers are as important as the children's parents, friends and relations in providing an example of being an enthusiastic reader. Similarly, Whetton *et al.* (2007) claim that it is essential that teachers convey positive attitudes by becoming model readers for and with their pupils, showing enthusiasm for the written word and allowing children to 'lose' themselves in the wonder of the tale.

During the twenty-first century, there has been a revival of interest in the use of phonics to underpin the act of reading and spelling. Enthusiasm for specific approaches such as 'synthetic phonics' mesmerised government ministers of every persuasion as they caught a glimpse of a seemingly infallible approach to reading that would boost test scores and raise standards. Understandably, practitioners tend to be suspicious of claims about foolproof methods for the effective teaching of reading, as over the years there has been no shortage of such claims for other approaches, notably the 'whole word' method that relies heavily on visual identification of words, and a 'whole language' approach, which emphasises the importance of contextualised learning. Although the teaching of reading is based around phonics, every possible method, technique and approach available should be utilised, as teachers enthuse about the joys and benefits of reading at every opportunity and use a mixture of methods and strategies to encourage children to become enthusiastic and competent readers. As the authors of one of the most comprehensive and respected publications about reading concluded a generation ago, there is no one method, medium, approach, device or philosophy that holds the key to the process of learning to read (DES 1975, 'The Bullock Report'). The report acknowledged that, although the teaching of reading is always open to improvement, the solution 'does not lie in the triumphant discovery or rediscovery of a particular formula' (p. 77).

Questions to consider and discuss

- What factors might be responsible for children acquiring a thirst for reading – or losing interest in it?
- What do you consider to be 'narrow' and 'broader' sets of reading skills?
- How might teachers convey positive attitudes to pupils about books and reading?

References

Department for Education and Science (DES) (1975) *A Language for Life*, The Bullock Report, London: Crown Copyright.

Mart, L. (2011) *A More Complex View of Reading: Teachers and Children as Readers Together*, Abingdon: Routledge.

Twist, l., Schagen, I. and Hodgson, C. (2007) *Readers and Reading: National Report for England 2006*, Slough: NFER.

Whetton, C., Ruddock, G. and Twist, L. (2007) *Standards in English Primary Education: The International Evidence (Primary Review Research Survey 4/2)*, Cambridge: University of Cambridge.

Section D: The teacher

Teaching and learning issue 31: Teachers as educational agents

It is undeniable that the most significant people in school are the teachers, though the teaching assistant's role is also important in helping to coach pupils who have fallen behind or are struggling, and guide them in the task completion. Teachers find great satisfaction in guiding children and seeing the 'light come on', as they intervene, explain and demonstrate the right way ahead. Nevertheless, the best quality primary education is created by teachers who maintain a balance between, on the one hand, intervening and, on the other hand, encouraging children to explore and interrogate the unknown or areas of knowledge in which they only have tentative understanding.

While it is true that teachers make a vitally important contribution towards children's education, they are not the only agents in the process. Parents, friends, the media and sources of information from books, the Internet and other incidental factors all subscribe to a child's total learning experiences. In fact, it is no exaggeration to say that, in every child's life, the first and prime educator is the parent. A distinction can usefully be made between influences that stem from 'natural societal setting' and those that emerge out of 'formal instructional setting', whereby the first influence (natural settings) is described as the everyday world of an individual child's experience at home, work and play – such learning is often referred to as 'incidental'. By contrast, the second influence (formal settings) refers primarily to schools, where a qualified or trainee teacher takes on responsibility for planning and managing instruction, such that the learner is guided towards and hopefully achieves specified objectives.

Based on a narrow definition, educational agents can be considered as people in the employ of a recognised educational institution (such as a school or early learning centre), who are paid to help pupils learn effectively by offering specialist expertise and guidance. An alternative definition of an educational agent is *anyone* who consciously helps another person to learn – whether that help is given directly (as in a lesson) or by creating an appropriate environment to facilitate learning (e.g. an imaginative play situation) or inviting questions (such as between a mother and child while they go shopping) or simply allowing the person to share and talk about an experience, predicament, concern or curiosity. Peer support and organising pupils in co-operative groups also contributes substantially to the educative process, as children learn from one another and gain confidence by being a member of a successful collaborative enterprise.

Questions to consider and discuss

- What characterises the process of teaching and being taught?
- What can a parent teach a child that a teacher cannot, and vice versa?
- How might a teacher exploit the expertise that resides in other educational agents, including children's peers and the media?

Teaching and learning issue 32: Gender, teachers and teaching

Around 80 per cent of primary teachers and the vast majority of teaching assistants are female. The number of male adults working in the early years is extremely small. Approximately one in four primary schools in England does not have any men on the staff, though a variety of government initiatives to encourage men into teaching, coupled with rising unemployment figures, have boosted numbers slightly, mainly in the secondary phase. Reasons for the under-representation of men in primary education range from public perceptions that women are better with younger children, to lack of remuneration as a teacher compared with other employment, to disquiet about instances of child abuse and fears that male teachers might be accused of wrong motives, to the overly prescriptive education system that conflicts with the spontaneity and need for flexibility that characterise most men.

A survey of six hundred eight–eleven-year-olds by YouGov for the Training and Development Agency (TDA) in 2008 suggested that many boys would welcome more men in schools. The survey found that 39 per cent of boys did not have any men teaching them and one in twelve had never been taught by a man, while 48 per cent of boys believe male teachers set good examples for them and 28 per cent said men understood them better. Just over half of the boys (51 per cent) said the presence of a male teacher made them behave better; just under half of the boys said men helped them enjoy school more (44 per cent), and 37 per cent said that male teachers help them to feel more confident about themselves. Over recent years the proportion of men teaching infant-age children has increased, though they still account for an extremely low proportion of total staff.

Gasnnerud (2001) interviewed twenty experienced women teachers in Sweden and identified six themes that were significant in their daily work:

1. Teachers saw their professional role as gender neutral, but also felt that being female affected their daily work.
2. Experiences of motherhood and of teaching as work and the meaning of a professional attitude were closely connected.
3. There was a need to balance the demands of private life and work life, in which both spheres are characterised by gender-specific responsibilities and an ethics of care.
4. The emotional demands were exhausting and time consuming, but also very important for work satisfaction and personal motivation.
5. Informal collegial ('non-hierarchical') interaction provided a source of emotional support as well as development of professional knowledge.

6. A perception of teaching as a low-status profession is linked in people's minds with the job being a suitable one for women.

While concerns have been raised about the dearth of male teachers, counter-arguments suggest that men are more likely to be favoured ahead of equally competent women and appointed to senior posts. It is also unclear whether the fact that pupils tend to remember their male teachers is due to their 'scarcity value' rather than expertise or ability to maintain discipline. There is also evidence that boys take their role models from other boys, slightly older than them, and not from teachers, celebrities or even sports personalities. (See Teaching and learning issue 5 earlier in this chapter.) Debate is likely to continue about the extent to which pupils need male teachers, but the incidence of family households with only one adult (usually the mother) has added weight to the argument that children from such backgrounds benefit from being taught by men as well as women.

Questions to consider and discuss

- How significant is the gender imbalance among primary school teachers in terms of: (a) children's academic progress; (b) boys' attitudes; and (c) staff relationships?
- What does Gasnnerud's research tell us about the role and motivation of women teachers, and the demands placed on them?
- What unique qualities do men and women bring to teaching, if any? Do schools or educational settings without any male teachers need to compensate for their absence? If so, in what ways? Would it matter if the staff were all male?

Reference

Gasnnerud, E. (2001) 'A gender perspective on the work and lives of women primary school teachers', *Scandinavian Journal of Educational Research*, 45 (1), pp. 55–70.

Teaching and learning issue 33: The consequences of labelling children

The use of stereotypes (applied to a defined group of pupils) and labels (specific to an individual) is to attribute characteristic behaviour to a group or individual in such a way that the description on the label is intricately bound up with the personality and existence ('being') of the child or children concerned. Common stereotypes are represented in expressions like, 'boys will be boys' or 'children from broken homes fall behind' or 'African children love to dance', all of which may contain elements of truth but, when applied generally, predispose teachers to expect less or more than is reasonable from each child in that category. As a result, labels start being attached to individuals such that the quiet, unassuming boy is referred to as 'unusual'; the successful child from a troubled background is considered to be 'an exception to the rule'; the West Indian child who prefers classical music to reggae is thought of as being 'untypical'. These examples point up an important distinction between 'inclination' and 'stereotyping', where inclination is an acknowledgement of commonly observed behaviour (e.g. most boys like to climb trees; most girls prefer pink), while stereotyping conveys that exceptions to the norm are peculiar. Thus, the minority of boys who like to keep their feet firmly on the ground and the minority of girls who choose brown above pink are treated as special cases instead of being commended for their individuality.

Labelling therefore has implications for children's learning if it acts as a constraint rather than an emancipator. The quiet boy is given mundane tasks because he is considered to be untypical; the child of a single parent is given simpler homework tasks in the belief that home life is difficult; the unassuming Nigerian girl is given a static role in the class production instead of being taught the dance steps.

Negative labelling and stereotyping children unfairly can have a lasting adverse effect that not only harms their self-esteem but also affect their adult lives. On the other hand, a *positive* label expressed regularly through the use of comments such as, 'He is a bright lad' or 'She is so friendly with everyone', can help to build confidence if used sincerely and appropriately. Nevertheless, when dealing with a class of children on a daily basis, bear in mind that these sorts of accolades must be employed for the benefit of every child, not the chosen few.

Hart *et al.* (2004) strongly oppose the use of ability labelling, arguing that explaining differences in terms of inherent ability is:

> not only unjust and untenable but also deprives teachers of the chance to base and develop their practice upon a more complex, multifaceted and infinitely more empowering understanding of teaching and learning processes and of the influences, internal and external to the school, that impinge upon learning and achievement.
>
> (p. 17)

The authors go on to explain that the use of ability labelling is based on a view that teachers cannot make a difference and are therefore powerless to change a child's intellectual limits, 'however lively and inspirational their teaching, however positive their relationships, however illuminating their explanations' (p. 18). They point out that reference to present attainment is a more satisfactory way of viewing ability in that it does not preclude future improvement.

Labelling is often linked closely with children diagnosed as having special educational needs (see also Chapter 3, Professional theme 9), and the use of 'statements' to describe the symptoms and desirable learning support for pupils with identifiable needs is commonplace, though the process can be ponderous and difficult to monitor. Ofsted claimed that thousands of children had been wrongly labelled as having special educational needs (SEN) because of systematic failures. The report, *A Statement is Not Enough* (Ofsted 2010) suggested that large numbers of children were being offered extra support for SEN when, it was alleged, all they really needed was better quality teaching. In schools visited by the inspection teams, an over-identification of SEN contributed to lowering expectations for pupils. In effect, an attitude prevailed that could be encapsulated by: 'They have special educational needs, so what can you expect?' By contrast, high-quality assessment of children's educational needs allows teachers to diagnose areas of weakness and put positive strategies in place to address them.

Questions to consider and discuss

- Why, despite an awareness of the possible damaging effects of labelling, do teachers continue to use expressions such as 'bright children' and 'slow learners' and 'average ability'? What alternative descriptors exist?
- What credence do you attach to Hart *et al.*'s view that 'the use of ability labelling is based on an opinion that teachers do not make a difference'?
- To what extent can special educational needs be blamed on (a) poor teaching and (b) other factors? How might teaching be adjusted to better accommodate a wide range of educational needs?

References

Hart, S., Dixon, A., Drummond, M.J. and McIntyre, D. (2004) *Learning Without Limits*, Maidenhead: Open University Press.

Ofsted (2010) *A Statement is Not Enough: Review of Special Educational Needs and Disability*, London: Crown Copyright.

Teaching and learning issue 34: Implementation of the ECM agenda

The Every Child Matters (ECM) legislation brought about changes in supporting parents and carers, and led to earlier intervention and more accountability and integration between services, together with enhancement of workforce reform in schools. The aim of the ECM agenda has been for all children to be supported in staying healthy and safe, achieving success, making a positive contribution to society and learning skills about handling their finances. As part of the process, every primary school is obliged to offer childcare provision between 8 am and 6 pm all year round, either on-site or in partnership with other schools and local providers. Schools also have a responsibility with respect to ECM and wider issues that relate to pupil wellbeing, including to:

- provide a bespoke approach to teaching and learning and social development;
- provide every child with a key adult who knows him or her well;
- identify children's needs early and respond to them appropriately;
- engage with and consult pupils about issues relating to their wellbeing and aspects of school life;
- engage and support parents in their children's learning and development;
- work in partnership with other organisations to safeguard and improve children's lives;
- take responsibility for improving children's lives in the wider community.

See Cheminais (2010 p. 2) for a fuller explanation of these conditions and their implications.

An in-depth study by Ainslie *et al.* (2010) about the implementation of the Every Child Matters agenda found strong evidence of effective multi-agency working, particularly in relation to children who are at risk or have special educational needs, and also in terms of contributions to the curriculum and life of the school for all pupils. There was solid evidence of a commitment from professionals to making ECM work, together with a genuine belief in its underlying principles. Concerns were raised that poor resourcing and a lack of practical support could hamper the embedding of the reforms. Teacher respondents in the study were exercised about the need to receive more support with their increased workload; specialised training; and stronger multi-agency working. A significant concern was the ways in which inspection and audit frameworks were perceived by teachers as largely threatening, rather than supportive, and designed to expose weakness and underperformance rather than highlight successes. The negativity tended to make staff defensive and inclined to protect the status quo rather than critically reflect on practice.

Questions to consider and discuss

- What are the practical issues that teachers need to deal with in implementing multi-agency liaison?
- How might the ECM agenda positively assist the curriculum and life of the school for all pupils?
- What could be done to help teachers become more reflective and less defensive?

References

Ainslie, S., Foster, R., Groves, J., Grime, K., Straker, K. and Woolhouse, C. (2010) 'Making children count: an exploration of the implementation of the Every Child Matters agenda', *Education 3–13*, 38 (1), pp. 23–38.
Cheminais, R. (2010) *Implementing the Every Child Matters Strategy*, Abingdon: Routledge.

Teaching and learning issue 35: Attitudes towards computers

Computers and related forms of technology appeal greatly to most children, but seem to have a particular fascination for boys, pupils with learning difficulties, and those who struggle to cope with regular routines. Many gifted pre-adolescent pupils become computer enthusiasts, especially about playing games. Some parents believe that it is never too early for a child to learn how to use the computer as it prepares them for school and the future workplace. There is some evidence to suggest that children use computers at home without the necessary guidance of an adult and fail to exploit their potential. The design of educational software programs for home use has been influenced strongly by computer gaming concepts, designed to be fun as well as educational. However, as far as possible a distinction has to be drawn between games in which there is a genuine educational element and software where the entertainment element outweighs the learning.

A whole category of educational software has grown up specifically intended to assist classroom teaching, including sophisticated software for teacher assessment and reporting. Typically, such software is projected onto a large whiteboard at the front of the class and/ or run simultaneously on a network of desktop computers, sometimes referred to as classroom management software. Although there is a danger of teachers using computers as a 'babysitting service' for unmotivated children, they provide a powerful incentive and learning tool for most pupils; for example, to access information, make choices, practise arithmetic, design and construct, complete exercises and respond to questions about specific subject content.

Concerns have been expressed about the adverse effect of excessive computer work on children's eyesight; on the degree of isolation it creates in the home environment; and the damage to physical posture. There is also some unease about the fact that children read at only half the speed from a computer screen and comprehend less when compared with the same words in traditional paper form. Evidence also suggests that children without access to the Internet in the evening are being increasingly disadvantaged in the classroom and liable to underachieve in examinations.

Mumtaz (2001) found that eight-year-old and ten-year-old children made more use of the computer at home than at school. The most popular activity on the home computer was playing games, whereas the most frequent activity in school was word-processing, which many pupils considered to be unappealing. Mumtaz also noted interesting gender differences, in that boys spent more time playing computer games, whereas girls spent more time e-mailing friends.

Enthusiasm among teachers about the appropriateness of computer technology for learning can also depend to an extent on the age range of pupils that they teach. Thus, teachers of younger primary age children, who tend to favour a more kinaesthetic ('hands-on') approach, seem to be more sceptical about incorporating computers into regular teaching than teachers of older age groups. Teachers of the youngest children resist using too much modern technology because: (a) they feel that concentration on the operating system detracts from the close intimacy engendered through adult–child relationships, so crucial in developing a positive learning climate; and (b) it deprives the children of opportunities to engage with tactile activities – touching and handling objects.

Hermans et al. (2008) found that primary teachers' attitudes towards the use of computers in teaching varied considerably, depending on their educational beliefs. Thus, teachers whose ideas were rooted in constructivism (i.e. that learners have to be helped to make sense of ideas through discussion, reflection, experimenting, sharing, etc.) were more positive about the classroom use of computers than teachers possessing more traditional beliefs (i.e. those who prefer to use more direct 'didactic' methods of teaching).

Questions to consider and discuss

- What is the relationship between beliefs about the aims of education and the use of technology?

- What practical considerations should teachers take into account when using computers in the classroom: (a) for teaching purposes; (b) for learning purposes? How real is the danger that the computer will become a 'babysitter' for troublesome or less able pupils?
- What account should teachers take of differences in computer preferences between boys and girls, and between less and more competent pupils, in their planning, organising and managing of learning?

References

Hermans, R., Tondeur, J., van Braak, J. and Valcke, M. (2008) *Computers and Education*, 51 (4), pp. 1499–1509.

Mumtaz, S. (2001) 'Children's enjoyment and perception of computer use in the home and the school', *Computers and Education*, 36 (4), pp. 347–62.

Teaching and learning issue 36: Reflective and self-reflexive practice

Top teachers think hard about their work and exercise professional judgement about classroom practice, rather than meekly complying with the status quo or externally derived priorities. If anything, most primary teachers are too self-critical and are always seeking to maintain their standards and, whenever possible, develop their expertise. Self-reflection is of limited use unless teachers are given opportunity to ponder, comment on policy decisions, challenge present practice, negotiate their working conditions and exercise professional autonomy with regard to teaching methods and discipline. An ordinary teacher is content to implement the latest national strategy or new initiative without question; the best teachers look for ways to be innovative while still formally complying with the latest demands. Schön (1991) proposed two types of reflecting: 'reflection-in-action' and 'reflection-on-action', the former denoting the sorts of thought processes that take place during an event (notably, during teaching) and the latter denoting a retrospective view about events that have passed (e.g. when writing a journal).

Reflexivity is sometimes used interchangeably with the concept of being reflective. It has been described as the process of being conscious, in any instance, of what is influencing the way that we respond, both internally (in our minds) and externally (in our actions). Fisher (1998) refers to 'metacognition', which is, broadly speaking, the process of deliberating upon one's thinking processes. It signifies a practitioner's ability and willingness to undergo a higher form of reflection ('self-reflexive') than would normally be experienced from casual thought or superficially pondering about events.

Moore (2004) makes the point that reflecting too deeply can sometimes lead to recrimination rather than the intended aim of improving practice. He advocates that a more reflexive approach (here defined as examining cause and effect) is the only way for teachers to resist undergoing an agonising retrospection about their shortcomings and, rather, to recognise the ways in which our lives and experiences shape the way we presently act. Once these underlying factors are identified, steps can be taken to correct and adjust our behaviour without unnecessary loss of self-confidence. It is worth noting that this very sound principle equally applies to pupil behaviour.

Marcos *et al.* (2011) evaluated studies that promote reflection, whereby teachers are encouraged to improve their reflective practice through programmes of professional development. (See Teaching and learning issue 37, below.) Findings indicated that there was a lack of agreement among teachers about how to conduct reflection, but noted a strong trend towards prescription (i.e. to be reflective you must do this and that) with little justification provided for the advice being advocated by the trainer. The authors concluded that teachers are provided with only limited information on how to improve their reflective practice, which can limit its use to something functional rather than innovative. Teachers in the study appeared to accept the ideas on reflection presented to them during professional development as if they represented valid practices that were embedded in real experiences and accompanied by evidence from participant appraisals. In reality, the reflective accounts did not provide precise descriptions of genuine practice, lacked affirmation, and were not accompanied by procedures or approaches to guide implementation. Referencing work by Edwards, Gilroy, and Hartley (2002), the authors concluded that a lack of practical support to facilitate practice was one of the reasons why reflective accounts offered as part of a teacher development programme are not effective in helping teachers to understand or modify existing teaching methods.

Questions to consider and discuss

- How might reflective practice be elevated to the more profound 'self-reflexive' practice that is more likely to have a direct impact on classroom practice?
- What steps can be taken to prevent reflective practice deteriorating into what is colloquially known as 'navel gazing' and thereby serving little useful purpose?
- What are the benefits of reflexive practice as a team, rather than an individual, endeavour?

References

Edwards, A., Gilroy, P. and Hartley, D. (2002) *Rethinking Teacher Education: Collaborative Responses to Uncertainty*, Abingdon: Routledge.

Fisher, R. (1998) 'Thinking about thinking: developing metacognition in children', *Early Child Development and Care*, 141, pp. 1–15.

Marcos, J.M., Sanchez, E. and Tilema, H.H. (2011) 'Promoting teacher reflection', *Journal of Education for Teaching*, 37 (1), pp. 21–36.

Moore, A. (2004) *The Good Teacher: Dominant Discourses in Teaching and Teacher Education*, Abingdon: Routledge.

Schön, D. (1991) *The Reflective Practitioner: How Teachers Think*, New York: Basic Books.

Teaching and learning issue 37: Shaping professional development

The old adage that teachers improve or get worse but never stand still is undoubtedly close to the truth. Keenness and enthusiasm can be swept aside by what seem to be endless demands. Creativity and imagination can be replaced by a need to 'survive' each day. Friday night becomes the happiest time of the week. Sunday evening feels very different! Trainee teachers have excessive amounts of paperwork to complete. Qualified teachers have less to do except for key times of the year, notably, completing reports, or in advance of an inspection, but still far too much. One way and another the everyday necessities of teaching can become totally consuming of time, energy and ambition. (See also Chapter 4, Challenges 2 and 3.)

Although it is a common experience to be overwhelmed in the early stages of your career, life as a teacher does not have to become a 'tail-chasing' exercise, nor does it have to deteriorate into dull mediocrity. Teaching is a craft, but it is also a profession, providing teachers with the benefits and challenges that any professional faces, not least the need to be a forward-looking person with well considered principles, a sense of purpose and a desire to learn and progress. There are ten key factors in ensuring that your life as a teacher is not only personally fulfilling (i.e. enjoyable and worthwhile) but also professionally enhancing (i.e. you become a more effective practitioner and valued colleague). The factors are, in no particular order, as follows:

1. Learn yourself and keep learning from others.
2. Get your regular priorities sorted through careful time management and making sure that you do what is *necessary* first and what you *feel* like doing second.
3. Take care of your wellbeing by eating well, getting enough sleep and taking regular breaks.
4. Stay up to date with the latest ideas about effective teaching by reading appropriate literature; absorb helpful tips into your portfolio of ideas, but beware of anything peddled as a simple solution to a complex problem.
5. Treat training exercises as an opportunity to improve and not as a necessary evil, even when you think you have better ways of occupying your time.
6. Read, think and reflect as systematically as the demands of the job allow, recording key points in a journal if possible.
7. Gain expertise in an area of academic interest over and above the regular teaching needs, gradually becoming very well informed in a way that will give you confidence and status and enhance your standing in the school.
8. Cherish your colleagues by taking an interest in how they are doing, feeling and coping, so that you avoid becoming introspective and self-absorbed.
9. Enjoy being with children and become an expert in observing them, interpreting their moods, responding to their needs and helping them along the journey of life. (See also Chapter 3, Professional theme 22.)
10. Enjoy contact with parents and view them as allies in the education and socialisation of their children.

As part of the process of developing more-effective teachers, the Government produced a White Paper (policy discussion document) in 2010 called *The Importance of Teaching*, part of which introduced a new competitive national scholarship scheme for teachers known as the Professional Development (PD) Scholarship Scheme, administered by the Training and Development Agency for Schools (TDA). The three aims of the scheme are:

1. To encourage serving teachers to pursue knowledge independently to Master's level and beyond.
2. To bring about a culture change to create expectations within the sector about the importance of scholarship throughout a teacher's career.
3. To share learning, knowledge and expertise across the school system.

In the same year, research was commissioned by the General Teaching Council for England to discover how teachers identify their strengths and weaknesses, and to whom they turn for support and ideas (Poet *et al.* 2010a, 2010b). Findings from the report, *How Teachers Approach Practice Improvement*, included the predictable fact that nearly all teachers were keen to improve their professional practice. Teachers also want to:

- do the best job they can and meet the needs of all the pupils;
- learn about effective ways of presenting information to children;
- improve their subject knowledge;
- utilise reflection and peer support in developing their practice;
- be observed and receive constructive feedback;
- collaborate with colleagues and also do independent research;
- access formal development through courses that address school-identified development needs;
- engage with development activities that have a positive impact on self, school and pupils;
- use colleagues as a source of first-hand support and inspiration.

(amended list)

It was also noted in the report that: (a) the ethos and style of senior staff have an impact on the type and level of support available; (b) the professional Standards are not widely used; and (c) lack of time is the biggest barrier to teachers, together with limited funding, the culture of the school and the attitudes of colleagues. One of the least contentious findings was that teachers' energy levels impacted on the motivation to improve their practice. An exhausting schedule led to a 'treading water' approach in which teachers were kept at full stretch in dealing with their regular commitments, let alone enhancing their practice through course attendance, further study and the like.

Finally, it is important to bear in mind that having a desire to develop professional expertise is not the same as aspiring to become a 'super-teacher'. According to inspection reports and feedback from head teachers, the vast majority of teachers do a decent job or better and work very hard. They sometimes make mistakes and have periods of time when their enthusiasm wanes. It is unlikely that you will be any different. There is, however, a sharp distinction to make between being a 'steady-as-a-rock' teacher and an indifferent or complacent one. In truth, there are very few of the latter type, so it is best to be positive and press ahead with confidence to be the best teacher you can be without injuring your health. In doing so adopt as your mantra: *Be informed; stay informed; inform others.*

Questions to consider and discuss

- On what grounds can teachers be confident that they are improving: (a) their practice; (b) their value as a staff member?
- Which of the bullet points listed above are of greatest significance to you? What principles or factors guide your choice?
- Is it reasonable to expect every teacher to be exceptional? What are the key arguments?

References

Poet, H., Rudd, P. and Smith, R. (2010a) *How Teachers Approach Practice Improvement*, London: General Teaching Council for England.

Poet, H., Rudd, P. and Kelly, J. (2010b) *Survey of Teachers 2010: Support to Improve Teaching Practice*, London: General Teaching Council for England.

Teaching and learning issue 38: Persevering as a teacher

Palmer (2007) argues that poor teaching is not because of poor technique but because teachers allow fear to stifle them. In fact, it takes a good deal of pluck to be a teacher. It takes courage to walk into a classroom and deal with up to thirty pupils, each with his or her personality and different learning needs. It takes courage to accept the challenge of planning, organising, teaching, managing and assessing. It takes courage to deal with parents, liaise with colleagues, meet expectations, cope with your emotions and handle criticism. Teacher courage is different from the bravery displayed by soldiers in battle, a lifeboat crew or an astronaut, where a specific task has to be accomplished at great personal cost. It requires a 'stickability' to persevere when children are restless, face up squarely to one's own shortcomings, refuse to compromise on core beliefs and show a willingness to deviate from the original lesson plans to accommodate pupil interest. So, if ever you feel a little apprehensive about the job, it is not an indication of your incompetence or sign of an impending crisis; it is simply the fact that teaching, as well as being fulfilling and thrilling, requires wholehearted commitment that can sometimes feel overwhelming.

Research by Smithers and Robinson (2009) found that more than a quarter of all trainee teachers never work in the classroom after qualifying and those that do experience a 'culture shock' of such intensity that 40 per cent leave after just a few years, citing poor behaviour among pupils and excessive workload as the main reasons. On the other hand, one of the greatest thrills of being a teacher is to see the satisfaction and pleasure that successful teaching and learning engenders in children. Happy teachers produce happy pupils.

While perseverance requires doggedness and a refusal to allow adverse circumstances to impede you, it should not, however, be equated with 'hanging on' or 'barely coping'. It involves using available resources, pieces of advice from colleagues and professional learning opportunities of varying kinds to facilitate your progress as a teacher. The passage of time and hard-won experience counts for a lot, but is no substitute for making a conscious resolve to be a top teacher through continually evaluating your practice, observing skilled practitioners and gaining insights from written sources, lectures and staff discussions.

Questions to consider and discuss

- To what extent does Palmer make a valid point in claiming that poor teaching is born of fear?
- What is unique about the sort of courage required by teachers? Where are your own weaker and stronger areas in this regard?
- What are the major differences between teaching before and after qualifying?

References

Palmer, P.J. (2007) *The Courage to Teach: Exploring the Inner Landscape of a Teacher's Life*, San Francisco: Jossey-Bass.

Smithers, A. and Robinson, P. (2009) *Good Teacher Training Guide 2008*, Buckingham University's Centre for Education and Employment Research.

Teaching and learning issue 39: Being observed teaching

Years ago, the only lesson observers were pupils in class! Today, lesson observation is seen as a vital element in making progress as a teacher and becoming a first-rate practitioner. Watson-Davis (2009) suggests various models of observation: (a) the observer as learner, also known as 'the worker bee model'; (b) paired, peer and trio observations; (c) the observer taking the role of coach; and (d) the performance management/ Ofsted model using the observer as assessor or judge. Targets play a role in teacher appraisal, adding to their significance for practitioners at all levels of experience; thus, the attainment of the children in their classes (improvement in reading age, results of tests, etc.) is also a major factor in determining teachers' suitability for in-school advancement or promotion. The need to demonstrate pupils' competence in passing tests is, of course, most sharply focused on teachers of Year 6 (ten–eleven-year-olds). From 2012, the Ofsted inspection framework has been based on four core areas: (1) pupil achievement; (2) quality of teaching; (3) behaviour and safety; and (4) the quality of leadership.

Revised performance management arrangements for *qualified* teachers (trainees and newly qualified teachers – NQTs – are assessed under slightly different criteria) came into force in September 2007 in England. The expectation is that classroom observations are to be developmental in nature (i.e. helping to improve practice) and multi-purpose in usage (see categories a–c in the Watson-Davis model, above). In reality, it is difficult for assessment of classroom practice to be both formative and evaluative, not least because teachers tend to make their lesson more elaborate and 'untypical' when an observer is present.

The period of classroom observation allowed per 'performance management cycle' can be up to three hours in total, depending on individual circumstances. All classroom observations should contribute to a teacher's professional development and be conducted in a way that promotes professional dialogue rather than the observer's judgement of competence. Oral feedback should be given within a day of the lesson being observed. A written report should be evaluative and describe both the strengths and the areas for development. There are separate procedures for the support and review of the work of newly qualified teachers, which do not fall under the auspices of performance management.

Lesson observations can be a valuable form of professional development for both the person being observed and the observer if approached in the right frame of mind. The teacher being observed should not try to impress the assessor but behave as naturally as possible; in turn, the assessor (probably a senior colleague) should undertake the task with humility and a genuine desire to help. The feedback from the observation is particularly important and should be as commending as possible. Areas for development are likely to fall into one or more of four areas: (1) lesson presentation – clarity of explanation; accurate transmission of information; disclosure of aims; specificity of expectation; (2) pupil response – quality of adult–child interaction; opportunities for the 'pupil voice' to be heard and acknowledged; enthusiasm for learning; (3) management of tasks and activities – appropriateness of the set work; differentiation of content and demands made of pupils; availability of resources; level of adult support; formative assessment; review of learning; and (4) behaviour management (see Teaching and learning issue 23 earlier in this chapter). Two key indicators as to whether the observation has been beneficial are as follows: (1) the teacher feels more confident about her or his teaching; (2) the relationship between assessor and assessed is closer following the lesson than it was beforehand.

Whether you are a trainee, NQT or more experienced practitioner, it is worth bearing in mind the following points about lesson observations. First, do your best to plan every lesson in the belief that it *might* be observed; in this way, you will be well prepared and 'in gear' for the real event. Second, when being observed, do not try to put on a spectacular lesson; instead, teach as you would normally do but ensure that you subtly 'tick the right boxes' (see previous paragraph). Third, don't be overly ambitious, but at the same time avoid playing safe and thereby failing to show your strengths; for instance, don't just use closed questions or provide work that merely keeps pupils occupied. Fourth, before being formally observed, be brave and find out in advance what a small number of sensible pupils and the assistant say about your teaching. Finally, view the feedback as a positive means of helping you become an excellent primary teacher.

As part of the preparation for being observed, and to check if your lesson planning (i.e. thinking through the conduct of the lesson or session in your head) is fully adequate, leave your lesson plans at home one day and see how well you cope without them. Alternatively, leave the detailed plans to one side, summarise the lesson elements in no more than ten points, and use those notes as your sole guide for a session. It won't be easy initially, but with perseverance you will teach more fluently and become less reliant on detailed plans, which is, after all, what nearly every experienced practitioner does.

Questions to consider and discuss

- How can you ensure that you 'tick all the right boxes'?
- What are the advantages and disadvantages of using a shortened version of lesson notes that contain only key points?
- Which aspects of your teaching need to be clearly demonstrated to the observer?

Reference

Watson-Davis, R. (2009) *Lesson Observation*, Southampton: Teachers' Pocketbooks.

Teaching and learning issue 40: Coping with setbacks as a teacher

There is a standing joke among teachers that the only perfect teacher is a retired one! It is certainly true that, in teaching, as in every profession, there are a small proportion of people who leave the classroom for more prestigious posts owing to the fact that they are unable to cope with the rigours of the job. The knowledgeable tutor might or might not be a more capable teacher than you. The seemingly 'divine' figure of the head teacher is as fallible as any other member of staff when working in the classroom, as 'teaching heads' in small schools will affirm. In truth, the concept of 'super-teacher' is a fiction; the vast majority of practitioners do their very best, with highs and lows, moments of inspiration and a good deal of gritty determination. This truth does not mean, of course, that you should not be striving for improvement. When a teacher gets in a muddle, the best ones seek advice and find strategies to adjust their approach. Only weak teachers look for excuses and try to shift the blame onto the pupils, parents, circumstances or lack of resources.

It is inevitably the case that trainee and new teachers stumble and go through phases when they feel that things are getting worse rather than improving. The reality is that you almost certainly *are* making progress as a teacher, but your expectations of what you can and should achieve have risen, so what was acceptable in the early days of a placement or with a new class is deemed unacceptable as time passes. Anyone who has stood on a beach when the tide flows in knows that the movement of water is backwards and forwards, sometimes surging, sometimes passive, sometimes retreating, but ultimately upwards and onwards. So it is with your progress as a teacher.

Negative thoughts about your competence might be due to exhaustion or feeling demoralised after a poor lesson; it might be after a critical comment from a tutor or in dealing with a child who seems determined to make your life miserable. It is surprising how an inexperienced teacher's fragile confidence can be undermined by a single bad experience that seems to herald the end of the world but often provides an unpalatable but necessary reminder that, however well you are doing, there is still much to be learned. A good night's sleep and discussion with a confidante works wonders. (See also Chapter 4, Challenge 2.)

Finally, it is worth noting comments made by Eady (2011) in promoting what she refers to as your personal professional development (PPD). Eady insists that PPD is not something that is done *to* you such that, by attending a professional development course, you somehow become a better teacher. Instead, she recommends that you actively engage in further study to structure your own learning and view it as part of the everyday role of teaching and reflecting. In practice, to recover from setbacks you need to step back from the situation, evaluate your strengths and less well developed areas, and modify your strategy after considering the circumstances and taking account of what others have said, written and advised. This professional approach, though challenging, is preferable to one in which you simply plan more of the same, work even harder in the classroom and compound the same errors.

Finally, on those rare occasions when teaching seems impossibly hard; the demands are unmanageable; parents complain; children misbehave; your body is spent and weary; the tutor or head teacher seems unaware of all your work and effort; and you want to crawl away and hide, bear in mind four things. First, in the intensive and person-oriented work of a teacher, there are bound to be periods of time when you feel as if you are stuck in deep mud with the rear wheels spinning. Second, it is often your *perception* or feelings about a situation rather than the reality, so don't let your imagination overrule your pragmatism. Third, it is useful to share your concerns with a friend, but don't talk yourself into a depressed state of mind when you do so. Fourth, each day provides a fresh start – don't allow the shadow of a past experience to blot out today's sunlight. Teaching is a vitally important job, but no one ever pretended it would be easy.

Questions to consider and discuss

- How helpful is it to represent progress as a teacher as a straight-line continuum? What are the alternative models?
- What criteria should be used to distinguish an outstanding teacher from a good one?
- To what extent does effective teaching reside in the emotions as much as in technical competence?

Reference

Eady, S. (2011) 'Personal professional development' in A. Hansen (ed.) *Primary Professional Studies*, Exeter: Learning Matters.

3

Professional themes

Introduction

This chapter contains forty-four Professional themes, intended to stimulate discussion and act as a springboard for in-depth study and research, especially for those pursuing a qualification or expanding their knowledge of education topics as a basis for whole-staff discussion and professional development. Each theme consists of information gleaned from a significant source, together with a key question; discussion points; and a suggested action plan to facilitate advanced classroom practice.

The two opening themes provide an introduction to education purpose and policy; the remaining forty-two themes address five areas: children; child development; teachers and teaching; discipline and behaviour; and curriculum practice. These main topics are discussed in the following order:

Section A: Education purpose and policy
Section B: Children
Section C: Child development
Section D: Teachers and teaching
Section E: Discipline and behaviour
Section F: Curriculum practice.

Section A: Education purpose and policy

Professional theme 1: The purpose of education

Key question: *What do children need to learn and understand to gain a complete education?*

A complete education is only achievable in a school climate where every person's rights are respected; where responsibility for oneself and others is promoted; and where everyone in the school community views positive self-worth, the need to fulfil potential, and a sense of belonging as essential prerequisites. Fully educated children are not just the ones who pass examinations and gain top marks, but also those who develop the skills, knowledge and abilities to foster their physical, social, mental and emotional wellbeing in all aspects of life, and help others to do the same. Such pupils have a desire to achieve their full academic potential but also a growing awareness of their responsibilities as significant members of a community. Eaude (2008) wisely comments that, although it is tempting to think of what happens in the classroom as being mainly about what you do as a teacher, education is about enabling children to learn. The big question for educators is, of course, *what* children should learn. Put simply, whatever teachers believe pupils should learn has a profound effect on what they teach them and the way they go about doing so.

Discussion points

Consider how much these three wise sayings reflect your own views:

> The main part of intellectual education is not the acquisition of facts but learning how to make facts live.
>
> (Attributed to Oliver Wendell Holmes)

> I cannot teach anybody anything; I can only make them think.
>
> (Attributed to Socrates, Greek philosopher)

> An educational system isn't worth a great deal if it teaches young people how to make a living but does not teach them how to make a life.
>
> (Source unknown)

A rounded education consists of more than gaining factual knowledge or academic knowledge or skills; it is also about learning to understand the world and the people in it, such that children will be better equipped to become morally responsible, caring and selfless adults. Although the phrase 'whole child' is ubiquitous in the education literature, as a teacher you need to consider the implications for your practice of 'educating the whole child'. Where does your role begin and end? What arguments can be marshalled to defend/ reject the view that you should concentrate solely on the academic element of education and leave the moral, spiritual and social elements to the child's family and friends? How will you evaluate your success as a teacher? (See also Chapter 2, Teaching and learning issue 9.)

Action plan

- In addition to the regular curriculum, make every effort to introduce and discuss topics that help to widen children's knowledge and engage their interest.
- Show by your words and deeds that you are a morally responsible, caring and selfless person.
- Give children practical opportunities to demonstrate compassion – for example, through instituting a 'buddy' system, assisting less able readers and supporting worthy causes through fund raising.
- Pay close attention to the needs of children as individuals and not merely as pupils or 'learners'.

Reference

Eaude, T. (2008) *Children's Spiritual, Moral, Social and Cultural Development*, second edn, Exeter: Learning Matters.

Professional theme 2: Education policy decisions

Key question: *What are the factors that influence the forming of excellent teachers?*

A White Paper was published on 24th November 2010 called *The Importance of Teaching* and that set out details of government commitments to pare unnecessary duties, processes, guidance and requirements, as a means of ensuring that teachers have more time to do what they do best: namely, to teach their pupils. The White Paper also promised a reform of school performance tables and a more transparent funding system. Under the heading, 'Teaching and leadership', the Government stated its intentions to implement five key policy decisions:

1. *Recruiting new teachers* by raising the quality of new entrants to the teaching profession; ceasing to provide Department for Education funding for initial teacher training for those graduates who do not have at least a 2:2 degree; and enabling more talented career changers to choose teaching.
2. *Reforming initial teacher training* by increasing the proportion of time that trainee teachers spend in the classroom, focusing on core teaching skills, especially in the teaching of reading and mathematics, and in managing behaviour.
3. *Developing a national network of 'teaching schools'* on the model of teaching hospitals to lead the training and professional development of teachers and head teachers.
4. *Sharply reducing the bureaucratic burden on schools* by cutting away unnecessary duties, processes, guidance and requirements, so that schools are free to focus on doing what is right for the children and young people in their care.
5. *Recognising that schools have good pastoral systems* and understand well the connections between pupils' physical and mental health, their safety and their educational achievement, and that schools are well placed to make sure additional support is offered to those who need it.

The extent to which these aspirations are fulfilled remains to be seen, though the trend is presently towards greater school autonomy in making decisions about education provision.

Discussion points

Governments come and go. Education policies change. Pupils arrive in school, grow up and leave for the next phase of education. Teachers remain, but are subject to government policy decisions and the implementation of strategies determined both inside and outside the school. Effective head teachers ensure that the staff are consulted about the implications of new legislation and missives for teaching. The notion that there is a 'best' way to teach has been replaced by a more pragmatic approach developed through the latest teaching standards, which do not set out to prescribe in detail what good or outstanding teaching should look like but provide a framework for practitioners to exercise their professional judgement in relation to context, roles and responsibilities. One challenge is that a teacher who succeeds with pupils in one class/age group/ school might not do such a good job with different children. Whatever the circumstances, however, it is painfully obvious that a proportion of pupils make the transition from primary without having a firm grasp of basic skills and adequate self-discipline. Although much of the responsibility for a poor attitude to learning and unsatisfactory behaviour must rest with parents, your role is vitally important in ensuring that all children are equipped with the academic and social qualities necessary for making progress and being a responsible member of society. It's a challenging task but one which can also bring you immense satisfaction.

Action plan

Discuss with colleagues those of the following that are essential qualities for all excellent teachers, regardless of teaching context or pupil intake, and the implications for classroom practice:

- being knowledgeable about the subject or topic being taught;
- being aware of strategies to assist pupils in acquiring and absorbing the knowledge;
- being firm about boundaries of behaviour and willing to enforce them through persuasion or, if necessary, use of sanctions;
- being a careful observer of the things that children say and do;
- being helpful in guiding pupils through their learning experiences;
- talking naturally to children and listening carefully to them;
- being systematic in maintaining records of pupil progress;
- being ready to learn from significant others, including the pupils;
- employing the full extent of their personalities to encourage, praise, rebuke or celebrate;
- showing that they care about their pupils as children in their own right;
- being willing to share their feelings, interests and talents where appropriate.

Section B: Children

Professional theme 3: Understanding children

Key question: *How do children perceive the world and their place in it?*

Children in school are referred to as pupils or students or learners but they are, of course, still children! School offers them the opportunity to be educated formally with reference to a specified curriculum and government ordinances. Pupils normally wear a school uniform, which identifies them as part of a named community. They learn facts, skills and ways to behave, think and respond. New entrants often find it difficult to make the adjustment from home to school; others make the transition without any significant discord from day one. Although you get to know 'your' pupils and see them on most days of your working life, they are not, of course, really yours at all. Long before they come to school, parents, friends, relatives and neighbours will have influenced them. They will have probably spent long hours in front of the television set, been taken to different places, talked to a variety of people about many aspects of life and asked hundreds of questions. These children are not simply grown-ups in the making, but human beings in their own right. (See also Professional theme 7 later in this chapter.)

Discussion points

Consider your response to the following questions. Do you know or have you had to guess?

- At what age do children separate fantasy from reality?
- Are fictional TV characters 'real' to a five-year-old?; to a ten-year-old?
- Why are stories so powerful for children?
- What motivates most five-year-olds?; seven-year-olds?; eleven-year-olds?
- Why are live 'Punch and Judy' shows so appealing to children?
- What kind of music do children hear (a) at home; (b) in school?
- At what age do children begin to doubt and question things that adults tell them?
- What might a child say to a parent when asked: 'What did you *do* in school today?'
- What might a child answer when asked: 'What did you *learn* today?'
- Which factors and strategies help children to relax in class yet remain alert and purposeful?

Action plan

- Encourage children to share something from their favourite books, TV programme or film with classmates.
- As in the first point, above, but using a favourite song or piece of music.
- Arrange a time when children can bring to school a photograph or item from holiday with special meaning for them. Make sure they have gained permission first.
- For children aged seven years and older, organise a 'tell a joke' spot, whereby each day a few children can tell the class a joke. (Check the jokes before use!)
- Ask younger children to write and draw a scene from their favourite fairy story; in the case of older pupils, emphasise that it is a fairy story they used to enjoy when younger, or that their younger brothers and sisters currently enjoy.
- With great sensitivity, discuss with the class issues of 'truth' in stories.
- Ask children to draw or write about the adventure they would love to experience.

- Raise questions that fascinate children, such as 'Why do cats lick their paws?' and 'Why do we call owls wise?' and 'Why don't raindrops hurt your head?'.

Professional theme 4: Pupil attendance in school

Key question: *How can reluctant pupils be encouraged to attend and enjoy school?*

The *National Attendance Strategy for England* emphasises the link between children's welfare and school attendance, and the importance of ensuring that all children have access to the full-time education to which they are entitled. Some parents have fallen foul of the law by failing to ensure that their children attend school; a number of local authorities have brought successful prosecutions against these parents, resulting in fines and even short spells of imprisonment for the offenders. From September 2007 a new law and revised statutory guidance on exclusions came into force in England; thus, *Improving Behaviour and Attendance: Guidance on Exclusion from Schools and Pupil Referral Units* gives parents a duty, for the first five days of any exclusion, to ensure that their excluded child is not in a public place during normal school hours. The law also requires schools (for fixed-period exclusions) and local authorities (for permanent exclusions) to provide suitable full-time education from the sixth school day of the exclusion. Such is the political fervour attached to absenteeism that school governors have to set targets for attendance and submit these to the local authority. Generally, there is a high level of attendance in primary schools, where it is normal to register in excess of 80 per cent of pupils being present on any one day.

Discussion points

There are many possible reasons for children's reluctance to come to school, some of which are rooted in external factors. Common school-related factors include: (a) an inability to cope with the work; (b) a fear of bullying; (c) a lack of close friends; (d) anxiety about pleasing the teacher; and (e) a fear of getting undressed for PE, games and swimming. Very occasionally, a child is afraid of an adult or another pupil. Sometimes a girl will be nervous about being taught for the first time by a male teacher, but this unease usually passes quite quickly. Other factors are located in home circumstances; some children simply enjoy being at home so much that school is dull and insecure by comparison; some children are concerned about instability at home and have an underlying dread that parents will separate or circumstances will change while they are in school. The start of term is a particularly difficult time for some children, as they sacrifice the freedom of holidays for the rigours and constraints of school life. (See also Chapter 4, Challenge 4.) For others, school provides a sanctuary and antidote from the harsh realities of family life or neighbourhood menace. Pupil dissatisfaction is not confined to absentees; it can apply to all pupils as a result of boredom; dissatisfaction with the lesson content; the amount of freedom to explore ideas; the pressure to meet targets; the teacher's personality; or an uninspiring routine.

Action plan

- Make learning as enjoyable as possible, and your welcome equally genuine, such that even the most reluctant pupil will want to come to school.
- If you suspect bullying, mention the fact to a senior colleague and take firm action, but avoid making accusations until the facts are fully known.
- Listen to and observe children at work and informally to find out if there are prevailing problems that might be having a negative impact.
- Be ready to discuss concerns with parents but, if you are inexperienced, make sure you get advice from a regular teacher first.
- Console yourself that, although you cannot alter home circumstances, you can make school, and your classroom especially, a haven for a bewildered child.

Professional theme 5: Developing a child's sense of belonging

Key question: *How can teachers help new children, including those new to this country, to settle into the new school and classroom environment with minimum distress?*

We all need to belong somewhere and to someone. Children belong at home; they belong in their community; they also need to belong at school. The process by which children become 'absorbed' into school life can be almost immediate or, at the other extreme, it becomes a long and tortuous procedure. Crosse (2008) emphasises the importance of developing all new children's sense of belonging, which provides a way of helping them to construct their identity ('who I am'). It is particularly difficult to achieve this state with newly arrived children, particularly those from other countries and cultures. New arrivals not only have to cope with a different language, but also with different norms and expectations, which account for the reason that many newcomers retreat into a defensive silence during their first days in school. The author argues that, when children know that their home culture, language skills and knowledge are valued, the conditions for future academic success have been laid. She focuses on the importance of providing a variety of opportunities to cultivate oral language skills, not least through the medium of play and active listening.

The following extract is a modified version of a more extensive list of questions offered by Watkinson (2003, p. 33). Examine the list and respond to the questions: (a) on the basis of what you have seen in school; and (b) on the basis of what you would *like* to see in school:

- What books are available in the school to show different cultures and ways of life?
- What books are there that show people with disabilities as heroes?
- What resources, in terms of musical instruments, fabrics, pictures or artefacts, does the school possess?
- Where does the recorded music that is played during assembly originate?
- What sort of artwork is displayed on the walls?
- What relationships does the school have with the local community, voluntary organisations, churches and other places of worship?

Discussion points

The following suggestions for schools in dealing with new arrivals provide the regular teacher or a trainee working in the class with a helpful framework for action:

- Taking the initiative to greet the members of the family.
- Planning an appropriate curriculum that relies on visual rather than verbal skills.
- Putting in place support systems such as class buddies, mentors and deployment of support staff.
- Taking account of the cognitive challenge of lessons; identifying next steps; scaffolding the child's acquisition of English.
- Providing ongoing support through target setting and tracking.
- Having access to an interpreter for families struggling with English.
- Showing awareness of the difference between social and academic fluency and the changing needs of pupils as they become more fluent in English.
- Encouraging pupils to use the first language as a tool for learning.

Based on *New Arrivals Excellence Programme* (DCSF 2007)

Note also two further points: (1) special arrangements can be made for new arrivals in respect of Key Stage 2 tests; and (2) the Early Years Foundation Stage Profile (EYFSP) assessments can, with a few exceptions, be made using the home language. Partnerships with parents are particularly important at this stage for gathering evidence about children's previous education and learning experiences.

Action plan

- Make yourself familiar with the DCSF guidance (above).
- Determine which of the above discussion points has relevance for your situation.
- Give children a chance to settle; don't expect too much, too soon.
- Concentrate on the child's practical, social and emotional needs initially.
- Don't confuse shyness with unwillingness, or tentativeness with inability.

References

Crosse, K. (2008) *Introducing English as an Additional Language to Young Children*, London: Sage.
DCSF (2007) *New Arrivals Excellence Programme Guidance*, London: Crown Copyright.
Watkinson, A. (2003) *The Essential Guide for Competent Teaching Assistants*, London: David Fulton.

Professional theme 6: Developing positive attitudes in children

Key question: What approach should teachers take to foster in children a positive attitude to learning and to people?

In recent years, there has been a lot of talk in education circles, especially from within the political milieu, about having 'high expectations' of pupils, as if that thought and attitude alone will cause standards in education to rise. It is, of course, better to have high expectations than low ones, but unless strategies are implemented to assist the process of achieving them, they remain little more than wishful thinking. The true meaning of high expectations is a situation in which the teacher says to every child, in effect, 'I value what you are doing but I believe that you are capable of doing better and I will help you to achieve it'. It is worth noting that a generation ago, in an in-depth study of what was happening in schools, Rutter *et al.* (1979) concluded that, 'Schools that foster high self-esteem and that promote social and scholastic success reduce the likelihood of emotional and behavioural disturbance' (p.83).

Discussion points

Conveying positive and high expectations to pupils can take place in a number of ways. One of the most obvious and powerful methods is through strong personal relationships with pupils, whereby you and your assistant communicate an upbeat message to the children and show a willingness to respond to their questions, concerns and confusions. As teacher, you are their major source of knowledge and the facilitator of their learning, so the more skilled you are in doing so, the more confident they will feel in you as class leader. You will succeed in motivating pupils if you refuse to label any of them as a hopeless case (see Chapter 2, Teaching and learning issue 33 and Professional theme 9 later in this chapter); instead, look at each child and see the potential that lies hidden, waiting to be released by your skilful teaching, engaging personality, good subject knowledge and an ability to convey the fact that it is worth persevering with less appealing parts of the curriculum. As you encourage critical thinking and a spirit of enquiry, you will not only capture children's interest but also be effective in communicating an expectation that children are capable of finding solutions to quite complex problems and making decisions that impact positively on their lives, both in and out of school. Finally, remember that encouragement (literally 'offering courage') and genuine praise for a job well done lifts children's spirits and makes them hungry for more success.

Action plan

- Approach your teaching driven by a belief that every child has the potential to lead a purposeful and useful life, regardless of his or her academic qualities or background.
- Promote the idea to pupils that every one of them is capable of being exceptional in some area of their lives.
- Make your classroom a place of optimism and hope.
- Train and trust children to make decisions for themselves.
- Give children the chance to flourish – and sometimes fail – in a risk-supported environment that values endeavour as highly as result.
- Consider how a pupil in your class might answer if asked by a younger child what it is like being in your class.

Reference

Rutter, M., Maughan, B., Mortimore, P., Ouston, J. and Smith, A. (1979) *Fifteen Thousand Hours*, Cambridge, MA: Harvard University.

Professional theme 7: Adult responses to children

Key question: *How can teachers respond to pupils in such a way that the children feel reassured and valued?*

Children use teachers as a source of reassurance, encouragement and admiration. Insecure and less mature pupils look to caring adults for affirmation, consolation and celebration as they grapple with disappointment and come to terms with setbacks. In doing so, it is essential that teachers see 'behind' the child's comment and understand the motive underpinning to a remark. As Mowat (2010) rightly argues, interpersonal relationships lie at the heart of a school community and determine the extent to which schools are inclusive in their practice. Consequently, adults can play a crucial role in determining outcomes for pupils. The extent to which teachers affirm pupils and the extent to which they are listened to and enabled to communicate in a safe and trusting environment are all key to success. The same author notes that, when teachers are willing to share with children the kinds of things that are expected of teachers and their responsibilities, it opens up a dialogue with both pupils and their parents. In particular, a teacher's willingness to listen to and respect a pupil's perspective on situations brought about a positive change in the attitude of the young people with social and emotional behavioural difficulties in Mowat's study.

Discussion points

Consider these comments from children, the adult responses and the extent to which they conform to the criteria of being positive, honest and encouraging:

CHILD 1: I'm rubbish at this.

TEACHER: Well, that's the best I've ever seen you run; I don't suppose you'll ever catch up with mile-a-minute Mandy, but even I can't run that fast.

CHILD 2: Sir, John only beat me 'cause he cheated.

TEACHER: Well, I'm sorry if that's true, but the important thing is that you didn't give up. You kept going and didn't cheat, so well done.

CHILD 3: Miss, I was almost last. That's the worst I've ever run.

TEACHER: Yes, I expect you feel quite disappointed. But I know that you can do better and you know that you can, so you'll just have to keep trying. What's more, you haven't made any excuses for doing badly, which proves to me that you're a good sport and makes you a winner as far as I'm concerned.

Action plan

■ Try to put yourself in the child's place when responding to situations and making decisions.

- Help children to understand that adults – even teachers – are not free agents and have responsibilities to fulfil.
- Help children to accept that not everything in life turns out well.
- Leave children feeling more positive and determined after your conversation than before.
- Offer not only sympathy but also suggestions and strategies for alleviating a difficult situation and coming to terms with the reality.
- Be sensitive to the fact that sometimes the best response to a child's heartache is to say little and support a lot.

Reference

Mowat, J.G. (2010) "He comes to talk to me about things": supporting pupils experiencing social and emotional behavioural difficulties – a focus upon interpersonal relationships' *Pastoral Care in Education*, 28 (3), pp. 163–80.

Professional theme 8: Pupils' moral perspectives during primary school

Key question: *How do pupils' moral perspectives alter during their time in primary school?*

It is hardly necessary to state that perspectives of five- and ten-year-old children are different – but in what ways do they differ, and what are the implications for teachers? In particular, how do children of different ages view issues that have a moral and spiritual dimension? In February 2011, the president of the British Medical Association, Sir Michael Marmot, claimed that 44 per cent of all five-year-olds in England were not considered by their teachers to be able to share, self-motivate, co-operate and concentrate by the time they started school. Nearly half of children in England were not reaching what teachers considered a good level of development by the age of five. Researchers advised that activities such as reading to children every day, regular bedtimes and cuddling children have a positive impact on their development. The research indicated that poorer families are less likely to engage in these kinds of beneficial activities.

Johansson (2002) found that teachers of young pupils relate morality to the children's emotional and cognitive ability; to their feelings of empathy, guilt and shame; and to their ability to understand other people's perspectives. The strategies used by primary teachers in the study were intended to help children understand others; to learn morally good strategies; to pay recompense for wrongdoing; to set limits for evil acts; and to avoid moral conflicts.

As a means of interrogating the above issues, to what extent do you agree with the validity of the following statements for: (a) five year-olds; and (b) ten–eleven year-olds?

- They see everything in black-and-white terms.
- They believe everything an adult tells them.
- They struggle to predict the consequences or seriousness of their actions.
- They regard secure friendships as being their absolute priority and will do or say almost anything to preserve them.

- They will happily lie if it assists in either (a) resolving conflicts with friends; or (b) bringing an accusation against an adversary.
- They can distinguish between good and evil, right and wrong.
- They believe in kindly mythical figures (e.g the tooth fairy).
- They believe in scary supernatural phenomena (e.g. ghosts).
- They have an understanding of transcendence (a power beyond themselves).
- They can grasp the significance of 'being alive' and 'being dead'.
- They appreciate other people's points of view.
- They are capable of selfless acts.

Discussion points

Morality principally arises through social relationships, such that rules of conduct, degree of care, selflessness, loyalty and so forth mirror the tone and content of human discourse. Children have a variety of social circumstances from which to draw lessons and select the way in which they behave and react. As they grow up, they find that parental expectations oblige them to behave in certain ways; by contrast, their friendship experiences offer different norms and ways of behaving, and they encounter yet another set of expectations from teachers and assistants when they enter school. All children share a sense of outrage at situations in which, in their eyes, a decision or action is 'not fair'; indeed, children use fairness as a mantra by which to judge the 'rightness' or 'wrongness' of actions.

The ability to take account of extraneous factors grows over time, though even older pupils seem to have a blinkered attitude to some topics, their viewpoints doubtless influenced by parents and close friends. On the other hand, in many areas of their experience, they find that life does not fall into such neat moral categories for children. They agonise over being 'found out' for minor transgressions. They observe a lonely child and worry that they, too, might end up without friends. They enjoy being mischievous if they think they can get away with it. They want to like their teachers and feel uneasy if they don't. They usually only tell their parents what they believe grown-ups want to hear – to gain approval, rewards or even affection. Younger children tend to accept what most adults say, though some new entrants can struggle to understand how others can possibly think differently from them and become genuinely upset when prevented from behaving in a certain way as a result. Despite the fact that children tend to adopt the norms and expectations from home life until they enter the 'rebellious stage' during adolescence, you still have a crucial part to play in shaping pupils' moral and spiritual awareness.

Action plan

- Listen to children's conversations and learn what is important to them.
- Use powerful stories appropriate to the age range with a strong moral dimension, and hear what pupils have to say about the relevant issues during the subsequent discussion.
- Be willing to explain patiently, especially with younger pupils, why a certain action or form of words is not permitted.

- Remind yourself often that you are dealing with immature (but perceptive) children who have limited life experience on which to base their beliefs.
- While modelling patience and tolerance for other opinions, don't be afraid to explain what you believe and why.
- Remember that children tend to behave one way at school and differently in the home.

Reference

Johansson, E. (2002) 'Morality in preschool interaction: teachers' strategies for working with children's morality', *Early Child Development and Care*, 172 (2), pp. 203–21.

Professional theme 9: Labelling children with special educational needs

Key question: *What are the problems attached to labelling children, especially those with special educational needs?*

A major conclusion reached from a study of forty-six English primary schools by Lupton *et al.* (2010) was that, although the SEN system introduced following the Warnock report was intended to move away from the identification of individual disabilities, its continued reliance on the identification of categories of need with the inevitable 'labelling' (see Chapter 2, Teaching and learning issue 33) and its individual-based funding model perpetuates a system in which the 'problem' is named as one of individual difficulty, rather than the inability of schools as currently designed and resourced to provide equitably for the needs of all children.

The problems attached to seeing pupils in terms of their special needs labels rather than as individuals are well documented. For instance, two groups of trainee teachers are shown the same piece of videotaped classroom activity. One group is asked to record what they saw without further guidance; the other group is told that some members of the class in the tape exhibit features of learning and behavioural difficulties. The first group is only aware of the normal classroom interaction, whereas the second group is able to identify a range of special needs, in line with the expectations that were planted in their minds beforehand. Such studies demonstrate that we tend to see what we believe or are told is present, rather than assessing the situation objectively. It points up the danger of attaching negative labels to aspects of behaviour in such a way that practitioners have preconceived ideas about children, and subsequently convince themselves that what they have been led to believe is genuinely so. On the other hand, it is important that teachers learn to identify genuine special needs and have effective strategies to support such pupils.

While it is necessary to gather information about pupils' needs and the impact on learning, teachers need to be cautious about adopting a negative mindset that perpetuates rather than solves a problem. Ellis and Tod (2009, see Chap. 12) offer an important perspective about labelling, namely that pupils diagnosed as having special needs are likely to have a complex mix of problems rather than a single one; concentrating too heavily on a single aspect (e.g. an inability to cope with failure) at the expense of the others (e.g. limited social skills) unsettles the child. The authors argue that teachers sometimes 'perceive SEN to be an area of practice in which a label or category carries with it a prescription for provision' (p. 225). In practice, the circumstances and prognosis are much more complex. It isn't simply a case of 'doing something' but of 'doing the right thing', which normally entails a consideration of the whole child.

Discussion points

Taylor *et al.* (2010) carried out a study that revealed fascinating insights into the impact of labelling and pupil self-esteem. The authors found that those referred to as having 'general SEN' had significantly *lower* self-esteem scores than those in the groups labelled 'dyslexia' (so-called 'word blindness') and those in the 'control' group (pupils with no special needs). By contrast, there was no significant difference between the self-esteem scores of the dyslexia groups and the control groups. On the basis of these findings, it was suggested that being labelled as having general SEN negatively affects children's self-esteem because, unlike the specific label 'dyslexia', a general label offers very little in the way of an explanation for the child's academic difficulties. Furthermore, being referred to merely as having SEN meant that targeted interventions were not so available as they are for those with a less generic (non-specific) label. On the basis of the study, it is surmised that educators should endeavour to identify the precise problems experienced by children as early on and in as much detail as possible. Such a proactive approach should assist you in protecting children's self-esteem and ultimately lead to a decrease in the problems that are associated with low self-esteem.

It is worth noting that dyslexia takes a variety of forms, some severe, others trivial. Consequently, it is more accurate if you refer to the position of a child on the dyslexia *spectrum* than using the all-encompassing word 'dyslexic'. Thus, many young children reverse the letters 'b' and 'd'; quite a few children struggle with spelling; but few experience difficulty in reading because they see the words 'dancing' on the page. Each type of pupil has a form of dyslexia, but while the phase of reversing letters normally passes and spelling problems can often be sorted out by good teaching, the problems caused by jumping words requires specialist help (e.g. use of coloured transparencies on top of the black and white page to minimise the vibration impact). The children's positions on the spectrum are, therefore, markedly different.

Action plan

- Resist using the damaging expression, 'an SEN child'.
- Adopt a positive attitude towards all children, regardless of their apparent educational disadvantage.
- While taking appropriate account of a child's learning difficulty, do not make it an excuse for low standards.
- Talk to a child about the nature of his or her problems with a view to addressing them rather than passively accepting them.
- Involve parents as much as practically possible to assist with targeted intervention programmes.

- Give children who struggle in formal work ample opportunity to make their mark in other ways.
- Seek advice from colleagues.

References

Ellis, S. and Tod, J. (2009) *Behaviour for Learning*, Abingdon: Routledge.

Lupton, R., Thrupp, M. and Brown, C. (2010) 'Special educational needs: a contextualised perspective', *British Journal of Educational Studies*, 58 (3), pp. 267–84.

Taylor, L.M., Hume, I.R. and Welsh, N. (2010) 'Labelling and self-esteem: the impact of using specific versus generic labels', *Educational Psychology*, 30 (2), pp. 191–202.

Section C: Child development

Professional theme 10: Child development and learning

Key question: *What should and should not teachers assume about younger children's competence and ways to address their learning needs?*

Many assumptions exist about defining childhood, the way in which children develop and their assumed capabilities and capacities. Traditional *stage theories* interpret child development in terms of a series of discrete stages, each stage being attached to an age range; these theories have strongly influenced the way in which we understand the process of childhood. At the same time, Smidt (2006) insists that it must not be assumed that childhood is a universal process as described by traditional child development theorists, who see children as progressing from dependence to adulthood in an ordered, predictable and rule-governed way.

There are basically three broad viewpoints about the way in which children develop and learn. (1) Children will acquire knowledge naturally and automatically as they grow physically and become older, provided that they are healthy and well taught. Consequently, a child's underperformance is interpreted as the child needing more time to acquire the knowledge and skills needed to perform at the level of his or her peers. (2) Children acquire new knowledge and learn best by repetition and rote activities, such as reciting the alphabet regularly, copying letters and tracing numbers. (3) Learning and development occur when children interact with the environment and those around them. Thus, when a child encounters learning difficulties, the approach is to give the child individual attention and modify the classroom curriculum to help address his or her difficulties. MacGilchrist (2003) makes five important points about the nature of learning that have implications for classroom practice. Thus:

1. *Learning is an active process of meaning making.* Learners construct and integrate new knowledge in a way that makes sense to them.
2. *Learning about learning (meta-learning) and making sense of experience is a hallmark of effective learners.* Learners become increasingly aware of the thinking and learning processes that are taking place and thereby assume greater control over them. Larkin (2009) argues that encouraging children to

reflect upon their thinking can help them to make wiser decisions in all aspects of their lives.

3. *The relationship between learning and performance is complex.* It is influenced by motivation and self-image. Some children are capable of completing tasks ('performance orientation') without thinking hard about the implications of the work and they gain personal satisfaction other than through a tick at the bottom of the page.

4. *Learning involves the understanding and mastery of emotions.* The emotions include both personal feelings and viewing situations from other people's perspectives. Learning can be enhanced through developing a variety of social skills and a willingness to persevere and stay on task.

5. *Learning is situational.* The social contexts of the school and classroom are significant in promoting or inhibiting learning. Creating a positive, affirming and purposeful environment encourages children to be bolder and more forward-looking in their work.

Discussion points

An ordered and sequential view of child development tends to give rise to a view that identifiable circumstances and attitudes about children are 'normal' and, by implication, that other circumstances are therefore 'abnormal'. For example, the oft-quoted exemplar of a family consisting of husband, wife and two or three children does not fit a sizeable proportion of households today. Childhood can also seem to be a process of acquisition of competencies and skills according to predetermined forces, a theory that fails to acknowledge the extent to which children have the capacity to influence their own lives and development, as well as making an active contribution to their social environments.

The way in which you respond to a pupil's learning difficulties will to a large extent depend on your beliefs about childhood development. For example, if you believe that children learn naturally as they mature, you won't be overly concerned with pupils who appear to be 'behind' their peers, as they will catch up eventually if given time and opportunities to explore and digest knowledge. If you believe that a major contributing factor in the way pupils learn is their readiness to adjust to regular classroom practices, you might place more emphasis on teacher-led activities, close monitoring of progress and more formal teaching. If you believe that effective interaction with other people and the surroundings is of paramount importance, you will probably promote dialogue, active ('discovery') learning and the incorporation of children's existing knowledge (including that gained from outside the classroom) into the regular curriculum whenever possible. In other words, your view of childhood is not a theoretical exercise; it actively impinges upon the way in which you teach and organise learning.

Action plan

■ Clarify your thinking about child development and factors affecting pupil learning.

■ Resist basing your decisions and expectations about children's competence solely on their background.

- Encourage pupils to contribute their ideas about ways in which the classroom can be a happier and more productive place to learn.
- Use and monitor the impact of a variety of teaching approaches: sometimes giving ample opportunity to enquire and investigate with minimal adult intervention; sometimes designing formal sessions; and sometimes organising work with partners or in small groups. (See also Chapter 4, Challenge 5.)

References

Larkin, M. (2009) *Metacognition in Young Children*, Abingdon: Routledge.
MacGilchrist, B. (2003) 'Primary learners of the future', *Education 3–13*, 31 (3), pp. 58–65.
Smidt, S. (2006) *The Developing Child in the 21st Century*, Abingdon: Routledge.

Professional theme 11: Forms of intelligence

Key question: *How can the different forms of intelligence be acknowledged and contribute positively to pupils' learning and self-esteem?*

The work of Howard Gardner (Gardner 1983, 1999) has been influential in alerting educators to the fact that it is unwise to use a single measure of intelligence from which to draw conclusions about an individual's competence and potential, and preferable to think of a range of 'intelligences', usually referred to as *multiple intelligences*. Garnett (2005) interprets the seven original forms of intelligence as described by Gardner in terms of the way they help pupils. The following suggests ways in which the possession of each 'intelligence' can assist pupils' learning:

- *Verbal/linguistic intelligence* helps pupils to communicate and make sense of the world through language.
- *Musical/rhythmic intelligence* helps pupils to create, communicate and understand meanings made out of sound.
- *Logical/mathematical intelligence* helps pupils to appreciate abstract relations, use deductive and inductive reasoning and critical thinking.
- *Visual/spatial intelligence* helps pupils to perceive visual or spatial information and to create visual images from memory.
- *Body/kinaesthetic intelligence* helps pupils to use all or parts of the body to create or solve problems.
- *Interpersonal intelligence* helps pupils to make and see distinctions in other people's feelings and intentions.
- *Intrapersonal intelligence* helps pupils to identify their own moods and feelings.

Note that *naturalistic* intelligence and *existential* or *philosophical* intelligence were added to the list later, though there is considerable debate over the appropriateness of their inclusion.

Discussion points

Although we tend to speak of a child being of 'high ability' or 'low ability', a more accurate description must also refer to the area of learning in which the level of ability is evident. For example, you might speak of pupil A being of high ability in mathematics but low ability in PE. Again, pupil B might be described as 'very bright' in the areas of reading and other aspects of language development but 'not very bright' in science. Of course, even these descriptions only tell part of the story – a more accurate assessment might reveal that pupil C has (say) an excellent grasp of arithmetic but is confused about spatial geometry. In other words, you should be careful not to identify pupils in terms of able and less able without qualifying precisely what you mean. Use of the word 'capability' allows you to refer to a child's *potential* as opposed to present achievements, bearing in mind that academically slow pupils may be capable in affective and social areas. Reference to capability acknowledges that a child's ability is not fixed but capable of being improved by appropriate teaching and high levels of motivation.

Action plan

- Use assessments and child observations to identify each child's 'intelligences'. (See Professional theme 26 later in this chapter.)
- Resist the temptation to define a pupil's ability solely on the basis of achievements in core subjects.
- Assume that every child has capability and can enhance their intelligences with good teaching and learning opportunities.
- Confidentially select a group of (say) six pupils and, using Gardner's list of intelligences above, allocate an appropriate grade on a scale of A–D; continue the process until you have covered the whole class. Review the issues attached to this (wholly confidential) procedure.
- Based on the results from the point above, pinpoint areas of intelligence that might be enhanced and strategies for doing so. For example, musical/rhythmic intelligence might be identified by playing a short piece of lively music at the end of a session and inviting children to respond by tapping out the beat using non-verbal means. Similarly, reading an emotive story and inviting children to express their feelings will give you insight into pupils' interpersonal intelligence.
- Be alert to the presence of gifted and talented children. (See Chapter 2, Teaching and learning issue 18.)

References

Gardner, H. (1983) *Frames of Mind: The Theory of Multiple Intelligences*, New York: Basic Books.
——(1999) *Intelligence Reframed*, New York: Basic Books.
Garnett, S. (2005) *Using Brainpower in the Classroom*, Abingdon: Routledge.

Professional theme 12: Forms of knowledge

Key question: *How can we help pupils to master and to understand the links between different forms of knowledge?*

Knowledge without understanding is mere information. The highest forms of knowledge involve levels of understanding that allow for its use in different contexts. Knowledge needs to be applied in a practical setting or it is only of theoretical interest. Walker and Soltis (1992) identify three forms of knowledge that they refer to as 'knowledge in use': associative, applicative and replicative. *Associative* knowledge allows links to be made with previous learning. *Replicative* knowledge is being able to remember and reproduce facts when required. *Applicative* knowledge is for use in solving questions. Walker and Soltis argue that applicative knowledge is the most significant of the three as it 'requires seeing the connection between what one knows and what one wants to achieve' (p. 41). Thinking about how knowledge is used allows pupils to move from basic comprehension to being able to analyse and evaluate situations.

Discussion points

The term 'knowledge' is used as if there were a shared understanding about its meaning. In fact, knowledge takes many and various forms, including factual information, insight, skills to resolve and solve problems, awareness of others and capability to undertake and complete a task. Some forms of knowledge need to become deeply embedded but instantly accessible; for example, the ability to read; awareness of health and safety procedures; and an ability to handle money. Other forms of knowledge need to be accessible after reflection, utilising a resource or weighing up options; for example, contacting someone by using a mobile phone; finding the place of a letter in the alphabet; and choosing one item in preference to another. Yet other forms of knowledge rely on well-honed skills (e.g. in gymnastics or drama); on intuition ('just knowing'); on awareness of social etiquette (e.g. eating with the mouth closed); on repetition (e.g. controlling a ball); and systematic procedures, such as memorising directions or using a computer program. All forms of knowledge need to be employable in practice; theoretical knowledge is only useful if it impacts on our actions and behaviour. As a teacher, you need to be sensitive to the fact that knowledge is a complex web and you have the vital job of helping pupils disentangle and make sense of it.

Action plan

- Distinguish between information (disparate facts) and knowledge (facts within a meaningful context).
- Make knowledge acquisition enjoyable by employing fun ways to learn: use of rhymes, pupils echoing your words, visual aids, quizzes, etc.
- Identify essential facts and make sure they are learned thoroughly.
- Emphasise relational knowledge concerning our relationships with others, as well as bare facts, techniques and technical skills.
- Make frequent reference to ways in which different knowledge components overlap.
- Reinforce learning at every opportunity and in any way possible.

Reference

Walker, D.F. and Soltis, J.F. (1992) *Curriculum and Aims*, New York, NY: Teachers College Press.

Professional theme 13: Combining knowledge, skills and understanding

Key question: *What strategies can teachers use in the classroom to present learning as an interrelated whole?*

Skills do not exist in isolation from knowledge and understanding. Children need knowledge and understanding in order to consolidate what they have already grasped and open up fresh areas for enquiry. For instance, the skill of being able to solve problems systematically can provide insights that might not be gained by other means such as direct instruction or information served up in neat chunks of content by a teacher. Huxtable *et al.* (2009) insist that we have an educational responsibility to enable our pupils to recognise the people they are and want to be, to grow in their understanding of a world worth living in and how they might contribute by living the best lives they can. Over time, pupils grow in confidence and develop skills of questioning, reasoning, evaluating evidence and articulating their thoughts in front of their peers. These attributes require a blend of skills, knowledge and understanding.

Discussion points

The curriculum is divided into subject-specific sections that assist teachers in two ways: (1) helping to organise programmes of learning; and (2) focusing on subject-specific concepts. In reality, however, subjects do not have impermeable boundaries; they are not entirely separate from one another. Knowledge consists of facts but, as we noted in Professional theme 12, earlier, it is more than mere information. Knowledge has to be understood and implemented using appropriate skills if it is to be of much practical use. It is probably fair to say that knowledge usually precedes understanding, which precedes the development of skills for applying what we comprehend. Two of the best ways to test that knowledge, understanding and skills have been adequately mastered are: (1) to use them in problem solving; and (2) to encourage pupils to explain and demonstrate to their classmates. Teaching others is the surest test of deep learning.

Action plan

- Decide how much factual knowledge pupils require and present it as imaginatively as possible (e.g. by using visual aids).
- Practise essential skills (e.g. working with the alphabet; sequencing of numbers).
- Move beyond knowledge in its 'raw' form and help pupils to see its application (e.g. elements of phonics form the basis for spelling; close familiarity with the alphabet is vital for using an index).
- Encourage children to ask questions of clarification, not merely for what tasks they have to do and how to go about them, but also their wider significance.

- Organise 'hot-seating', whereby a volunteer pupil sits facing classmates and answers questions on his or her chosen topic.

Reference

Huxtable, M., Hurford, R. and Mounter, J. (2009) *Creative and Philosophical Thinking in Primary Schools*, London: Optimus.

Professional theme 14: Working atmosphere and learning climate

Key question: *What factors should be considered in an evaluation of a classroom's learning climate?*

The significance of the classroom's working atmosphere or 'learning climate' has received considerable attention in recent years as an important factor in facilitating a high-quality education. Haydn (2012) produced a ten-point scale to identify the working atmosphere in the classroom, ranging from Level Ten in which teacher and pupils are working together, enjoying the experiences involved, to Level One in which the teacher's entry into the room is greeted by jeers and abuse. Haydn explains that the scale was

> originally devised to encourage trainee teachers to think about the degree to which teachers are in relaxed and assured control of their classrooms and can enjoy their teaching, and also, the extent to which there is a 'right to learn' for pupils, free from the noise and disruption of others.
>
> (Haydn 2012, p. 2)

The scale is not for the purpose of judging teachers, but a means of helping them to evaluate the factors affecting classroom climate and its impact on teaching and learning.

Discussion points

It is an odd phenomenon in schools that a visitor can walk into two adjacent classrooms in which pupils are busily engaged in similar tasks and feel relaxed in the one and uneasy in the other. A number of factors contribute to the difference in atmosphere, including: (a) the teacher's demeanour – pleasant and cheery or dour and complaining; calm and consistent or liable to flare up without warning; (b) the adult–child relationship: relaxed and respectful or tense and turbulent; (c) the pupil–pupil relationship: happy and tolerant or tetchy and complaining; (d) the teaching approach: varied and interactive or pedestrian and wholly didactic; (e) the level of pupil independence: tightly monitored or generous; (f) the competitiveness: good-humoured and courteous or aggressive and ungracious; and (g) the extent of encouragement: everything praised, or nothing praised, or selective praise for genuine effort and achievement. In primary schools, the decorativeness of your room also impacts upon the impression created; thus, tidy without being prim; evidence of pupils' achievements; areas to stimulate interest, and so forth.

Action plan

- Use approving comments to commend sensible behaviour more than disapproving comments to criticise poor behaviour.
- Avoid confrontation with pupils whenever possible while maintaining order.
- Smile, laugh and generally enjoy being in the classroom.
- Be firm and rigidly stern with disobedient and naughty children.
- Celebrate small achievements, especially in the case of children who struggle academically.
- Be welcoming and unfailingly courteous to all visitors, whether adults or children.
- Treat learning as an adventure.
- Make every child in the school have a secret wish to be in your class!

Reference

Haydn, T. (2012) *Managing Pupil Behaviour: Improving the Classroom Atmosphere*, Abingdon: Routledge.

Professional theme 15: The impact of an objectives-driven agenda

Key question: *How can teachers encourage pupils to value the process of learning as much as they value the product?*

Experience shows that most pupils have a 'product' attitude to learning, often abetted by adult expectations and the demands made by teachers. Thus, they are set tasks for completion or activities to perform, and they strive to finish the work to the teacher's satisfaction. Children soon become aware that they will be rewarded with praise and approving comments from adults if they accomplish precisely what is expected of them. By contrast, if children deviate from the set task or insist on pursuing their own agenda, they are guided back onto the right path or scolded. In the light of these trends, Fisher (2005) argues that, if children become obsessed with an objectives-driven agenda, they tend to display some of the following characteristics:

- *Success is viewed as absolute, being either achieved totally or missed completely.* There is no halfway position for such children and they become upset if they do not fulfil or exceed expectations.
- *Excuses are given to explain away shortcomings in their work.* Children view anything less than perfect or below the achievements of their rivals as a personal affront.
- *Ability to learn certain things is seen as fixed rather than something to be improved.* Children will say that they are no good at some things and brilliant at others. In response to a teacher's prompting they will resist being coached or trained to get better at an area of learning they struggle to master.
- *Difficulties rather than possibilities and solutions dominate their thinking.* Two men looked through prison bars; one saw mud, the other saw the stars (attributed to poet Frederick Langbridge). Such children see the mud.

■ *Initial failure or problems result in depression.* Children with a product orientation evaluate success only in terms of achieving the objective. They do not
regard the process as significant; only the end result matters. Such children
quickly become downcast and dispirited if things don't go smoothly.

Discussion points

Achieving the correct result and finding the right answer are obviously very
important in learning, but the process of discovery, trial and error, and grappling with difficult concepts are also significant. Children can become anxious
if they do not do things correctly; this unease is exacerbated if you focus
exclusively on getting the right solution and only reward (verbally or through
merits) those pupils who do so. Focusing on an objectives-driven agenda to the
exclusion of other learning possibilities can lead children to be fearful of making
errors, which tends to narrow their thinking and creates a form of mental stag-
nation, as they are reluctant to think creatively and opt for the regular and 'safe'
option. It is easier for you to tell them what to do to get a correct result than for
them to feel liberated and apply their minds to a problem. You have the challenging job of helping pupils to accept their limitations, persevere to overcome
difficulties and keep setbacks in perspective. In doing so, it is of course essential
that misconceptions and misunderstandings are not allowed to take root. Ultimately, pupils have to learn what needs to be learned. You have to decide
whether, in any particular case, you are acting as guide, mentor, facilitator or
'rescue worker'; that decision will impact on the latitude in learning that children are allowed. Having said all this, it is nevertheless a fact that all children
need to experience the thrill of success. The learning process is only valuable if
it leads to a successful outcome. Process and product are interdependent.

Action plan

■ Clarify learning objectives but welcome diversions if they appear to be
academically fruitful.
■ Avoid giving the impression that the first pupils to get the 'right' answer are
the only ones deserving of approval.
■ Include a range of collaborative investigative or problem-solving activities into
the schedule in which there exist a variety of possible solutions and from which
less capable pupils can share and celebrate success with their more capable peers.
■ Do not allow children to flounder and become agitated; scaffold their
learning in stages by offering a small amount of guidance initially and increasing the specificity if it becomes clear that the child is still uncertain about the
way forward.
■ Regularly discuss with pupils the nature of their errors in a calm manner rather
than merely correcting them and moving on; thus, in a non-threatening and
sincere tone, 'I am interested to know why you did it this way'.

Reference

Fisher, R. (2005) *Teaching Children to Learn,* second edn, Cheltenham: Stanley Thornes.

Professional theme 16: Personalised and individualised learning

Key question: How can teachers ensure that each pupil's learning needs are met without creating an unmanageably complex system?

One of the terms that has entered the education vocabulary in recent years is that of 'personalised' learning in which each pupil's specific needs are catered for rather than each being seen as one of a group of children with similar needs. Personalisation as a term is sometimes used interchangeably with 'individualisation' and sometimes defined separately as referring to the operation of an individualised programme of work. However, some teachers have raised five concerns. First, that personalised learning is an unattainable ideal because no teacher, however skilled and knowledgeable, can offer a bespoke education to each pupil in the class. Second, that learning does not depend solely on teaching methods, so even the most carefully targeted programme cannot guarantee learning outcomes. Third, personalised learning that seeks to remedy a pupil's weaker areas rather than building on strengths can become unduly rigid in format, thereby constraining creativity and innovation. Fourth, the constant detailed assessment of each child's needs is burdensome on teachers. Finally, any approach to learning, regardless of its fine intentions, has to be cognisant of the need to achieve good pupil test results and satisfy inspection criteria. Interestingly, the Government's Pupil Premium (introduced in 2011) aims to provide head teachers with the money they need to offer an excellent and *individually tailored* education for pupils as a means of raising school results. Whether or not this aspiration proves to be an unattainable ideal remains to be seen.

It has been argued that there might be merit in restoring the system that existed in the past, especially in mathematics, whereby each child worked through a series of tasks and problems from text books at his or her own pace, using adult expertise and guidance as necessary. However, in making such a decision, Davies (2006) advises that tasks are not there to occupy the pupil, but should develop the pupil's learning further and enrich their learning experiences. Such an individualised learning system places heavy demands on the teacher as she or he attends to each child separately and, inevitably, repeats explanations as different children reach the same point in the textbook. Furthermore, the system can only work with pupils who are capable of such independence.

Discussion points

All teachers want every pupil to benefit from their teaching, make optimum progress and enjoy learning, and an important element of success is to provide work appropriate to each child's needs, assess their knowledge and understanding, and plan lessons that facilitate these aims. In your desire to help children individually there are a number of factors to take into account. First, there is one of you (the teacher) and up to thirty of them (pupils). There is no way in which you can attend specifically to each individual by providing a personalised programme of work, dealing with questions, providing guidance about the way forward, assessing work outcomes in detail and recording in depth the level of attainment. Any attempt to do so would result in exhaustion and high levels of stress as you attempted to maintain such a manic approach. (See also Chapter 4, Challenge 2.) What you *can* do, however, is to differentiate work in your planning, such that it is relevant to the needs of groups of children; attend to problems and misunderstandings; assess selected items of work; and keep records of noteworthy work outcomes. In the case of young children, the records will also refer to their social competence.

Occasionally, a pupil will have specific learning needs or traits, such that closer monitoring is necessary, but you should not attempt to replicate the special attention paid to these exceptional cases across the whole class. It is also helpful for you to respond to individual pupil interests and build on talents, encouraging pupils of all abilities to extend and deepen their learning. Importantly, however, remind yourself that you cannot learn *for* each child; you can only provide pupils with the opportunity to do so with your considerable assistance and support. Personalised learning is a tacit acknowledgement that learning is 'personal' but not 'private'. In other words, while children learn as individuals, the process of doing so is in large measure a public one, through adult intervention, co-operation with other pupils and sharing experiences with classmates, friends and parents.

Action plan

- Make a brief note of your initial impressions of each child – attitude to work; confidence; social skills; willingness to persevere; and broad areas of strength/difficulty.
- Consider ways of grouping pupils on the basis of (a) friendship; and (b) academic ability. See if there is any compatibility across the two groups.
- Involve the children in evaluating the areas of knowledge and understanding in which they feel: (a) very confident; (b) confident; (c) unsure; and (d) bewildered.
- As you set work for groups of pupils, note the ways in which children respond by using the following categorisation: (a) forging ahead without assistance; (b) progressing steadily with occasional support from an adult or classmate; (c) proceeding hesitantly. On the basis of your observations, begin to categorise children into these three groups.
- Start to identify areas of uncertainty *within the group* that you can follow up and clarify with them.
- As you get to know the children better, begin to identify the specific areas of uncertainty *for each pupil*.
- On the basis of the fifth point above, adjust your planning to take account of the areas you have identified.
- On the basis of the sixth point above, discuss with the tutor, mentor or colleagues ways in which individual needs can be addressed.

Reference

Davies, S. (2006) *The Essential Guide to Teaching*, Harlow: Pearson Education.

Professional theme 17: Competitiveness between pupils

Key question: *How can pupils' competitive instincts be channelled constructively?*

There are two broad types of competitiveness; the first is *external* competition that takes place between two persons or across a group of people; the second is *inner* competition, which might be described as self-motivated learning. While excessive competition can create unpleasantness, it is equally true that a lack of competitive stimulus leaves pupils intellectually dissatisfied and underachieving and can just as easily damage their self-esteem as enhance it (Davies 1998). Healthy competition and a desire to win are commendable, as they provide a conduit for enthusiastic endeavour and important training for the realities of life in the adult world. However, fierce competitiveness can be damaging to children's wellbeing if it denies them opportunities to enjoy participating for its own sake or fosters a 'winner-takes-all' mentality.

Discussion points

Most children are naturally competitive, sometimes aided and abetted by ambitious parents. This inclination becomes more noticeable as children grow older and seems to be particularly acute among boys. If allowed to grow unchecked, competitiveness can become obsessive and lead to an unhealthy aggression between different individuals, teams or factions. If used constructively, rivalry can heighten the desire to succeed, strengthen children's determination and provide a springboard for achievement. Only one pupil or group of pupils can ever be right at the top, so a child's willingness to be resolute, persevere and not afraid to fail must receive as much commendation from you as you give to the one who is the outright winner. Nearly all children are knowledgeable about or good at something, howbeit not directly under the remit of the formal curriculum; it is part of your job to draw it out. (See also Professional theme 11 earlier in this chapter.) You have the task of developing a classroom climate that facilitates co-operation while exploiting the natural competitiveness that exists among children.

Action plan

- Make your commendation for effort as common as your approval of achievement.
- Avoid reserving all your accolades for pupils who complete the work fastest (other than in a fun time).
- Foster a spirit of 'competition with self' such that each child strives to improve his or her own performance or quality of work, regardless of how others are doing.
- Give the greatest praise to children who succeed after struggling to do so and minimal praise to those who cruise through because they find the work easy. (Make certain that, on the next occasion, you increase the demands placed on such pupils.)

- Discuss with children in as natural a way as possible how they evaluate the quality of their own work.
- Encourage pupils to establish and monitor learning targets, but resist creating such a narrowly focused system that other learning possibilities become stultified.

Reference

Davies, N. (1998) 'Teaching for self-esteem versus behaviourism and competition', *Prospero*, 4 (1), pp. 18–27.

Professional theme 18: Benefits and disadvantages of homework

Key question: *How can homework be used constructively to advance children's knowledge and understanding without becoming burdensome?*

It is widely accepted that there are benefits to children if they continue learning beyond the immediate school day, notably by the setting of tasks to be completed at home, a process that has become known as 'homework'. The structure of the school day with its sessions, lessons, breaks and other regular events such as assembly does not allow uninterrupted learning. The timetable places constraints on the way learning occurs, such that teachers are obliged to plan lessons of a specific duration and children have to work at a particular pace to complete the tasks and activities attached to the curriculum element presented to them. In the past, some schools have experimented with a system of 'learning without walls' whereby the artificial constraints of lessons that last a specified time have been replaced with a more flexible system in which pupils can pursue their learning with minimal time barriers. Unfortunately, such innovations proved unworkable and so schools reverted to the familiar pattern of timetabled lessons. Nevertheless, the fact remains that pupils work at different speeds and take varying amounts of time to absorb and digest the knowledge associated with the regular curriculum; hence the introduction of homework as a means of: (a) allowing children to complete work remaining from lessons; or (b) developing their understanding through applying what they have learned during the school day.

However, Kohn (2006) questions why teachers and parents continue to insist on overloading children with homework when there are no definitive studies proving its overall learning benefits. Indeed, Kohn argues that homework can be detrimental to children's development by robbing families of quality evening time together and not allowing a child time to enjoy basic childhood pleasures. Similarly, Bennett and Kalish (2007) claim that excessive homework robs children of the sleep, play and exercise time they need for proper physical, emotional, and neurological development. Controversially, the authors insist that homework is a hidden cause of childhood obesity and is helping to create a nation of what they describe as 'homework potatoes'.

Discussion points

It might be the case that your school has a homework policy requiring you to set tasks for pupils at home, or you may believe that homework is beneficial and choose to set it regularly of your own volition. Either way, you are advised to take account of six points. First, homework should be manageable; there is little point in making the tasks unreasonably burdensome. Second, homework should either be a natural extension of class work and/or a simple investigation – in which case children must have the necessary resources available to complete it. Third, as far as possible, homework should be differentiated in a similar way to lessons. Fourth, homework that requires marking should ideally be marked the morning after it is completed, preferably by 'peer marking' so that you don't have to undertake a lot of additional work. Fifth, take account of the fact that, if school books are taken, there is no guarantee that children will remember to bring them back the next day, so close monitoring is essential. Sixth, homework of the 'project' type allows you to set a task that is ongoing rather than having to think constantly of something new for them to do. Bear in mind, too, that parents take homework tasks very seriously and can get anxious if, for whatever reason, their children are unable to complete them or are unclear about what they are supposed to do. In such circumstances, you can expect occasional calls or visits from parents to clarify matters.

Action plan

- Decide on the purpose the homework is serving.
- Only set homework when it is relevant to do so and not as a wearisome necessity.
- Think through the resource implications for children in completing the tasks you set them.
- Keep the process of setting and assessing homework straightforward, but also purposeful.
- Avoid the situation in which homework invariably consists of finishing off uncompleted class work, as this places an undue burden on slower workers and fails to stretch quicker ones.
- Use reading a portion from the child's 'reading book' as a regular homework task.
- Avoid making homework a millstone around your neck by generating a lot of marking.
- Make some homework open-ended – perhaps in the form of a project – and some of it in the form of specific tasks that are easy for children to moderate or mark themselves.

References

Bennett, S. and Kalish, N. (2007) *The Case Against Homework: How Homework is Hurting Children and What Parents Can Do About It*, New York: Three Rivers Press.

Kohn, A. (2006) *The Homework Myth*, Cambridge, MA: Da Capo Press.

Professional theme 19: Parental involvement in learning

Key question: How can teachers build effective home–school partnerships with parents to enhance children's education?

Parents are the first educators; but some are more competent than others. Recent studies suggest that a minority of children arrive in school with poorly developed social skills, weak language ability, erratic behaviour and an aversion to discipline. Other children are articulate, confident, socially competent, eager learners and adept at identifying and responding to school and classroom norms of behaviour. The majority lie at various points between the extremes. You might also have one or two children who have been traumatised by their experience of adults and will require a great deal of patient work to build their esteem, trust and confidence. It is likely that all shades of pupils from varied backgrounds will be represented in your class, which means, of course, that you will have a similar range of parents.

Demie and Lewis (2011) found evidence that low achievement levels of many White working-class pupils had been masked by the success of middle-class children in the English school system. The data confirmed that the White British working class is one of the biggest groups of underachievers, their results at each key stage being considerably below those achieved by all other ethnic groups. The authors suggest that the main reasons for such poor results are (a) the low aspirations of parents about their children's education; and (b) social deprivation. Page and Millar (2009: 4) suggest ten ways to build effective school–parent partnerships:

1. Appoint dedicated link staff members to liaise between parents and the school.
2. Improve communications in both directions – listen to parents and they will listen to you.
3. Develop one-to-one relationships between parents and staff – talk more, write less.
4. Help parents understand more about what their child does at school.
5. Involve more parents more often in decision making.
6. Develop and encourage parent support groups, social events and holiday schemes.
7. Celebrate success – tell parents about the good things as well as the bad.
8. Help parents to build their own confidence and skills.
9. Take advantage of the skills and experience parents can offer.
10. Have a clear complaints policy in place and treat criticism positively.

Discussion points

The most effective tools for successfully involving parents seem to be located in three approaches: (1) being a welcoming face and voice at the classroom door and, as time permits, in the playground; (2) sending children home happy and contented after spending the day in school; and (3) working closely with the teaching assistant. It has also been suggested that schools can and should support parents in developing their children's skills by making packs and videos available as a means of explaining what their children are learning at school and how they can be helped at home. These time-consuming but worthwhile initiatives are normally supported by training sessions in school for parents in subjects such as mathematics and computer literacy. The vast majority of parents desperately want their children to be happy in school, to do interesting things, to make friends and, crucially, to learn to read well. Remember that if pupils love you as their teacher, there is a strong chance that the parents will do so, too. (See also Chapter 2, Teaching and learning issue 4 earlier in this chapter.)

Action plan

- Look and sound as if you are pleased to see your pupils and their parents.
- Be positive but realistic with parents about their children's progress.
- Keep parents well informed about what is happening.
- Resist patronising parents by using false voices, forced laughter or simplistic explanations. They might not be teachers, but neither are they easily fooled!
- Make positive comments to parents in their children's presence.
- Set homework tasks that involve parents or grandparents; for example, relating their happiest childhood memories; sharing the funniest thing that ever happened to them; helping the child to compile newspaper cuttings about local events.

References

Demie, F. and Lewis, K. (2011) 'White working class achievement: an ethnographic study of barriers to learning in schools', *Educational Studies*, 37 (3), pp. 245–64.
Page, A. and Millar, C. (2009) *School-Parent Partnerships: A Short Guide*, London: Family and Parenting Institute.

 ## Section D: Teachers and teaching

Professional theme 20: Attributes of good teachers

Key question: *What characterises exceptional teachers and how are they recognised?*

In the Introduction to this book, we saw how difficult it is to describe and define an excellent teacher. If asked, every teacher would, of course, claim to be 'at least average' and aspire to be 'above average', which is, of course, a statistical impossibility – just as it is ludicrous to claim that all pupils can achieve above-average results. Moore (2001) claims that there is a tendency to describe teachers in terms of personality and charisma rather than academic prowess; the implication being that good teachers are 'born' rather than 'made'. In a later publication (Moore 2004) the author suggests that the simple use of the expression 'good teacher' fails to do justice to the threefold nature of the role:

1. The *competent craftsperson* – a concept currently favoured by Governments.
2. The *reflective practitioner*, which continues to get widespread support among teacher trainers and educators.
3. The *charismatic*, whose popular appeal is revealed in film and other media representations of successful teachers. That is, the teacher using his or her personality in ways that fascinate and engage children in their learning, the said person often referred to as being a 'natural teacher'.

In addition to possessing secure subject knowledge and being able to plan, teach and assess competently, an essential element of being a good teacher is to create the type of working conditions that facilitate what is sometimes described as an effective learning environment or climate: relaxed yet purposeful; achievement oriented without being unduly competitive; strongly motivating and encouraging. (See also Professional theme 14.)

Discussion points

Pupils need to have faith in you and be engaged in the lesson process and their own learning as closely as possible; that is, learning should happen with them and not be done to them. Children are unlikely to make strong progress if they are expected to go passively through the motions of being taught; rather, they need to be active learners who are grappling with concepts, ideas and situations, trying hard to make sense of them, and fitting them into their existing frame of understanding. In doing so, they need to be interested and occasionally fascinated by the curriculum, drawn into the lesson through your enthusiasm and sincerity, and invited to contribute to the proceedings by making suggestions, asking questions and proposing innovative ideas. You have the difficult job of ensuring that pupils are at ease in the classroom while working purposefully to advance their learning. In addition, monitoring of progress and occasional assessments of specific aspects of learning (e.g. level of fluency in reading) allow you to help children target, address and reinforce less well developed areas of their understanding and skills. While you will always want to explain what the lesson is about, why it is necessary and what they are likely to learn, it is also important to retain a slight sense of mystery about what might emerge from their endeavours to keep them on their toes and avoid a 'here we go again' reaction.

As a top teacher, you will need to be wise and exercise your professional judgement in determining your reactions to the many situations that arise throughout the day. Consider how you would act wisely in the following circumstances:

- The more assertive children are dominating the use of equipment during collaborative activities.
- Freda, aged nine, tells you that she does not have to do what you say because you are 'only a student'.
- The same two children are always last to be chosen by their classmates as members of teams for games activities.
- You are told a racist joke by a child in the class.

- You are asked by a senior teacher/mentor/parent to make sure that the books on the classroom shelves are suitable for the children in your class.
- Meena, aged eight, comes to you in tears because no one wants to play with her.
- A child confides in you that his parents are separating.
- Some children in your class complain that a girl who is new to the school had been swearing openly at other children. (Would it make a difference if you knew that the girl was from a very unsettled background?)
- A parent tells you that she does not want her five-year-old sitting next to a particular child because the child smells.
- A parent tells you that she does not want her able ten-year-old son sitting by a less able child because the child is always asking him questions when he is trying to get on with his work.

Action plan

To develop an effective learning environment that is relaxed, but purposeful, you might aim to achieve the following:

- Learn each child's name quickly and use it respectfully.
- Look and sound as if you are enjoying teaching by smiling a lot, laughing at humorous situations and welcoming pupil queries.
- Encourage children to ask questions and express their opinions courteously.
- Promote an 'all-for-one-and-one-for-all' attitude by accentuating positive things and celebrating achievements.
- Use vocabulary appropriate to the maturity and experience of pupils.
- Speak clearly, engagingly and precisely.
- Use a natural tone of voice and avoid strained speech.
- Get down to the child's eye level and make 'soft' eye contact where practically possible.
- Explain and 'lightly' enforce classroom rules by issuing reminders about appropriate action rather than operating heavy sanctions.
- Help children to take some ownership of the situation by establishing a system of elected monitors whereby children have small but significant responsibilities.

Reference

Moore, A. (2001) *Teaching and Learning: Pedagogy, Curriculum and Culture*, Abingdon: Routledge.

Moore, A. (2004) *The Good Teacher: Dominant Discourses in Teaching and Teacher Education*, Abingdon: Routledge.

Professional theme 21: Teachers' beliefs about teaching and learning

Key question: *In what ways do teachers' beliefs about education impact on their classroom practice?*

Your beliefs about education and the way that children learn best will strongly influence the way that you teach. Consider the extent to which you sympathise with the following statements and the implications of your answers for: (a) your attitude towards pupils; (b) your teaching approach.

- Each child learns in a different way from every other child.
- Boys' learning and girls' learning needs differ from each other.
- Teachers can constrain children's learning by poor teaching.
- Children need time to observe, think, try and experience things first hand.
- Teachers' enthusiasm has a positive effect on pupil behaviour and determination to learn.
- Effective teaching relies heavily on being a skilled observer of children.
- Pupil self-confidence is a necessary prerequisite for effective learning.
- Pressure on children to learn benefits some pupils and disadvantages others.
- Children's imaginations need to be activated for effective learning.
- Pupils need to feel that they have ownership of their learning.
- Effective teachers make it clear to children that they like them.
- Criticism of children is more likely to be damaging than helpful.
- Children need to have something to hope for and look forward to.
- The best teachers have deep personal humility.
- Children are more likely to succeed if they feel welcome and valued.
- Children have many things to teach one another.
- Children benefit from having an accurate assessment of their progress as learners.
- A fear of consequences if pupils get things wrong constrains their learning.
- Children learn better if they understand how they learn.
- Teachers need to have hard centres and soft exteriors.

Discussion points

You might believe that children learn best when their learning is closely controlled and monitored by the teacher. You might be comfortable when the class is sitting quietly and completing formal tasks; or perhaps you feel uneasy unless pupils are active and 'buzzing' with eagerness to complete an activity. You might favour group work or paired or individual work or a combination of the three, depending on the occasion and subject matter. Nearly all inexperienced teachers struggle initially to find a way of working that suits them best and is also appropriate for the pupils in the group or class; over time, a pattern of organising and managing pupil learning emerges that takes account of both education ideals and the realities of daily work as a teacher.

Your beliefs about education and the teacher role are a major factor in shaping the sort of teacher you become but they are not the only contributors. Your personality makes a difference to the way you behave in the classroom; the preferred teaching methods by other teachers inevitably influence your style; and the general class behaviour affects the freedom that you have to teach in the way that you want. Sometimes, the time of day or week or even the weather can affect your teaching, not to mention your state of health and prevailing confidence level. Even so, it is worth taking time to consider your response to the twenty statements above, as it is surprisingly easy to fall into ways of working that emerge randomly rather than being moulded by your beliefs. It is essential that in the hurly-burly of school life and the intensity of planning, organising, managing, assessing, liaising and extending your knowledge, you take time to consider what you really believe and the implications for practice. You may not be able to introduce every aspect immediately, but it pays to have ideals to which you aspire if you are to avoid being blown this way and that by the latest education fad.

Action plan

- Reflect carefully on each of the above twenty statements.
- Discuss them with a colleague, tutor or friend.
- Monitor whether your actions as a teacher accurately reflect your beliefs.
- Consider what changes might help you to align your beliefs and practices.

Professional theme 22: Observing children at work

Key question: In what ways can teachers use child observations to assist learning and promote classroom harmony?

By contrast with formal assessments, child observation is non-judgemental and serves to provide descriptions to inform teaching and adjust classroom practice. In this regard, Fawcett (2009) emphasises the importance of valuing children, recognising their abilities and listening carefully to what they have to say; she also stresses the significance of taking account of the wider setting when observing a child: family, community, culture, economics and geographical location. In other words, pure observation is more meaningful when placed in context, rather than in isolation, though creating a synergy between these elements is far from easy. Close observations of children not only provide information for teachers about academic and social development, but also might occasionally alert them to serious concerns about child welfare issues. It is also worth noting that children are *close observers of grown-ups*: parents, friends, relatives, teachers and support staff. Adults need to maintain a high level of integrity between what they say and what they do, as even very young children are quick to point out inconsistencies. As educators, we should provide role models that will have a positive influence on young people's attitudes and behaviour, rather than some of today's celebrities, who seem to be rewarded for behaving badly (Hallam and Rogers 2008). (See also Chapter 2, Teaching and learning issue 5.)

Discussion points

You need to become an expert observer of pupils for four principal reasons: (1) it provides you with insights into children's patterns of behaviour and their socialising – notably their friendship patterns; (2) it indicates their attention span, on-task focus and concentration level during lessons; (3) it allows you to see if a child is looking eager, anxious, guilty, uncertain, bold, assertive, tentative or unenthusiastic; and (4) it facilitates eye contact, warm smiles and nods of encouragement between you and the children. During question-and-answer sessions, it is useful to take careful note of which children contribute answers; which ones never respond; and which ones rely on their friends for support. Your teaching assistant is sometimes available to record the observations.

While formal means of assessment are normally attached to pupils' academic achievements, notably the ability to complete tasks and activities successfully, focused observations offer opportunities to see 'beyond' the immediate work completion and glimpse some of the factors impinging upon and directly influencing that process. In practice, the sheer busyness of classroom life makes systematic observation over even a few minutes almost impossible. You will need to make effective use of your assistant to 'hold the fort' during those times and also to take time out as described in Chapter 4, Challenge 5. In the process of doing so, you need to decide how to record your observations: whether in freehand form; using a checklist; taking photographs; or making audio/ video recordings (consulting the school policy about producing visual images of children before doing so). Don't underestimate the time and skill required to analyse such data; it is one thing to observe children, it is quite another to draw accurate conclusions.

Action plan

- Make it your aim to be a professional observer of children.
- Listen to what children say, but also pay close attention to their body language.
- Give free choice of partners from time to time and note the pupils who work best together, the ones who need to be kept apart, and which children are marginalised.
- Monitor children's responses to success and lack of success in lessons; talk to them about their feelings as well as the content of their work.
- As with other assessment data, keep all observation information confidential.

References

Fawcett, M. (2009) *Learning Through Child Observation*, second edn, London: Jessica Kingsley.

Hallam, S. and Rogers, L. (2008) *Improving Behaviour and Attendance at School*, Maidenhead: Open University Press.

Professional theme 23: Questions asked by teachers

Key question: What sorts of questions allow teachers to assess pupil's knowledge and understanding and promote further learning?

Teachers use hundreds of questions, which serve one or more of five broad purposes. First, questions offer teachers an opportunity to engage directly with pupils and establish a positive rapport with them. Second, posing a variety of questions that elicit considered responses stimulates pupils to think hard. Third, on the basis of their answers, teachers have an opportunity to assess pupils' depth of understanding. Fourth, questions help children to learn from others as they listen to what is said and adjust or evaluate their own understanding. Fifth, questions allow teachers to identify areas of pupil misunderstanding for clarification or remedial action. When dealing with a wide ability range, most teachers find that it is preferable to start with more straightforward questions as a means of involving all pupils, rather than beginning with conceptually challenging ones that limit the number of children who can participate. Myhill and Dunkin (2002) found that speculative questions were much more frequent in literacy than in numeracy. Thus, in literacy, 21 per cent of all questions asked were speculative, compared to 6 per cent in numeracy. In literacy, there were very few occasions when children were asked to articulate their thinking processes or their understanding (5 per cent of the total questions); by contrast, these were more frequent in numeracy (23 per cent of the total).

Discussion points

If you pose different types of questions, rather than concentrating exclusively on those that require a single yes or no response, children benefit in three ways:

1. Questions that start with 'Why?' help them get more information and knowledge about the area of learning, as they try to make sense of situations.
2. Questions that start with 'What do you mean?' and 'What about?' help them to clarify and gain greater understanding about the issues being raised through the subsequent discourse.
3. Questions that offer alternatives help them to think deeply and recognise that multiple perspectives on a topic exist.

For children to answer your questions successfully, they need rapid access to what they already know and the confidence to risk being incorrect. Your response to their answers will transmit a message to children about your expectations, mood and priorities, so be careful what you say and how you say it. You should also take account of the fact that a child who appears unable to answer may have stored the knowledge away and, in the pressure of the moment, been unable to draw it out of his or her memory bank, or may be weighing up other options rather than offering a predictable response. There are occasions, therefore, when you need to slow down the pace of the lesson to allow pupils opportunity to think before answering. In the case of more-probing questions, you might also wish to employ a strategy of 'discuss with your partner before deciding your answer'.

Children will sometimes ask you an 'obvious' question to confirm that they are doing things correctly; commend such questions as a positive sign that children want to get things right, rather than rebuking them for not listening or a similarly irritable remark. As part of this teacher–pupil dialogue, it is essential for you to encourage children to ask their own questions, as it acts as a spur to broaden their horizons, look at life from different positions and make sense of experiences that they are struggling to fit into their existing framework of understanding.

Action plan

- Monitor the types of questions that you use; divide them into: (a) interrogative questions requiring a specific, correct answer; (b) questions that offer children an either/or option; (c) probing questions that require children to think carefully before answering; and (d) profound questions that oblige children to make ethical or moral choices. The teaching assistant might be able to keep a tally.
- Try to increase the percentage of open questions (i.e. with more than one suitable answer).
- Increase the number of probing questions that you ask in mathematics lessons.
- Follow up answers to questions and discuss their implications.
- Adopt a responsive and encouraging reaction to questions asked by pupils.
- Organise question-and-answer sessions in which one child is 'the expert' (on, say, a hobby or special interest) to field questions from classmates. Ensure that the whole experience is positive and elevates the participant's confidence.

Reference

Myhill, D.A. and Dunkin, F. (2002) 'What is a good question?' *Literacy Today*, 33, pp. 8–9.

Professional theme 24: New teachers' rite of passage

Key question: *How can new teachers adjust to the demands of the job and expectations of colleagues while retaining their individuality and professional integrity?*

The rite-of-passage concept is based on the principle that the possession of teaching ability alone does not guarantee that new teachers will be accepted into the social fabric of school life and make a valuable contribution to the corporate endeavour. A new teacher also needs to respond appropriately to the expectations of personal behaviour demanded by existing cultural norms, in as much as all new personnel are required to demonstrate a willingness to learn about the school's procedures and priorities, and affirm the shared practices. The attitude and behaviour of trainees and new teachers after their arrival is, of course, noted and evaluated by the indigenous staff. This monitoring is prominent in primary schools, which are intimate working environments and where agreed forms of conduct and staff relationships are essential to maintain harmony. When the head teacher and governors make an appointment, one of their prime considerations is how well the new staff member will fit into the existing situation.

Going through stressful and challenging experiences is not pleasant but might be necessary if new teachers are to make progress as a practitioner. Results from a study in the Netherlands by Meijer *et al.* (2011) suggest that most teachers in the early stages of their career do not perceive their development as a steadily ascending line but as an undulating path with highs and lows and transformative moments or periods of time. Somewhat perversely, perhaps, it was during these times of crisis that new teachers explicitly reconsidered their connections to teaching and regained their motivation for the job. During such events, support from mentors and colleagues could make the difference between despair and a determination to continue.

Discussion points

Twiselton (2006) claims that new teachers tend to pass through three stages in their knowledge and understanding of teaching:

Stage 1: As *task manager* during the early stages of learning to teach, in which they view their role in terms of ensuring that pupils complete set tasks.
Stage 2: As *curriculum deliverer*, as they see themselves supporting pupil learning by following a designated scheme, curriculum or lesson plan.
Stage 3: As a *concept* and *skill builder*, in which they are aware of the need for pupils to develop a wider and deeper understanding of knowledge and develop appropriate skills to facilitate learning.

The aim is for you to reach the third stage as quickly as possible without losing your grip on stages 1 and 2, but also to be aware that there are no shortcuts to achieving full competence as a teacher and there will be setbacks during the process. Eisenhart *et al.* (1991) suggest that, to be accepted by the existing staff, new teachers have to pass through at least three stages, which they refer to as: (1) separation; (2) transition; and (3) incorporation. A new teacher sometimes has to loosen his or her fixation on the way that things were done in the previous school at which they worked, grapple with the demands and requirements of the new situation during a transitional adjustment period, and finally become assimilated into the new culture.

There are a number of situational factors that affect the process of being encultured. The first and most significant factor is the effect of existing practices that are taken for granted by the existing staff but are largely unknown by newcomers. The quicker you become aware of, and accept, the stated code of conduct ('the way it is done here') and work out the *unwritten* code (the assumed procedures, priorities, shared beliefs and opinions), the easier the rite of passage will be. The second concerns the different personal factors reflected in the images that new teachers have of themselves and their beliefs about teaching. Thus, if you come across as arrogant because you think that you have all the answers and nothing to learn, your passage will be much less comfortable than if you exude confidence but do so with a due sense of humility, and accept that you have a lot to learn. The third factor relates to the methods and strategies used in teaching. Classroom approaches employed by colleagues that make little sense to you when you arrive in a new school become clearer over time, so it pays to avoid being dismissive of them or unduly sceptical, whatever your initial misgivings. More-experienced teachers have usually found ways to draw the best out of the pupils while maintaining discipline, so watch, listen and learn. The fourth factor is the quality of mentoring transmitted through coaching, discussion and the provision of emotional support. Your tutor's role is crucial in this regard to guide without being intrusive and advise without being dogmatic. With so many diverse factors to consider, it is not surprising that new teachers, whether trainees on placement or NQTs in their first post, require time to acclimatise to the prevailing school ethos before they can make significant headway in their teaching and become wholly integrated into the staff. (See also Professional theme 32 later in this chapter.)

Action plan

- Adopt a positive approach to the new situation and do not allow negative thoughts or anxious fears to dominate.
- Show a willingness to learn from every situation and every person, including assistants, administrative staff and parents.
- Do not try to impress anyone; be natural and sincere and a person of integrity.
- Be prepared to offer your expertise generously but with due humility.
- Take account of every comment made to you by more-experienced colleagues and weigh up the advice carefully.
- Show by your commitment and thoughtfulness that you are worthy of respect.
- Listen intently (and discreetly) to all staffroom conversations as a way of gaining insights into school life.
- Look and sound as if you are enjoying your time in school even if you are experiencing some unease.
- Studiously avoid gossips, complainers and cynics (if any exist); gravitate towards people who smile a lot.
- Remind yourself constantly that you are a valuable member of staff – simply less experienced than the others.

References

Eisenhart, M., Behm, L. and Romagno, L. (1991) 'Learning to teach: developing expertise or rite of passage?' *Journal of Education for Teaching*, 17 (1), pp. 51–71.

Meijer, P.C., de Graaf, G. and Meirin, J. (2011) 'Key experiences in student teachers' development', *Teachers and Teaching*, 17 (1), pp. 115–29.

Twiselton, S. (2006) 'Developing your teaching skills', in J. Arthur, T. Grainger and D. Wray (eds) *Learning to Teach in the Primary School*, Abingdon: Routledge.

Professional theme 25: Accountability and autonomy in teaching

Key question: *How can teachers retain a healthy degree of autonomy while remaining accountable to others?*

One of the much-valued dimensions to the job of teacher is the relative freedom that being alone in the classroom with a group of pupils confers. While schools are now more open establishments, it is nevertheless true that a good deal of a teacher's work is detached from having direct contact with other adults except, perhaps, the occasional presence of an assistant. As part of the Government's attempts to raise standards in teaching, professional standards for teachers in England were introduced in 2012. The standards state that teachers must show tolerance and respect for the rights of others and not undermine what are referred to as fundamental British values. The values include upholding democracy, the rule of law, individual liberty and mutual respect and tolerance of those with different faiths and beliefs. The new code requires that teachers must uphold public trust in the profession and maintain high standards of ethics and behaviour in and out of school. Teachers should make sure their personal beliefs are not expressed in ways that might exploit pupils' vulnerability or might encourage them to behave recklessly or break the law. Nearly all teachers would agree that such sentiments are valid but that they hardly need expressing formally.

In a White Paper published in 2010 called *The Importance of Teaching* it is argued that too much professional development involves compliance with bureaucratic initiatives rather than working with other teachers to develop effective practice. (See also the Introduction at the start of this book.) In this regard, it is interesting to note the conclusions reached by Wilkins (2011) after interviews with newly qualified teachers about their understanding of professionalism. Thus, the 'improvement agenda', which he defines as a remorseless focus on increasing the quality of teaching and learning and the standards of attainment by pupils, is more or less taken for granted by them. Such an agenda dominated their own schooling, which has led to new teachers having a more relaxed approach to balancing accountability (being judged on results) with autonomy (freedom to make decisions about how they teach). It appears that younger members of staff are more willing to accept the strictures of accountability than their older colleagues.

Discussion points

Teacher autonomy has been the subject of considerable discussion over the years, not least at the commencement of the National Curriculum in 1988/89, and the imposition of the 'literacy hour' with its prescribed format at the end of the 1990s. Furthermore, many teachers have expressed unease with the way in which the results of national curriculum tests and associated end-of-year tests in Key Stage 2 have dominated educational policy and practice in schools. Increased rights for parents, embodied in legislation, community involvement in the schooling process and, more recently, pressure to teach reading by using designated methods, have combined to create a situation in which teachers have been wary of straying too far from what they perceive as the 'official line'. Consequently, there has been an increase in didactic (direct teaching) methods (see Chapter 4, Challenge 5) and an emphasis on teachers in schools and across schools collaborating to implement common practices and share expertise. The evolution of a new brand of advisory teacher ('advanced skills' or 'expert' teachers) spreading advice among local school cohorts has added to the sense that teachers are expected to teach and behave in specific ways. As a result, a rather disdainful view of professionalism has developed, loosely defined as 'closely adhering to other people's expectations' including, in some cases, the whims of a few outspoken parents. On the other hand, once the classroom door is literally or metaphorically closed, the vast majority of teachers are still given licence to teach and organise learning in a way that fits their beliefs about education. With rare exceptions, they do so with relish!

Action plan

- Do what you are obliged to do with good grace; do what you have the freedom to do with integrity.
- View your colleagues as a potential resource for you, and yourself as a resource for them.
- Do not allow your fear of doing the wrong thing to cramp your teaching style and creativity.
- Observe others teaching and find out not only *what* they do but, if possible, *why* they do it that way.
- Embrace new ideas (rather than being cynical about suggestions), but interrogate them thoroughly before attempting to implement them.
- Listen closely to criticism of your performance in case there is some truth in what is being alleged, but continue to do what you believe to be in the pupils' best interest.

Reference

Wilkins, C. (2011) 'Professionalism and the post-performative teacher: new teachers reflect on autonomy and accountability in the English school system', *Professional Development in Education*, 37 (3), pp. 389–409.

Professional theme 26: Differentiating for learning

Key question: *How can teachers differentiate for learning in a way that benefits all pupils?*

Segregating pupils into 'sets' on the basis of ability has become increasingly common in recent years; separating children into classes (Class A, B, C, etc.) is still uncommon (though see Chapter 2, Teaching and learning issue 21). It is almost universally agreed that it is educationally appropriate to differentiate work in core subjects on ability, such that the slower and less competent pupils are given less demanding work, together with lower teacher expectations about the quality of the end product, and academically brighter pupils have to tackle more demanding work, together with higher teacher expectations. However, there are a number of practical issues attached to class-based segregated education ('setting'), which can be summarised as follows:

- Because a group of children share some difficulties (e.g. poor readers), it does not follow that they require the same kind of education provision for every area of work.
- Children who are separated from classmates have limited exposure to a model of classroom behaviour experienced by their peers and can feel disenfranchised.

- When children are extracted from class they are falling further behind in the normal class work and may miss out on access to the full curriculum; they also have to spend time on 'catching up' and thereby lose out on the chance to undertake more appealing activities.
- The work that children do under segregated conditions tends to be in the basic elements of a subject or to involve an excessive concentration on the use of worksheets or other easy-to-organise practices, which thereby neglects opportunities for collaborative problem-solving and investigations with their peers.
- There is evidence to support the principle that children learn most effectively through group interaction, so the efficacy of 'one-to-one instruction' is questionable.

Discussion points

It doesn't take sophisticated assessment techniques and arduous testing for teachers to discern that pupils vary considerably in their level of intellect, skill acquisition, ability to understand concepts and application to tasks. If you were to ask each child the same questions and give every child the same work to do, it would immediately become apparent which ones were capable and which were strugglers by the nature of their responses. Some pupils try to disguise their lack of knowledge or understanding by being silly, hiding behind other children or pretending that they knew the answer but had 'just forgotten'. To allow for these differing abilities, you are required to plan work in such a way that every child is able to grapple successfully with the demands of the tasks or activities, and to find success. It all sounds easy in principle but, as every practitioner knows, it is far harder in practice.

The concept of differentiation was devised as a method of educating children of similar age in the same class, regardless of their academic standing. The reality is that, in attempting to provide a socially harmonious environment by keeping children of mixed ability working together, you have to face the challenge of providing explanations, questions and tasks that in some mysterious way 'match' the abilities, capabilities and supposed learning style of each child, every single lesson! To cope with this requirement, teachers often spend as much time in planning, preparation and assessment as they do in actively teaching, not least because of the inclusion of children with special needs into mainstream classes and the additional demands this places on the teacher. Differentiation is not confined to setting appropriate tasks but needs to be reflected in the types of questions that you ask – always involving less able children by using uncomplicated questions – and the vocabulary you employ. (See Chapter 2, Teaching and learning issue 16.)

When allocating tasks and activities, you can differentiate in one of four ways: (1) group children of roughly comparable ability on nests of tables and allocate them co-operative activities to complete together; (2) as in option (1), but give tasks that have to be completed individually, though they can discuss with others in the group; (3) give pupils the same set of tasks initially, but 'stage' the remainder of tasks so that there are always further, more demanding ones for brighter children after they complete the easier elements; and (4) plan (say) three separate, but related, sets of work for the top-/middle-/lower-ability ranges to work on independently. In practice, there is a limit to the amount of differentiation possible with a large group of pupils, as their needs are invariably wide and extensive. You can only do your best to ensure that pupils are engaged with a form of work that promotes their learning and provides challenges, without overwhelming them or causing them to pepper you with questions about how to complete the tasks.

Action plan

- Get to know the children intimately before making crucial decisions about work content and groupings.
- Remind yourself often that, although you can adjust your teaching approach to accommodate different pupil abilities, you cannot learn *for* them.
- Take into account the fact that learning is not linear; it is cyclical and requires regular revision, regardless of the child's ability.
- Concentrate your efforts on excellent classroom teaching more than any other single aspect of the job.
- Make sure that every child succeeds at something and goes home feeling satisfied.
- Avoid being locked into a mind-set that regards less capable children as inferior to their classmates.

Professional theme 27: Effective public speaking

Key question: *How can teachers improve their delivery and clarity of speech to convey meaning and help children to learn?*

Any form of public speaking relies on effective communication. Whether in a secluded area of the classroom, on stage in assembly, addressing a staff meeting or speaking to parents, the quality of your delivery requires adherence to five principles:

1. *Know to whom you are speaking.* Whether a speech is formal or casual, its target is the audience, so you have to consider what will interest them and persuade them.
2. *Know who you are.* Good public speaking is about being genuine and credible, using your own voice and ideas rather than repeating someone else's thoughts.
3. *Know what you want to say.* Good, logical reasons why what you say is correct, supported by evidence and illustrations, are at the heart of any talk.
4. *Know where you are going with the talk.* Even the best ideas are forgettable if they do not possess a structure: beginning, middle, end, in a logical progression.
5. *Know the full range of arguments.* By listening to others, whether opponents, questioners or colleagues, you can adjust your ideas to be more relevant and address the issues of importance to an audience.

Discussion points

It is remarkable that competences required by trainee teachers do not emphasise an ability to speak effectively and clearly communicate meaning through the use of words. You will never become a top teacher if you are weak in this vital area of public speaking. It is not only in front of pupils that you need to be proficient, but also in talking to colleagues and addressing an audience of parents. Whatever the specific circumstances in which you speak, there are four factors to consider:

1. You must overcome shyness, which is largely due to a lack of self-confidence. To do so, you must first convince yourself that you have as much worth as anyone else and, to use a cliché, learn to like yourself. Focus on the people in front of you, not on how you look or feel. Take several slow deep breaths and release the air gradually. Stop thinking about yourself as being shy; instead, tell yourself that you are a positive, happy and capable person. It has a remarkable transforming effect.
2. Order your thoughts so that it is possible to list the main headings from your talk on a single page of a notebook. While it is good to make detailed plans and think through their implications, you must ultimately be able to look up and engage the eyes of the listeners. If you need to quote something it is, of course, perfectly in order to have the quotation on a separate piece of paper and read it verbatim.
3. Practise, practise and practise. If you are an inexperienced teacher, it is worth recording what you intend to say to the children. If possible, record yourself while sitting in front of a mirror, so that you can also observe your non-verbal behaviour.
4. Put yourself in the place of the listeners and try to see things from their perspectives. Neither pupils nor adults have heard what you are saying to them before you start speaking, so slow down and concentrate on getting the message across, rather than worrying about how impressive you are sounding. Although most teachers improve the technical quality of their delivery over time (articulation, pace of speech, use of pauses, etc.) they do not necessarily improve as *communicators*, so keep persevering not only to speak clearly but also to be clear in your mind about what you are attempting to convey.

Speaking to children is less daunting than facing an audience of adults, but doing so still requires attention to the basic elements described above. As a rule, speak more slowly to younger children and avoid innuendo. All children enjoy listening to a teacher who has a pleasant voice and a 'sing-song' tone rather than a dull one. Naturally, use of gesticulation, varying facial expressions and good eye contact assist in engaging the audience. (See also Chapter 1, Learning skill 9 about pupils' public speaking.)

Action plan

■ Approach the improvement of your public speaking with the same dedication you would give to practising the piano or honing your sports skills. You can do so by reciting tongue twisters; improving enunciation by 'exaggerated' reading aloud; employing singing techniques to strengthen the larynx; and facing a mirror when you practise speaking.

- Find useful advice through the Internet or other sources using key words such as: voice, diction, clarity, speaking.
- Record your voice using a variety of texts (e.g. reciting a poem, or reading cookery instructions, or describing an object, or speaking above loud music) then ask a friend to comment on the clarity of your words and what they convey.
- Warm up for speaking by breathing slowly and naturally, buzzing your lips, gently massaging your cheeks and making a circular movement of your jaw.
- Elevate your voice by imagining that the words are coming out of the top of your head.
- Make effective use of pauses; link body movement (especially the eyes) with variations in voice tone.
- Avoid being defensive or ridiculing yourself.
- Acknowledge courteously the existence of contrary viewpoints and alternative positions.
- Conclude positively and cheerfully.
- Give listeners time to absorb the implications of what you have said and ask questions to clarify issues.

Professional theme 28: Fostering creativity in teaching and learning

Key question: *How do teachers foster creativity through their teaching in a way that enhances pupil learning and promotes innovation?*

Inspection reports about creativity in schools agree that it is most likely to be found in classrooms where teachers do not feel bound by orthodox teaching methods, but rather make use of cross-curricular themes and spend time developing an enlivened physical environment. Creativity does not emerge by simply giving children time and space to 'create something', but by generating enthusiasm and offering appropriate adult support within a culture of self-expression where new ideas are actively sought and encouraged. Grainger (2003) argues that teachers should spend more time on discussing literature, oral storytelling, poetry performances and improvised drama if children are to be offered the chance to 'interpret, communicate and *create* meaning for themselves' (p. 44, author's emphasis) in their learning. She stresses that a willingness to take risks with creative and artistic activity enhances teachers' confidence and pupils' imaginative engagement. Teachers who are excited and personally involved are much more likely to communicate joy and wonder than those who work through a plain transmission of facts.

Discussion points

Every teacher wants to be creative. There are a number of challenges attached to this aspiration, however, including the following requirements: (a) to be clear what you mean by 'being creative'; (b) to shape creative teaching strategies; (c) to understand how to promote creative learning; (d) to decide whether creative teaching results in creative learning; and (e) to distinguish between focused creativity and random creativity. Thus, in point (a), you might define 'being creative' as 'the freedom to choose'; or 'doing things in an unconventional way'; or 'finding solutions to complex problems'.

To shape creative teaching (b), you might reorganise the lesson format; or use a range of visual aids; or incorporate drama and puppetry; or heighten the level of teacher–child and pupil–pupil interactivity; or increase the competitive element. (See also Professional theme 17.)

In devising strategies for point (c), you might decide to develop collaborative working; or provide investigative problem-solving activities; or encourage pupils to find their own solutions and ways of working. (See also Professional theme 30 later in this chapter.)

To monitor the effectiveness of your creative teaching on pupil learning (d), you might take account of pupils' so-called learning styles – auditory (speaking); visual; kinaesthetic ('hands-on') – in determining which approach stimulates and raises the level of enthusiasm and imagination. (See also Chapter 2, Teaching and learning issue 14.)

Finally (e), to ensure that your creativity does not deteriorate into gimmickry or become an entertainment, reflect on how you would justify your teaching approach to a parent or inspector. (See also Chapter 1, Learning skill 10: Being imaginative and creative.)

Action plan

- Initially develop lesson plans in the usual format.
- Envisage ways in which you might introduce and explain the lesson content and purpose to pupils using imaginative means (e.g. through visual aids, computer images).
- Formulate tasks and activities in such a way that they contain an open-ended element (i.e. where children have to think hard about how they proceed).
- Develop collaborative tasks as a means of promoting pupil involvement and stimulating ideas.
- Encourage pupils to think laterally and suggest or find different methods of solving problems and finding answers.
- Introduce a wider range of key words and phrases (including subject-specific ones) to facilitate discussion and enlarge their vocabulary.

Reference

Grainger, T. (2003) 'Creative teachers and the language arts', *Education 3–13*, 31 (1), pp. 43–47.

Professional theme 29: Reflective practice and teaching

Key question: *How can teachers ensure that reflective practice actively influences the quality of their teaching?*

One of the earliest proponents of the concept of reflecting about practice was John Dewey (1859–1952) as he studied actions involved in learning new skills.

Dewey concluded that there are two basic sorts of actions, the first type being *routine* action, governed by habit or expectations; the second type being *reflective* action, involving flexibility and self-appraisal, influenced by the social conditions. Reflective practice in teaching is, of course, broadly posited on the second type, though reflection can be applied to any action. Dewey's original publication, *How We Think*, was written for teachers, and the first edition became the reference book of progressive educators (Dewey 1910, 1997). In more recent years, Donald Schön has argued in his seminal work, *The Reflective Practitioner: How Teachers Think* (Schön 1983, 1991), that professionals who receive coaching and encouragement to think carefully about what they do, while they do it, learn more deeply than those who merely perform their duty in a perfunctory fashion.

Discussion points

In the United Kingdom, Andrew Pollard and Sarah Tann popularised the concept of teacher-reflection by means of their much-acclaimed publication *The Reflective Practitioner* (Pollard and Tann 1987) by suggesting that reflective teaching is characterised by four elements (amended):

1. An active concern with the aims and consequences of an action, as well as with its means and technical efficiency.
2. Combining implementation skills with attitudes of open-mindedness, responsibility and wholeheartedness.
3. A cyclical or spiralling process, in which teachers continually monitor, evaluate and revise their own practice on the basis of what they perceive to be its strengths and shortcomings.
4. Decisions and actions based on teacher judgement – partly by self-reflection and partly by insights extracted from other areas of education.

In a wide-ranging review, Larrivee (2008) argues that the aim of reflective practice is to think critically about your choices and actions in teaching. Consequently, teachers should interrogate the goals, values and assumptions that guide their work. In reality, most teachers are so preoccupied with implementing the latest government initiative and ensuring that they comply with the head teacher's demands that they scarcely have time to stop and think about fundamental education issues. As a trainee or newly qualified teacher, your knowledge and insights can awaken fresh awareness and enthusiasm in your jaded host, so take time to raise interesting questions and courteously offer your own perspectives. See also Mattheson (2008) for a useful overview of key issues.

Action plan

- As you reflect upon each session and each day in school, divide your thoughts into three sections: first, those things I've done well; second, those things I could have done better; last, those things that went badly wrong. The chances are that nearly everything will fall into categories 1 and 2 so, while addressing issues of substance, don't waste your time agonising over matters of little consequence.

- Write down every day one important lesson and one teaching tip that you have learned at school. Do it systematically and you'll be amazed at the cumulative effect.
- Stick to your principles about the best way to educate children but also be willing to amend your beliefs in the light of hard-earned experience. Remember that, while it is true that our beliefs drive practice, the reverse is also true, namely, that practice influences beliefs.
- Consider frankly the extent to which you are trying to implement someone else's convictions about teaching and the extent to which they are your own.
- As much as lies within your power, and after considering all forms of advice, behave in the way that you think is *right* in the classroom.

References

Dewey, J. (1910/1997) *How We Think*, New York: Dover Publications.
Larrivee, B. (2008) 'Meeting the challenge of preparing reflective practitioners', *The New Educator*, 4 (2), pp. 87–106.
Mattheson, D. (2008) *An Introduction to the Study of Education*, London: David Fulton.
Pollard, A. and Tann, S. (1987) *The Reflective Practitioner*, London: Continuum.
Schön, D. (1983/1991) *The Reflective Practitioner: How Teachers Think*, New York: Basic Books.

Professional theme 30: Teaching methods and co-operative learning

Key question: *How do teachers teach so as to inculcate a spirit of collaboration and mutual endeavour among the children?*

It is possible for teachers to provide information, explain procedures, give directions, organise work and use teaching techniques in such a way that the relationship between them and the children is of little significance. Thus, a complete stranger could come into the room and manage the learning process efficiently without forming a bond of trust with the pupils or gaining their respect. However, as we have noted elsewhere in this book, to foster ongoing effective learning, teaching primary-age pupils relies heavily on the creation and maintenance of a secure relationship between children and teacher. To increase levels of motivation and ensure a purposeful classroom climate, interactive teaching requires that both the teachers and pupils be at ease with each other and willing to contribute to the learning process. Furthermore, the most productive learning climate necessitates active co-operation between pupils and a strong sense of togetherness.

A study of more than three thousand primary-age children in the Netherlands by Thoonen *et al.* (2011) showed that teachers who made an effort to be connected to the children's personal world and employed co-operative learning methods had a positive effect on pupil motivation. By contrast, too much direct instruction by the teacher had a negative impact on children's enthusiasm for learning and a detrimental effect on behaviour. (See also Chapter 4, Challenge 5.) Teaching based on collaborative principles appears to have appreciable benefits for both teacher and learner (though note the information and guidance in Chapter 1, Learning skill 4).

Discussion points

Naturally, you want the pupils in your class to co-operate and work together harmoniously to complete tasks and learn from one another. You may feel that organising for learning is best served by creating opportunities for children to pool their ideas and develop solutions. On the other hand, you might prefer a more individualised approach, whereby every pupil is solely responsible for his or her own learning and does not rely on others to achieve a successful outcome. It is probable that you combine the two forms, that is, you expect each pupil to be independent-minded, yet willing and able to work as part of a team.

In addition, however, you, the teacher, also form part of the collaborative endeavour, as you are rightly viewed by children as an integral part of the learning community and the key person in their school world. Your attitude – whether aloof and stern or, by contrast, communicative and responsive – will determine in large measure the way that pupils approach learning and respond to one another. The very best teachers know that it is less a case of 'me and them' as 'we and us'. Setting an example and insisting on courtesy and mutual endeavour instils in children the knowledge that co-operation is ultimately in everyone's interest. It is up to you to set the right example in this regard.

Action plan

- Act and behave as if you were the leader of the class – because you are!
- Distinguish between co-operation, which is a social requirement, and colla-boration, which is a learning strategy.
- Make every effort to explain (but not to justify) to pupils the rationale underpinning classroom procedures and organising learning.
- Stress frequently to pupils that each child is ultimately responsible for his or her own learning, aided by you and other adults.
- Modify your teaching approach by introducing small but significant changes over time. For instance, you might allocate a larger percentage of the lesson to enquiry, or choose some sensible children to co-ordinate feedback from classmates towards the end of the session, or incorporate a short quiz into the proceedings.

Reference

Thoonen, E.J., Sleegers, P., Peetsma, T. and Oort, F.J. (2011) 'Can teachers motivate students to learn?' *Educational Studies*, 37 (3), pp. 345–60.

Professional theme 31: Teachers' duty of care

Key question: *How can teachers safeguard children's welfare while allowing them opportunities to explore, experiment and take reasonable risks?*

There is no single definition of what constitutes 'a child' or when childhood ends. The United Nations Convention on the Rights of the Child, ratified by the UK Government in 1991, states that a child is defined as every human being below the age of eighteen years unless, under the law applicable to the child, the age of majority is attained earlier. In child protection terms, England, Wales, Northern Ireland and Scotland each have their own regulations that set out the duties and responsibilities of organisations to keep children safe, but they agree that a child is anyone who has not yet reached his or her eighteenth birthday. The Department for Education (DFE) in England defines safeguarding and promoting the welfare of children in three ways:

1. Protecting children from maltreatment.
2. Preventing impairment of children's health or development.
3. Ensuring children are growing up in circumstances consistent with the provision of safe and effective care.

The DFE legislation explains that child protection is a part of safeguarding and promoting welfare. It refers to the activity that is undertaken to protect specific children who are suffering, or are likely to suffer, significant harm. It can be seen from these comments that the concept of 'welfare' has grown beyond *in loco parentis* and now has to take account of issues of law and criminal responsibility. Nixon (2007) warns that, as parents and carers become more aware of their rights under law, the actions of teachers, school governors and local authorities will increasingly be tested for evidence of negligence. Depending on the age of the children, the person with a primary duty of care (notably the teacher) must ensure that all reasonable precautions have been taken to safeguard their welfare, but it is far from easy to know at what point 'being careful' lapses into being 'unduly cautious'. Children need opportunities to explore, to experiment and occasionally to take risks, howbeit within a controlled and, crucially, a disciplined environment.

Typical of the dilemmas faced by teachers are the results of a survey of sixty-three practising primary teachers conducted by Owen and Gillentine (2011), which indicated that, although teachers of younger children understood the benefits of touching, they were fearful of being falsely accused of inappropriate behaviour. The problem is especially acute for male teachers and assistants. Regrettably, the teachers surveyed had begun the process of resolving the problem by restricting the nurturing practice of touch. The authors argue that teachers must be given the freedom to safely and appropriately touch children, as children have a basic need for such contact as a form of reassurance and approval.

Discussion points

Every adult in school has a moral responsibility towards pupils in school to ensure that they are kept safe from physical harm, protected from emotional damage and not placed under unreasonable psychological pressure. At the same time, teachers are required to exercise discipline and promote good behaviour, based on the fact that children are happier and learn more efficiently under orderly conditions. Safeguarding children must not, however, be confused with mollycoddling them, so ensure that you build plenty of opportunities for the pupils to design and build with materials, create their own games in PE and on the computer, and show initiative through engaging with collaborative problem solving and investigations. Naturally, you will want the pupils in your care to learn in a positive and secure environment; in view of this, you will need to make a habit of checking regularly that your words as well as your actions are consistent, blameless and in the children's interest. In particular, it pays to be alert when excitement is high and children are more animated than usual, and when you are tired and grumpy, as it is on such occasions that you are more likely to make errors and utter irritable comments that cross the boundary of appropriateness.

Action plan

- Check that equipment is in good condition and is used appropriately, especially large-scale items such as those for PE.
- Clarify the way that you expect children to behave towards you and one another.
- Have high but realistic expectations of what pupils can achieve in their academic work such that you support and encourage them rather than browbeat them.
- Show by your words and deeds that children are valued for who they are, and not merely for their academic prowess.
- Discuss children's welfare regularly but discreetly with colleagues and, where appropriate, with the parents of any vulnerable child.
- Maintain an accurate record of notable incidents.

References

Nixon, J. (2007) *Teachers' Legal Rights and Responsibilities: A Guide for Trainee Teachers and Those New to the Profession*, Hatfield: University of Hertfordshire Press.
Owen, P.M. and Gillentine, J. (2011) *Early Child Development and Care*, 181 (6), pp. 857–68.

Professional theme 32: Professional learning communities

Key question: *What steps can be taken to facilitate the development of a professional learning community?*

Professional learning community (PLC) is an expression used to describe collaborative learning among colleagues in a particular work environment. Thus, teachers and co-workers in school with shared interests might combine as a team for a specific purpose – for example, discussing ways to enhance the social experiences of young children; strategies to promote problem-solving techniques in learning; guidelines for dealing with distressed children, and so on – though head teachers, especially of smaller primary schools, also like to promote a 'whole school staff' ethos to offset the possibility of factions developing. Norwood (2007) comments that, although collaborative efforts might be hard to organise and maintain initially, smaller sub-groups can work together as, for example, academic or grade-level teams, or any other sub-group that works well within the framework of what the school community is hoping to accomplish.

Discussion points

Ideally, a learning community should include staff, pupils, parents and the wider community in the education of the young. In practice, it is far from easy to achieve this ideal. Classroom teachers are primarily responsible for the academic, social and emotional development of pupils in their classes, rather than being instrumental in promoting a wider societal ethos. On the other hand, every adult in school benefits from being part of a friendly, interactive and loyal team, so time spent in fostering good relationships and helping everyone to feel involved at some level in determining the future direction of school policy can only be beneficial.

More difficult for new teachers and trainees is the relatively rare situation in which other people – colleagues, head teacher, governors, parents or even pupils – try to dictate professional skills, such as teaching methods, or impose a code of behaviour that sits uneasily within the belief framework of the person concerned. If you are a trainee teacher, you have to adjust to and accommodate the regular teacher's teaching approach initially, but are expected to gradually assume control over the prevailing style. It is fair to say that this issue can sometimes be a contentious one and requires openness and ongoing discussion between you and the host teacher.

In practice, you will not become a member of the community until you have successfully negotiated the rite of passage, but it is fair to say that some newcomers never quite fit in with the existing staff. The process of adjustment usually takes several weeks and the occasional misjudgement is inevitable, but colleagues are nearly always forgiving if they see your sincerity and determination to adjust to the prevailing norms. (See also Professional theme 24 earlier in this chapter.) One way and another, you have to demonstrate that you are doing your best and are willing to learn from others. Every time you set foot in school, you have a responsibility towards every other member of the community. Conscientious people with a ready smile and a due sense of humility (not to be confused with servility) are always welcome.

Action plan

Through the learning community, play your part in helping to develop some or all of the following:

- Making every effort to learn about the norms and expectations of the school community.
- Fostering an ethos of aspiration, success, achievement and wellbeing among learners, staff and the wider community.
- Supporting children in achieving a lifelong love of learning.
- Sharing knowledge, resources and skills with others in the community.
- Offering expertise and fresh perspectives about aspects of teaching and learning; for example, subject knowledge and practical ideas for its implementation.
- Creating the conditions for continuous improvement in academic standards, social concord and behaviour among the pupils.

Reference

Norwood, J. (2007) 'Professional learning communities to increase student achievement', *Essays in Education*, 20, pp. 33–42.

Professional theme 33: Achieving peace of mind as a teacher

Key question: *How do teachers maintain a positive view of life when things get tough?*

The motivation to teach primary-age children is multifaceted and powerful. Sinclair (2008) suggests that the most common reasons for trainees choosing to teach include a positive self-evaluation regarding their own attributes and capabilities to be teachers, a desire to work with children and the intellectual stimulation that teaching provides. She also notes that trainee teachers modify their level of motivation and commitment to an extent during the period of time spent on school experience. Her research revealed that, for the most part, the placement in school showed trainees what the job of being a teacher was really like, and confirmed or negated their choice of teaching as a career. The small percentage of the trainee respondents who became disillusioned about teaching after school experience cited factors such as tensions emanating from school politics, poor relationships with supervisors and difficulties in implementing what they had learned from coursework in their classroom practice. Ho and Au (2006) found in a survey of two hundred and twenty primary and secondary teachers that teaching satisfaction correlated positively with self-esteem but negatively with psychological distress and teaching stress. In other words, ease of mind and heart were essential prerequisites for fulfilment and satisfaction in the job.

Research by Moriarty *et al.* (2001) discovered that most teachers of younger children found their work both satisfying and rewarding. However, teachers also felt they were being impeded by external factors, such as educational change and current curriculum initiatives, which made the job more demanding and increased the stress and strain. In particular, the teachers in the survey expressed frustration in having to implement policies that they felt were contrary to their own understanding of effective and appropriate pedagogy and professional values.

Discussion points

Peace of mind is not a cosy option for inadequate teachers, but a vital necessity to ensure that you are operating at optimum efficiency and taking a daring approach to the job rather than behaving altogether predictably. Doubts about personal competence can embed themselves in your mind, lower your morale and constrain innovative practice as you opt for a 'safe' but uninspiring teaching approach. Peace of mind is engendered through knowing what you are doing; doing it as well as you can; focusing on your achievements, not your shortcomings; and refusing to lapse into a pessimistic state of mind. If at any time you find that you are starting to doubt your own abilities or wonder if you are, after all, capable of succeeding, put up a 'no entry' sign to such negativity and refuse to contemplate failure. At the same time, seek advice from those who can help you to use your perceived failings as a launch pad for improvement; suffering in silence serves only to deepen your anxiety. Teaching has a nasty habit of permeating your life in such a way that you begin to confuse your worth as a person with your competence as a teacher. You would not judge the worth of a child solely on the basis of her or his achievements; extend the same generous principle to yourself.

Action plan

- Take control of the factors that influence your life; don't develop a victim mentality.
- Remind yourself often that no one in any job at any time is totally successful.
- Have a number of close confidantes outside school in whom you can confide.
- Adjust your thinking in such a way that you look to help and support others first and foremost, as this approach acts as an antidote to self-pity.
- At the start of each day say, in your own words, 'Today will be a great day!' emphasising the word 'great'.
- Just as you try to value each child for the person she or he is, adopt the same perspective towards yourself.
- Laugh often and freely.
- Read the suggestions made in Challenge 2 and Challenge 3 found in Chapter 4.

References

Ho, C.L. and Au, W.T. (2006) 'Measuring job satisfaction of teachers', *Educational and Psychological Measurement*, 66 (1), pp. 172–85.

Moriarty, V., Edmonds, S., Blatchford, P. and Martin, C. (2001) 'Teaching young children: perceived satisfaction and stress', *Educational Research*, 43 (1), pp. 33–46.

Sinclair, C. (2008) 'Initial and changing student teacher motivation and commitment to teaching', *Asia-Pacific Journal of Teacher Education*, 36 (2), pp. 79–104.

Section E: Discipline and behaviour

Professional theme 34: Pupil compliance

Key question: *How can teachers create a learning climate that encourages pupil enthusiasm for learning and counteracts indiscipline?*

Fisher (2011) investigated the views of Year 6 pupils (ten–eleven years old) concerning factors that influenced the way in which they conducted themselves during uninteresting lessons. She found that they were strongly inclined towards compliance because it did not pay to be confrontational. Pupils were generally eager to please the teacher and did not want to damage the relationship. Thus:

The majority of children engaged in behaviours, sometimes complex, to avoid reprimand and to conceal their dissatisfaction within a lesson. They were aware that their behaviour did not expose their dissatisfaction with aspects of the curriculum; however, they were keen to retain their metaphorical veil to avoid upsetting their teacher. Dissatisfied children appeared to face a dilemma: express your dissatisfaction and risk alienating the teacher – with no evidence to suggest that non-compliance alerted the teacher to adjust their teaching – or conceal your dissatisfaction and continue to please the teacher.

(p. 136)

Fisher concludes that there is a danger of teachers promoting compliance with regard to the ground rules that operate in the classroom at the expense of children having opportunity to share their perspectives about learning. In other words, pupils' positive co-operation could quickly degenerate into lifeless conformity.

Discussion points

Most lessons are reasonably interesting for pupils but, inevitably, some parts of the curriculum will be less engaging than others. While most teachers genuinely want to hear the 'pupil voice', they cannot build their teaching solely around those things that appeal to the children. It is also undoubtedly true that some lessons will appeal more to some children than to others. However, it is not simply the curriculum content that matters, but also the *manner in which it is taught* that provides the key to satisfaction. Even at a time when topic work was commonplace in British schools, Gunning *et al.* (1981) warned that organising learning on the basis of children's interests could be deceptive, as teachers 'find in children what they hope and expect to find' (p. 21). Furthermore, it is unlikely that all the children in a class or group will share common interests; consequently, teachers 'may seize upon the interest of one child but be unable to find any expressed interest in particularly apathetic and unresponsive children who are not prepared to initiate activity' (p. 22).

You will doubtless wish to strike the perfect balance between compliance ('do what I say') and encouraging initiative ('do what you think is right'). Most new teachers wisely opt for more of the compliance than the initiative during the settling-in period at the start of a school placement or first post. If you are a trainee teacher, you have to take careful account of the regular teacher's style and philosophy, as too much deviation in the early stages might be viewed as counterproductive and unsettle the children. Gradually, however, you must make some tough decisions about when it is appropriate to allow pupils greater freedom in making decisions about their own learning. If you permit freedom of choice too soon, it can result in confusion because pupils won't have the skills and strategies to use their time constructively; if you wait too long, you risk preventing more adventurous children from exploring new avenues of learning and causing frustration. It is far better if pupil compliance is a voluntary act on their part than imposed by you through forceful means, but make sure that you don't give the impression of being a weak and compliant teacher! (See also Chapter 2, Teaching and learning issue 23.)

Action plan

- Assume and expect that children will behave well, but be ready to respond decisively if they do not. Avoid saying 'shh'.
- Do not be discouraged or distracted if some children grumble about the work they are doing; stay cheerful and hold out the prospect of something more engaging to come when they have completed the work satisfactorily.
- Give pupils the benefit of the doubt if their inappropriate behaviour appears to be as a result of your poor explanations or badly framed instructions rather than their wilfulness.
- Make it clear from the outset that, while you will be accommodating and helpful, you will not tolerate poor behaviour or disobedience from anyone.
- Designate specific times – perhaps last thing on Friday afternoon – when children are invited to talk about the 'best' thing they did during the week. Don't be surprised if they focus on aspects of the curriculum other than the core subjects!
- Create an atmosphere in which children feel comfortable in asking (courteously) about the reason they have to learn that part of the curriculum. Have some good answers ready!

References

Fisher, H. (2011) 'Inside the primary classroom: examples of dissatisfaction behind a veil of compliance', *British Journal of Educational Studies*, 59 (2), pp. 121–41.

Gunning, S., Gunning, D. and Wilson, J. (1981) *Topic Teaching in the Primary School*, London: Croom Helm.

Professional theme 35: Dealing with indiscipline

Key question: *When should teachers use a light touch and when should they exercise tight control?*

All new teachers struggle with issues relating to pupil behaviour and exercising discipline. Regardless of all the advice they receive during training, all the reading, all the reflection about strategies, methods and principles of maintaining order, each group of children raises fresh challenges. There are no absolutes; no electronic aid to inform teachers whether their response to a pupil is appropriate; no immediate feedback about whether a particular action, sanction or form of words will assist or hinder a resolution. To add to the complication, a technique that worked well with one class seems relatively ineffective with another. Only time will tell whether or not your methods are appropriate in the situation.

One recalcitrant pupil can cause a teacher to agonise over her or his capability. By contrast, a response that brings about a more settled learning climate raises teachers' spirits and revitalises their teaching. Jacques (2007) comments that trainees and some experienced teachers tend to blame the children when behaviour difficulties arise. Jacques emphasises the point that different circumstances simply mean that different discipline strategies have to be employed.

While in the normal run-of-the-mill times, a teacher can rely on the existing good relationship with pupils to allow simple tactics such as a shake of the head to diffuse the situation, on other occasions some tight control strategies have to be employed. There is no single technique that brings about the desired outcome.

Adams (2009) explores the concept of 'behaviour for learning' (that is, attitudes towards learning) linked to the *Every Child Matters* agenda, with particular emphasis on the significance of relationships with self, with others and with the curriculum, together with children's social knowledge. The author emphasises the importance of self-reflection and notes that academic factors can affect behaviour for learning. Adams also highlights the need to consider the 'whole child', including wider social factors (e.g. the situation at home) in attaining positive behaviour. In this regard, children with autism provide particular challenges, as the condition is not only stressful for the individual and adults in school but also for the parents (Langan 2011). In this regard, Muller (2010) comments from a parental perspective:

> I just want my child to have friends – this is a common hope for families who have a child with autism spectrum disorder or Asperger syndrome [a form of autism but with which children have fewer problems speaking and are often of average or above-average intelligence]. Parents can feel despondent when they watch their child wandering around the playground alone, and frustration when their child walks off in response to a child asking them to play. Similarly, when their child thinks it is fun to punch, hit and kick other children, the resulting isolation from their peers can be frightening for many parents.
>
> (p. 331)

(See also under Chapter 1, Learning skill 9.)

Discussion points

Faced with silly behaviour, inexperienced teachers are sometimes tempted to ignore it or hope that by sounding fierce they can minimise the disruption. In fact, ignoring the behaviour is rarely effective (though there are exceptions to this rule) and indicates to the class that the teacher is not in control of events. Similarly, severe comments often make matters worse in the long term and, although temporarily effective, they lead to exhaustion and distress if used over a prolonged period. The problem with harsh reactions is that they deal only with the symptoms and not the underlying causes such as boredom, bravado, inappropriate lessons, inadequate lesson management, and so on. It is axiomatic that the few do not dictate your agenda or unduly influence the teaching approach at the expense of the majority, but the reality is that they often do so. The manner in which you handle the difficult cases will determine your overall effectiveness in maintaining discipline. Ideally, every child should learn to be self-controlled, but a small number of hardy cases need strong action and, if necessary, the application of sanctions. (See also Chapter 2, Teaching and learning issue 23.)

Action plan

- Check that pupil restlessness is not due to lesson tedium.
- Endeavour to develop a more upbeat approach to your teaching.
- Expect good behaviour and do not countenance disobedience.
- Make it clear to the children whether you are giving commands ('you must do this') or offering them a choice ('do this or that').
- Make it a rule never to overreact to indiscipline but, none the less, to react!

References

Adams, K. (2009) *Behaviour for Learning in the Primary School*, Exeter: Learning Matters.

Jacques, K. (2007) 'Managing challenging behaviour', in K. Jacques and R. Hyland (eds) *Professional Studies: Primary and Early Years (Achieving QTS)*, Exeter: Learning Matters.

Langan, M. (2011) 'Parental voices and controversies in autism', *Disability and Society*, 26 (2), pp. 193–205.

Muller, R. (2010) 'Will you Play with Me? Improving Social Skills for Children with Asperger Syndrome', *International Journal of Disability, Development and Education*, 57 (3), pp. 331–34.

Professional theme 36: Coping with restless pupils

Key question: *What can teachers do to assist restless children to learn and behave appropriately?*

At one time, restless children were referred to as 'having ants in their pants' because they seemed unable to sit still for long. More recently, it has been recognised that restless behaviour sometimes has a more deep-rooted genesis. Blythe (2009) stresses the significance of what she refers to as the ABC of attention (A), balance (B) and co-ordination (C) with respect to specific learning difficulties that are linked with common motor skills resulting from deficiencies in a child's brain function. Hannaford (2005) argues that, contrary to popular opinion, the development of nerve networks which constitutes learning never stops. She suggests that children with attention disorders, who move around a lot in class, are just doing what is natural to them and trying to stimulate the part of the brainstem that wakes them up. The author also insists that expecting children to learn when they are under stress – for example, when told to be quiet and not allowed to move from their place at a time when they desperately need to talk and move about – can be counterproductive and damaging. In practice, teachers have to find ways of accommodating children's need to be active while maintaining order, being able to teach without constant interruption and protect other pupils from being harassed. No easy task.

Discussion points

Unsettled pupils, who seem to have been born under a wandering star, can become a source of considerable irritation to teachers, who expend a lot of energy trying to keep such children on task. An important element of behaviour management resides in your ability to prevent difficulties by utilising a variety of verbal and non-verbal cues. By exercising these cues skilfully, problems are less likely to occur in the first place. For instance, you might develop a long stare at the child and continue to do so until he has returned to his seat. Again, you might have a small tinkling bell that you sound when the child needs to pay attention. Such strategies do not eliminate the underlying problem, but offer a framework for the child to use in tempering the off-task tendencies; they must, of course, be used alongside high-quality classroom practice, not as a substitute for it.

If the child also has symptoms that include a short attention span, being disorganised and impulsive, it is possible that he or she (usually he) will be diagnosed as having attention-deficit/hyperactivity disorder, commonly referred to as ADHD. In fact, very few children have this condition; many more children who fail to concentrate are simply unconditioned to sitting still, paying attention and completing their work. It is part of your job to help them improve and learn self-discipline, but you normally have to reach a compromise whereby the child is allowed some scope for moving around on the proviso that he does not disturb the others. You can gradually tighten the restrictions on movement and reward compliance; but don't expect miracles. The school SEN co-ordinator (SENCO) will advise about such matters, but it is also important for you to develop your own skills and strategies for coping with this kind of restless pupil. Unfortunately, the child's progress is likely to be slow and erratic with numerous instances of non-compliance. Simplistic solutions so beloved of politicians and theorists rarely prove successful.

Stemler *et al.* (2006) suggest that you need to take account of two components. The first component involves understanding the kinds of actions you need to take in order to *prevent problems from arising*; the second component involves understanding appropriate action to take *once a challenging situation has to be dealt with*. The authors recommend that you use one or more of seven practical strategies, which can be viewed as a sine curve, with the first two options being 'inactive', the last two options being 'overactive' and the middle three being 'reactive'. Thus: (1) avoid; (2) comply; (3) confer; (4) consult; (5) delegate; (6) legislate; and (7) retaliate. The implications for your classroom practice can be summarised as follows:

1. Avoiding confrontation is different from ignoring the behaviour, which usually means that it will worsen over time.
2. Complying means that you accept the child's behaviour in the belief that it cannot be changed, which is a defeatist approach.
3. Conferring means that you determine your response and inform other adults (e.g. teaching assistant) of your intentions.
4. Consulting involves discussing the situation with a more experienced colleague and taking advice about appropriate action.
5. Delegating usually means giving the main responsibility to another adult or even, in part, to a small group of sensible pupils (providing it does not interfere unduly with their studies or undermine your authority).
6. Legislating is a strategy whereby you impose rules, regulations and sanctions for transgressions, regardless of the pupil in question.
7. Retaliation is when you use your authority to impose order fiercely – an approach that brings short-term results but fails to address the underlying problems and can create animosity.

It is not difficult to see that the middle three of the above strategies (3–5) are likely to form the core of your response, though occasional use of the other, more extreme options is sometimes justified. For example, there will be occasions when you are in full flow and, despite the child's misdemeanour, you decide to ignore the behaviour until you have concluded your presentation. At the other extreme, there will be times when you need to be extremely insistent; for instance, if the child's actions are causing distress to others, your assertive intervention is essential. These decisions require professional judgement and wisdom and there are bound to be occasions when you select the wrong option. Don't despair! Some things only come with experience and you will gradually make fewer errors as you progress.

Action plan

- Regularly remind the class about the agreed rules.
- Allow a restless child some leeway to move about but draw the line when he interrupts other children.
- However annoyed you feel, always give the impression of being calm and unperturbed.
- If other pupils protest about the child's behaviour, thank them but also ask them to allow you to deal with the situation.
- Set the child specific short-term targets with a very simple 'cumulative' reward system (points, stars, etc.).
- Keep parents and the SENCO informed: parents largely about commendable things; SENCO about both positive and negative trends.
- Be very strict at the first sign that the child (or any other) is taking advantage of your reasonableness. When you insist on something being done, speak strongly but keep your voice at a normal pitch.
- Seek help and advice if the child's behaviour deteriorates; it is not shameful or a sign of failure to do so.

References

Blythe, S.G. (2009) *Attention, Balance and Co-ordination: The ABC of Learning Success*, London: Wiley-Blackwell.

Hannaford, C. (2005) *Smart Moves: Why Learning is Not All in Your Head*, Marshall, NC: Great Ocean Publishers.

Stemler, S.E., Elliott, J.G., Grigorenko, G.L. and Sternberg, R.J. (2006) 'There's more to teaching than instruction: seven strategies for dealing with the practical side of teaching', *Educational Studies*, 32 (1), pp. 101–18.

Professional theme 37: Managing disruptive behaviour

Key question: How should teachers interpret and respond to cases of insolence and wilful disobedience?

Rudeness to adults in primary schools is rare. Children will only make cheeky remarks if: (a) they believe that they can get away with saying them; or (b) they feel that the rebuke or sanction is a price worth paying. Impertinence can take a variety of forms, the most common being pulling silly faces when asked to do something by an adult (younger pupils); making 'clever' comments (older pupils); or feigning confusion (any age). Some children become adept at teasing adults yet remaining on the right side of insolence. Chaplain (2010) advises that teachers should keep things in perspective and not lose their sense of humour or take the behaviour as a personal 'attack' on them – though this attitude is far from easy to adopt when it happens! Importantly, Chaplain goes on to say that it is not uncommon for teachers to reach the point of questioning their own ability and losing confidence when faced with disruption. This loss of confidence is reflected in the teachers' tentative behaviour; mischievous pupils soon detect the insecurity and take full advantage. It is important to add, however, that the vast majority of children have neither the courage nor desire to be rude or disruptive, and want to enjoy a harmonious relationship with the teacher and get on with their work.

Discussion points

It is important to stay completely calm when dealing with transgressions, yet without ignoring them. You have to strike a balance between remaining unflustered and showing your displeasure. If you underreact, the children get the impression that you are unable or unwilling to exercise correct discipline. If you overreact, you can alienate not only the transgressor but also the sensible pupils and thereby make matters worse. Some inexperienced teachers view naughty behaviour as a slight on their characters and respond punitively; a small percentage of teachers laugh it off as unimportant – both reactions are unhelpful. You have to decide whether your response is: (a) primarily to punish; or (b) to educate about the right way to behave; or (c) to correct the child. Any hint of pleading on your part will be interpreted as weakness and ruthlessly exploited, especially by an older, badly behaved pupil.

Action plan

- Learn to distinguish between friendly banter and impertinence.
- Make it a golden rule that you do not make the whole class pay for the misdemeanours of the few.
- In dealing with a transgression, allow the lesson to flow with the minimum of interruption unless you judge that a failure to intervene immediately will lead to further problems.
- Use a 'warning → second warning → sanction' approach unless the child is a regular offender and knows full well the consequences of an action; in such cases, implement the sanction immediately and irrevocably.
- Never threaten to do something unless you are sure you can carry out what you say.
- Avoid falling into the trap of 'I can make more fun of you than you are making of me'.
- Never set up a fierce public dialogue with an individual miscreant.
- Don't expect an unreasonable child to suddenly act reasonably; perseverance is needed.

- Follow through your intentions to issue sanctions where appropriate, regardless of how a child suddenly becomes 'reformed' after you have issued the edict.
- Try not to personalise the situation, especially with a child who gets under your skin.

Reference

Chaplain, R. (2010) 'Managing classroom behaviour', in J. Arthur, T. Grainger and D. Wray (eds) second edn, *Learning to Teach in the Primary School*, Abingdon: Routledge.

Section F: Curriculum practice

Professional theme 38: Negotiated meaning for effective learning

Key question: *How can teachers best communicate meaning to pupils?*

Pupils, teachers and teaching assistants are constantly interacting as a way of understanding one another better. Thus, children talk to other children; adults talk to children; and children talk to adults. The words that are used, together with body language and intonation, convey meaning to the recipients. Children speak rapidly to their friends, using short sentences, slang expressions and expressions of intent. Adults tend to speak more slowly to pupils than they do to other adults; children respond by speaking even more slowly in response, as they seek to grasp what the adult says and, crucially, what the adult *means*. On the assumption that a satisfactory definition of curriculum resides in all the things that children learn in school, both formally in terms of schemes of work and informally in terms of information, insights and understanding gained through a variety of other means, teachers have to ensure the effectiveness of communication channels (verbal and non-verbal) between participants in the learning process.

Issitt and Issitt (2010) take the view that, in the processes of adult–pupil communication, the exchange and production of meaning is never simply a transfer from one mind to another – meaning is in some senses always 'negotiated'. This process of negotiated meaning provides the intellectual space for the creative act of mutual understanding. The authors pay particular attention to the innovative use of poetry with children. Children share their ideas and feelings with an adult, who then shapes them into a poetic form as a means of helping pupils to transform their view of themselves and the world. Poetry and other forms of creative expression enable children to look afresh at ordinary things, affect their emotions and make them think more deeply about the significance of life events.

Discussion points

Children often ask of adults, 'What does this mean?' or, more significantly, 'What do *you* mean?' The first question is asking for clarification (e.g. understanding the nature of the task). The second question is more profound; it indicates that the child is grappling to 'get inside the head' of the adult and make sense of what she or he is thinking and saying. As the conversation flows between child and adult, the child asks further questions, the teacher checks the child's understanding and eventually a 'meeting of minds' takes place, such that the child is able to proceed confidently without adult 'scaffolding'. Such negotiations occur frequently throughout the day and form an integral part of the learning process. As children grow older, you need to help them develop the ability to negotiate meaning in their own heads without reference to others; that is to say, to develop a capacity to ponder, reflect and draw conclusions that guide their actions.

Another significant point for you to note is that studies indicate that child–adult conversations are not necessarily a search for negotiated meaning but rather the child's attempts to grasp what needs to be done to please or placate the teacher. In this regard, negotiated meaning has an important power dimension in that the large majority of pupils recognise that, whatever their feelings and preferences, the teacher nearly always has the final word. A similar situation can be observed when groups of children collaborate to reach an agreed solution. The less confident children accede to the opinions expressed by their more dominant classmates in the full knowledge that their dominance will eventually overrule other points of view. Negotiation is different from 'clarifying from the teacher what is expected', the former being achieved through dialogue, the latter through specificity of command.

Action plan

- Always be aware of the fact that pupils might be more eager to please you than to properly understand what they are doing.
- Teach children how to listen for meaning by using questions to clarify points.
- During your explanations, offer alternative perspectives by prefacing statements with phrases such as, 'What I am trying to say is … ' and 'Another way you can think about this matter is … '.
- Try to see 'behind' children's questions. After answering, it is sometimes appropriate to explore further by enquiring why the child asked that particular question.
- Keenly observe the significance of power issues as pupils collaborate, and intervene in such a way that assertive pupils are encouraged to take account of other children's ideas.

Reference

Issitt, J. and Issitt, M. (2010) 'Learning about the world of the student: writing poetry for teacher-student understanding', *Education 3–13*, 38 (1), pp. 101–09.

Professional theme 39: Effective learning environments

Key question: *What can teachers do to ensure that their classrooms not only look good but also provide a healthy learning environment?*

Teachers of younger children often establish different areas to stimulate the children's imagination: a *story corner* surrounded by lavishly painted pictures of characters from fairy tales. A *writing corner* separated from the rest of the room by curtains from which hang samples of completed stories and pictures. A *mystery corner* with unusual items of interest. A *home corner* full of household items. The same classroom may have a number of tables with specimens from walks, maths equipment and small-scale construction materials to handle, play with and enjoy. Cards with carefully framed questions or challenges will be placed alongside the displays, prompting children to extend their thinking by handling the objects and talking about them to their friends. The pupils in these classrooms encourage their parents to come and admire their contributions. The class teacher is known throughout the school as having a 'fantastic class-room'. Even though head teachers sometimes worry that time spent on display can mean time lost in promoting standards in the core subjects, the best schools are able to combine high academic standards with creativity reflected in the appearance of the building.

Discussion points

Whatever the age of pupils, a pleasant and well-ordered work environment is always preferable to a dowdy and chaotic one. Children prosper when the stimulating classroom combines with your positive attitude and purposeful approach to teaching and learning. Naturally, you want the room for which you have responsibility to be organised in such a way that children have easy access to key facilities and that resources are available, correctly stored and properly labelled. Whether or not the classroom is set out as described above will depend to a large extent on four factors: (1) whole-school policies about classroom layout; (2) the physical size of the room and space factors, which will affect the siting of desks, tables and display areas; (3) your teaching approach – tables and desks are often more formally arranged for direct teaching, whereas greater emphasis on exploratory (enquiry-based) learning leads to a more 'zonal' layout and combinations of tables; and (4) the age range of pupils – teachers of younger children tend to organise using nests of tables rather than the more individualised approach often employed by teachers of older pupils.

Action plan

- Organise your learning area with regard to its aesthetic appearance, accessibility (e.g. to resources) and in a way that fits your teaching approach.
- Divide the display space into: (a) examples of pupils' work; (b) informative posters plus, perhaps, a linked display table; (c) semi-permanent items, such as rotas, lists of birthdays and photographs of children.
- Pay as much attention to 'comfort' factors as to any other concerns; for instance, ensure that every pupil is comfortably seated, has sufficient light, can see the board or screen without twisting around, is able to leave his or her seat without disrupting others, and has sufficient space to work.
- Take special care to cater for the needs of left-handed children by trying to seat them at the left-hand end of the table.

Professional theme 40: Targets for learning

Key question: *How can learning targets become liberating, not constraining?*

The issue of targets and target setting has been and remains contentious. There is some validity in the claim that the original intention of learning targets being a helpful strategy for focusing on educational priorities and monitoring children's progress so as to enhance learning has been hijacked by linking target setting with political aspirations. Thus, Isaacs (2010) argues strongly that successive Governments have increasingly and unhelpfully intervened directly in curriculum and qualifications development. It is undoubtedly true that, over the course of the second half of the twentieth century and into the twenty-first, both the national curriculum and its attendant assessments have benefited from and been hampered by the governmental pursuit of improving national standards in education attainment.

Targets have become an integral part of school life at every level, especially those attached to national curriculum tests. It is useful to distinguish between targets *in* learning, which are externally imposed by Government and related to the ages of pupils, and targets *for* learning, which form an integral element of lesson preparation. Clarke (2001) suggests that there are three broad types of target:

1. *Quantitative targets* using numerical data (such as a percentage of children to reach a particular pass rate).
2. *Qualitative targets* based principally on written evidence (such as children's ability to spell certain words correctly in different contexts).
3. *Non-recorded* targets based on children's self-evaluation of their progress (such as those resulting from informal conversations between teacher and taught).

Wyse (2001) refers to the complexity of setting targets and subsequent assessment, notably the amount of interaction time with pupils that is required to plan future targets in literacy. He suggests that, for the processes that he observed to be purposeful, then 'high levels of skills and understanding were required to be coupled with the ability to develop strategies to improve management of the process' (p. 16). By contrast, he argues, unachievable targets are demotivating for children and result in slower academic progress. Wyse also noted the following points from his study of final-year trainee teachers (paraphrased and amended):

- Accurate target setting has to be based on a clear understanding of previous development and attainment.
- It is important to recognise that children reach the same targets at different rates.
- Targets should not be too numerous or difficult.
- Frequent reference to targets is necessary, supported by maintaining target sheets, cards or notices for each child.

- Targets need to be discussed orally to support understanding and to assess progress.
- It is important to identify the nature of what the target is related to (level descriptions, SATs educational assessments, framework for teaching, etc.).
- A lot of marking can be replaced by oral discussion with children.
- Specific marking is more productive than making general summary comments.
- Formative assessment (feedback and intervention during lessons) is particularly useful for the purpose of setting and monitoring targets.
- Self-assessment is a useful tool to enhance pupil participation.
- Extra adult support is often necessary to enhance target setting.

Discussion points

In some teachers' minds, targets have become synonymous with external pressure to achieve narrowly defined academic results at the expense of a fuller and more rounded education. Other teachers view them as an incentive to spur pupils on to achieve the best possible academic results by whatever means. No doubt the majority of teachers tend to think of targets as one of those facts of life in school, so make the best of doing the best they can with the children for whom they have responsibility. It is certainly true that government targets distort priorities and, for Year 6 teachers and pupils in particular, create a high degree of anxiety lest the national test results are disappointing and school inspectors employ punitive measures. At the micro-level, however, targets have the potential to be powerful tools in helping children to identify areas of learning that require improvement. The discussions that take place between you and the pupils are valuable in themselves, as they strengthen the adult–child bond and facilitate an on-going dialogue about ways in which learning might progress. Furthermore, establishing targets requires that strategies be employed to achieve the goals, such that learning becomes more tactical and less random than might otherwise have been the case.

In 'teaching to the test', teachers tend to adopt a more didactic (transmission) style of teaching and stop employing more exploratory, enquiry-based methods. They justify this change of technique with reference to four reasons:

1. *A pragmatic reason:* they are anxious to ensure that the children do well in the tests, regardless of the temporary loss of pupil autonomy.
2. *A philosophical reason:* they believe that repetition and reinforcement will almost certainly increase test success.
3. *A professional reason:* they don't want to be the teacher responsible for a class of children viewed as 'failing'.
4. *A personal reason:* they want to feel that they have done their best for the children and their parents.

Targets also have a number of possible disadvantages. First, they can be too broad and make the task of achieving them an unreasonable one, or too narrow and create a form of 'academic tunnel vision' whereby other avenues of learning are ignored in the quest to reach the specified target. Second, targets place pressure on pupils and teachers that can easily lead to damaging levels of stress.

Third, targets can lead to a rigid task-completion mentality, whereby inability to meet the target is viewed as failure rather than an important part of the learning process. Finally, targets emphasise the strictly measurable and take no account of effort, determination and special circumstances, which you should always take time to acknowledge in your dealings with children. An indication that target setting is becoming more of a burden than a benefit is if you spend almost as much time in devising and monitoring targets as the pupils do in attempting to attain them. Remember, too, that learning requires reinforcement and practical application, so be cautious about referring to a pupil as having 'fully met' the target. (See also Professional theme 15, earlier in this chapter.)

Action plan

- Use targets as *part* of a comprehensive learning strategy rather than its core.
- Use a mixture of short-term targets (lesson by lesson; day by day) and longer-term targets (e.g. over a half-term).
- Link targets with formative, rather than with summative, assessment.
- Discuss targets with the children in a natural manner, stressing the excitement element and adopting a 'you-can-do-it-with-my-help-plus-your-determination' attitude.
- Avoid any inference that initial failure to 'meet' the target in a given time equates with being unable to reach it; instead, view it as *delayed success*.
- Always acknowledge a child's hard work in the process.
- Offer specific guidance and 'targeted' support rather than merely facilitating learning.
- Continue to use a full range of teaching methods, including repetition and rote learning as supplementary strategies.

References

Clarke, S. (2001) *Unlocking Formative Assessment*, London: Hodder & Stoughton.
Isaacs, T. (2010) 'Educational assessment in England', *Assessment in Education*, 17 (3), pp. 315–34.
Wyse, D. (2001) 'Promising yourself to do better. Target setting and literacy', *Education 3–13*, 29 (2), pp. 13–18.

Professional theme 41: Encouraging children to write

Key question: *How to help pupils acquire writing skills that can be utilised to communicate information and ideas effectively.*

A hundred years ago, pupils wrote with chalk on slates. A generation ago, the only significant writing that children did was carried out using a pen or pencil on paper. Today, writing takes many forms, including the traditional 'on paper' tasks, together with keyboard skills, texting and other technological means. There have been countless books and articles published about writing skills, but five things stand out. First, that only a minority of children enjoy writing; in the early stages it takes a lot of effort to progress beyond their first attempts to form individual letters and, gradually, to write whole words; later on, it is far easier to use a keyboard than a writing implement. Second, moving children from printing letters to cursive (joined-up) writing is a major step. Third, more boys seem to experience difficulty than girls. Fourth, formal letter writing has largely been superseded by e-mail. Fifth, and most importantly, the mechanics of writing must develop alongside forms of thinking; that is, the written word must *convey meaning* to a reader. It is this final point that provides another major challenge, as teachers help pupils to put their thoughts in written form.

Palmer (2010) advocates the use of 'speaking frames' as a means of teaching talk for writing. She advocates a four-step process whereby children first *listen* to adult speakers; then *imitate* elements of their speech; then begin to *innovate* on these language patterns; and finally use this language data to *invent* their own expressions. The author insists that in the listen-imitate-innovate-invent process, teachers should pay far closer attention to the first three. The variety of pedagogical strategies involving talk can be summarised as follows:

- *teacher-led talk*: children respond as directed;
- *child-led talk*: collaborative groups to share ideas; investigate; and solve problems;
- *teacher–child dialogue*: opportunities for both teacher and pupils to initiate discussion; ask questions; and raise issues.

Discussion points

Many teachers encourage children to express their thoughts out loud as a means of clarifying their thinking. Sometimes, a pupil struggles to articulate ideas verbally, but the very process of doing so helps to cement ideas. In addition to the physical process of writing (by hand or keyboard) the order of action must be *think-articulate-write*. Less-competent writers will often benefit from being given prompts in the form of a list of relevant words, phrases and sentences, either suggested by the children or provided by the teacher. Ideally, writing must always be for a specified purpose, though the incentive for early writers who are mastering basic skills is likely to be task completion rather than communicating with an audience. There is no reason why you, as teacher, should not be the audience, but more meaningful targets are likely to appeal to older children, such as other children in a different class or a different school; local councillors; school governors; local celebrities; and so forth. Teachers of younger pupils have sometimes used a soft toy or puppet as the recipient.

It is perfectly possible to create a class letter by inviting all the children to suggest contributions and for you to type the key points onto the computer as they arise. Alternatively, each child can compose his or her own letter (with appropriate drawings) and place them all in a folder to be sent to the relevant person or persons. Although what used to be known as 'creative writing' (i.e. fictional writing produced by children with minimal teacher direction) has become neglected in recent years, it still provides opportunities for more capable pupils with a fertile imagination to develop a longer, sequenced piece of prose.

Action plan

- Link talking and writing closely.
- Ensure that, through regular practice, younger pupils are correctly forming letters and older pupils are developing an appropriate written style.
- Take account of the needs of left-handed children.
- Provide support for pupils who struggle to get their ideas down on paper or screen by using a variety of prompts.
- Stimulate children's imaginations through the use of gripping stories, cartoon characters, favourite TV shows, class drama, visits from interesting people and other shared experiences.
- Give pupils time to think, reflect, ask questions and formulate ideas before launching into a writing exercise.
- Read back samples of writing, being careful not to embarrass any child. (Note that asking a poor reader to read aloud his or her work can be counterproductive.)
- Demonstrate how an extended vocabulary can enhance written work; for instance, suggest alternative verbs as substitutes for the ones used by the pupil.

Reference

Palmer, S. (2010) *Speaking Frames: How to Teach Talk for Writing Ages 10–14*, London: David Fulton.

Professional theme 42: The educational value of play and drama

Key question: *How can play and drama be used most effectively to advance children's learning?*

Smidt (2006, p. 48, adapted) offers four explicit characteristics that define the concept of play: (1) play is something the child has chosen to do; (2) play is often pleasurable and always deeply engrossing, and we tend to see children enjoying their chosen activity; (3) in play there is no risk of failure, as the child simply changes the agenda; and (4) the emphasis is on the process, rather than on the product. Robson (2006) argues that what she refers to as 'pretend play' may be particularly significant for the development of theory of mind because, in pretend play, 'children step in and out of role, represent situations and transform objects, talk about mental states ... and have to negotiate meanings and actions with others' (p. 79). Cohen (2006) insists that, in the playful state, the child is able to build up a stockpile of habits, skills and knowledge that is more extensive than it would have been in the goal-orientated state alone.

Discussion points

Children of every age play, though some inhibited individuals might find difficulty in co-operating with other children of similar age. A very small percentage struggle so badly with social situations that they decline any offer to play and remain aloof; such children require specialist help. If you teach young children, your principal decisions are: (a) when to allow play opportunities; (b) how

much direction to offer; (c) the extent and type of intervention; (d) whether to use play as an incentive after task completion. Close observation of children playing will give you insights into their social interaction, language use and capacity to use their imaginations.

Older pupils are more likely to engage with play in the form of drama, in which interpreting and acting out scenes forms an integral part of the experience, howbeit more teacher-controlled than the spontaneous sorts of play associated with young children. It is worth persevering to promote dramatic interpretations of events but to do so gradually and teach appropriate skills rather than assume that pupils will have an in-built capacity to develop them. Although few drama sequences end up as public performances, you might inculcate into children some of the basic skills, such as clear speech, use of facial expression, gesticulation and bodily expressiveness. These skills cannot be assumed; they have to be taught, practised and put into action. You don't need to be a drama expert to introduce children to the wonders of 'play as drama'. (See also Professional theme 43, below.)

Action plan

- Be clear in your own mind about the value of play in children's learning and social development, not least in explaining your reasons to parents.
- Avoid giving the impression that play is something that happens after the 'real work' has been completed.
- Design collaborative play/drama activities – perhaps based on exciting stories – that stimulate use of children's imaginations.
- Have a systematic approach to teaching drama skills.
- Prepare a dramatic presentation for a class assembly using mime, scripted dialogue, poems and choral speaking.

References

Cohen, D. (2006) *Social Skills for Primary Pupils*, Birmingham: Questions Publishing.
Robson, S. (2006) *Developing Thinking and Understanding in Young Children*, Abingdon: Routledge.
Smidt, S. (2006) *The Developing Child in the 21st Century*, Abingdon: Routledge.

Professional theme 43: Organising large-space lessons

Key question: *How might teachers develop a large-space session that reflects some or all of their organisational preferences?*

Dean (2008) suggests that teachers need to look closely at their 'organisational preferences' and lists fourteen significant areas: (1) pattern of daily programme; (2) the teacher's use of time; (3) the children's use of time; (4) choice of activity; (5) curriculum content; (6) use of competition and co-operation; (7) grouping of children; (8) use of space; (9) use of furniture; (10) use of resources; (11) records and assessment; (12) work with other teachers; (13) work with parents; and (14) equal opportunities.

The *stepped approach* is commonly used for organising and managing large-space lessons (PE, gymnastics, games and drama) based on specific and detailed explanations and demonstrations by the teacher, followed by independent activities undertaken by pupils. In the stepped approach, all the children are introduced to an elementary task, which they then explore or practise for a given length of time, followed by introductions to increasingly complex tasks, each of which the children engage with as individuals, pairs or small groups. An example from movement and drama will help to illustrate the above approach using the theme of *the impact of heat on life forms*.

1. As the class has been working on the cross-curricular topic of 'heat and cold', noting the variations in climate in different countries and the effects of extreme temperatures, the teacher uses the phenomenon of melting ice as the basis for the drama lesson.
2. In the hall, the children warm up 'on the spot' individually by stretching and moving different parts of their bodies to raise awareness of the movement possibilities and limitations, guided through each step by the teacher. Children with limited mobility are encouraged to contribute at their own level of physical comfort. The teacher concentrates the children's attention on fine motor skills and less obvious body movements, such as use of fingers, facial muscles, shoulders, hips and toes. Children are asked to 'melt down like a snowman in the heat' as a task that will enable them to practise the movements. Initially, the children just collapse in a heap, but the teacher uses a tambourine to sound out first five, then ten, then twenty beats as the time frame for the action.
3. After a minute or two of individual endeavour, the teacher asks the children to work in pairs and rehearse the 'melt down' while facing each other, again using a twenty-beat time frame, trying to co-ordinate their actions so that they finish simultaneously (as puddles on the floor).
4. The teacher asks for volunteer pairs to demonstrate their actions to the rest of the class and selects three of them, commending and pointing out significant features of their actions.
5. While the children sit and listen, the teacher plays some music from the film *The Snowman* (based on the book by Raymond Briggs) to remind them about the dance scene and the melting that happens to the main snowman character at the end of the film. The teaching assistant is responsible for controlling the CD player, so that the teacher can concentrate on class management.
6. The children individually explore larger movements associated with the dancing, each child in a separate area of the hall to avoid accidentally colliding with one another. The teacher moves about commenting on the actions, suggesting alternatives and offering advice.
7. The teacher asks the children to explore movement in pairs, then in double-pairs to create a foursome.
8. The teacher asks for volunteers to demonstrate their ideas to the rest of the class.
9. Finally, the teacher asks the children to combine their dance and the 'melting down to a puddle' movements, first individually, then in pairs, then in groups, using the same piece of music.

10. The children remain in their prostrate positions while the teacher moves quietly around the room, sprinkling some 'magic dust' on them as a signal that they are to 'come alive' and sit up straight.

11. Before returning to the classroom, the teacher spends the last two minutes raising some of the issues from the movement and drama, praising their hard work, inviting comment about the impact of heat and cold on life forms, and linking the comments to work being undertaken for the topic.

12. The children return to the classroom as silently as snowmen gliding through the night sky.

Discussion points

Before the next lesson, you can spend a short time reminding the children about the previous session, rehearsing some of the movements associated with melting and introducing the associated theme of 'fire and burning'. You can stress the importance of fire safety issues and the devastation that can occur when people are careless, but also explain that burning can also destroy pests and reinvigorate growth. The lesson can follow a similar pattern to the one described above, but the emphasis is now on the effects of wood as it turns to charcoal/ ash 'from the tips of fingers (twigs) to the ends of toes (roots)'. In the later stages of the lesson, you might put the children into groups to explore fire spreading across a forest, tree by tree, until all the children have become piles of charred and smoking charcoal/ ash. The process is then reversed as the 'new growth' eventually creates young saplings that bend and sway in the breeze as they reach for the sky. Finally, the process is brought together in an extended performance, with appropriate supporting music, from the first burning to the final resurrection.

The above descriptions offer a model for a range of sessions based on whatever theme you happen to be pursuing in the classroom. Note the importance of combining the development of specific skills with opportunities to explore the theme within explicit guidelines, rather than allowing pupils to explore ideas randomly.

Action plan

See the detailed example described above.

Reference

Dean, J. (2008) *Organising Learning in the Primary School*, Abingdon: Routledge.

Professional theme 44: Transition from primary to secondary school

Key question: What can teachers do to prepare children for the move to a different school?

The final year of primary school is always hard work, both for pupils and for teachers. Children have to spend many months preparing for the national curriculum tests and are often required to 'get their heads down' and concentrate on formal tasks. Teachers have to persevere in keeping an increasingly lively group of pre-adolescents on the straight and narrow, sometimes employing very firm tactics to maintain discipline. After the tests, the final weeks of the year tend to be less pressurised and teachers often introduce more topic-based (cross-curricular 'thematic') work.

In truth, the majority of final-year pupils are looking forward to moving on to the next school, while at the same time fearing the prospect. A major study of primary–secondary transition in state schools in England indicated that the experiences of economically poor pupils at age eleven are often very different from their more affluent peers (Burgess *et al.* 2008). Results from the study show that poor pupils' peer groups in primary schools are more fractured at the age of eleven years; after transition, these pupils subsequently find themselves concentrated within lower-performing secondary schools or allocated to lower sets.

Zeedyk and Gallacher (2003) undertook a survey to ascertain the views of primary pupils, secondary pupils, parents and teachers in regard to the transition process. They found that bullying was a major concern for all groups, followed by fears of getting lost, increased workload and peer relationships. The authors argue that the views of both primary pupils and their parents need to be considered if the experience of transition is to be improved. It is inevitable that in every class there will be those pupils who have outgrown primary education, either physically or emotionally or both, while others view the prospect of leaving the familiar setting of their present situation with a mixture of excitement and foreboding.

Discussion points

You might not teach a 'transition' class, but as a staff member you still have a responsibility for every child's welfare, including the occasionally bumptious group of pupils referred to as the 'school leavers'. If you work in an infant, first or middle school, the leavers will be children of a different age from Year 6, but the principles of preparing them for the move upwards are similar. First, you owe it to your pupils to give them the best possible education and strengthen their skills in key areas of learning (notably reading and comprehension) such that they will get off to a good start in their new school. Second, the move from one school to another is a huge emotional wrench for some children, especially if they are to be separated from their friends, so emotional preparation is as significant as academic preparation. Third, the prospect of facing significant change has a powerful effect on vulnerable children and can lead to an intensification of behaviour patterns, so you need to exercise forbearance while insisting that good behaviour is maintained. One of the main challenges is to remain calm, solid, reassuring and decisive, both for pupils and, on occasions, their anxious parents. It is vitally important that you do not allow yourself to be swept up in the turbulence but are a 'rock' in the midst of choppy waters.

Action plan

- Make time to talk at length about the transition process – not only the practical issues, but also how the children feel, their concerns, expectations and anxieties.

- Chat informally with parents about their perspectives on the transition procedures and suggestions about strategies to assist the process. (Don't be surprised if some parents ask you pointed questions about the practicalities attached to the transfer and advice about strategies to ensure that their children get a place at the preferred school.)
- As ten- and eleven-year-old girls and boys are becoming increasingly self-conscious, insist on a strict code of ethics, but make allowance for maturation factors.
- Reward sensible behaviour with high-status privileges; notably, giving, and trusting pupils with, responsibilities.
- In all your decisions about pupils, bear in mind that big children make more noise and occupy more space than little ones, so be careful not to blame them for things over which they have no control. (See also Chapter 2, Teaching and learning issue 26.)

Reference

Burgess, S., Johnston, R., Tomas, K., Propper, C. and Wilson, D. (2008) 'The transition of pupils from primary to secondary school in England', *Transactions of the Institute of British Geographers*, 33 (3), pp. 388–403.

Zeedyk, M.S. and Gallacher, J. (2003) 'Negotiating the transition from primary to secondary school', *School Psychology International*, 24 (1), pp. 67–79.

Challenges for teachers

Introduction

The need to make correct decisions and judgements forms an integral part of every teacher's day. Long before you set out for school, you will have been faced with a variety of choices: whether or not to take in that interesting story or leave it for another occasion; whether or not to approach the teacher in the class next door about the possibility of planning a joint educational visit; whether or not to confront the naughty child about his behaviour in class, seek help from a colleague or contact his mother; whether to reorganise the monitoring system; whether to begin practising for the approaching class assembly or to wait until a couple of key children return to school after illness; and numerous others. Once in school the fun really begins, as your eyes and ears pick up cues about what is taking place, how you ought to respond and selecting the right action from numerous options.

This chapter consists of six challenges and associated dilemmas that confront most teachers at different times during their careers. The six cases outlined below do not, of course, cover all eventualities, but provide an opportunity for you to engage with some of the educational and moral decisions that have to be made by practitioners, regardless of experience or circumstance. Each case consists of an introduction, a scenario and a selection of factors for considera-tion; these elements are accompanied by a discussion of the things you might need to take into account in making a correct decision or finding a satisfactory way forward. There is also an Activate your thinking, a Top tip and one or more additional references for information and study.

Many years ago, educationist Evelyn Rogers (Rogers 1946) wrote of the challenge of 'adapting the subject matter to the needs of forty different children in forty minutes' (p. 178) and the tension that exists between following a pre-scribed pattern of teaching and responding to each pupil's individual interest and enthusiasm. In her article, 'Progressive ideals in practice: the teacher's dilemma', she makes special note of the way in which some less able children are more comfortable with a predictable lesson format that minimises thinking and emphasises 'doing', while more-able children benefited from being obliged to engage their minds. Such a dilemma and many similar ones will doubtless resonate with modern-day educators as they respond to the challenge to ensure that every child is given opportunity to fulfil his or her potential.

As the teacher, you are faced with the need to make instant decisions in the classroom. At the same time, you have to establish procedures and rules of conduct that are gradually embedded in the warp and weave of classroom life, such that they become an integral and natural way of teaching. Creating a shared understanding with pupils about 'the way we do things here' means that you don't have to expend energy in providing explanations to children as to why such-and-such a thing is acceptable or unacceptable. Nevertheless, one of the key skills that all teachers have to develop is an ability to evaluate a situation rapidly and make a response that is not only fair but also seen to be fair by the other party, be it pupils, colleagues or parents. Teachers are not judges in a court of law handing down sentences regardless of whoever stands before them. They must exercise wisdom in the way that they approach encounters with others and respond appropriately to events that form an integral part of the daily routine.

Some issues require especially careful consideration and decisions about priorities, reactions and strategies for coping with the associated challenges; they can only be shaped over a longer period of time and honed by experience. It is sometimes difficult to know just how to react to specific instances, not least when you are new to the situation and still coming to grips with the prevailing classroom ethos and norms. There are simply no 'quick fixes' in teaching, but the sooner you can adjust to what is expected, the easier life becomes. (See under Chapter 3, Professional theme 24 for details about a new teacher's rite of passage.) It is also worth noting that Tirri (1999) found that, in virtually all categories of moral dilemmas, teachers used the best interest of a child as the key determinant in their thinking and decision making. Although you undoubtedly support this principle, it is also necessary to take account of the impact your decisions have on your *own* wellbeing and attitude to the job.

References

Rogers, E. (1946) 'Progressive ideals in practice: the teacher's dilemma', *Educational Research Bulletin*, 25 (7), pp. 178–82.

Tirri, K. (1999) 'Teachers' perceptions of moral dilemmas at school', *Journal of Moral Education*, 28 (1), pp. 31–47.

The challenges

The six challenges that are discussed in detail below are as follows:

Challenge 1 **Maintaining a calm working environment**: the challenge of ensuring that noise remains at an appropriate level without curtailing work-related discussion.

Challenge 2 **Protecting your own wellbeing**: being an enthusiastic teacher while avoiding the fatigue that results from continuous dynamic teaching.

Challenge 3 **Fitting it all in**: how to have sufficient time during the day to achieve all that is required of a teacher.

Challenge 4　**Starting with a new class**: the beginning of a new school year brings stresses and strains, but it is also an opportunity for a fresh start.

Challenge 5　**Achieving a balanced teaching approach**: how to use creative methods as well as formal teaching to enhance children's learning.

Challenge 6　**Teaching mixed-ability, multi-age classes**: ways to organise and manage learning for two or more year groups in the same class.

Challenge 1: Maintaining a calm working environment

The challenge of ensuring that noise remains at an appropriate level without curtailing work-related discussion.

Introduction

Teachers want pupils to be active and involved in the lesson, but sometimes find that noise level becomes a problem. Most of the sound is due to the children's enthusiasm and eagerness to find the answer or share ideas, but a few pupils use it as an excuse for chatting and some seem almost incapable of remaining quiet for more than a few seconds. While teachers try to encourage co-operation and collaboration, they are uneasy about the effect of noise levels on learning and on their reputation as someone who can maintain discipline. (See also Chapter 2, Teaching and learning issue 23.)

Scenario

The children are attentive when the teacher is introducing the lesson and they talk quietly at the commencement of the activity; however, the passivity quickly evaporates and the volume of noise becomes progressively higher. If the activity is in pairs or small groups, the teacher welcomes and encourages discussion, but is also anxious that the volume is rising and aware that off-task conversations are taking place. The teacher keeps reminding the class that it is too noisy and the level drops for a time but soon swells again. Awareness of the variations in noise level proves to be distracting and worrying for the teacher, who becomes more concerned with controlling it than with assisting children's learning. Eventually, the teacher starts raising her voice to rebuke the children, but merely succeeds in adding to the cacophony. Finally, she insists on complete silence, which is almost impossible to maintain and does little to promote a vibrant learning climate.

Factors for consideration

1. To distinguish between disruptive noises and constructive talk.
2. To distinguish between quietness and passivity; and between rowdiness, exuberance and hyperactivity.

3. To weigh up the benefits of collaborative work, which tends to be noisy, and solitary work, which is easier to control but often inappropriate for enquiry-based activities.
4. To balance the deep learning that takes place through healthy verbal interaction against the potential disruption that talk can generate.

Discussion

A peaceful and attentive class is generally much happier than a noisy and chaotic one. Children become unruly as a result of one or more of five factors: (1) excitement or overexuberance; (2) lack of respect for the teacher; (3) boredom and low motivation; (4) uncertainty about the lesson purpose; and (5) lack of concern about the consequences. It is therefore essential for you to take charge of the situation in a firm but reasonable way and insist on compliance through: (a) clarification of what is admissible; (b) making the lesson as interesting and visually engaging as possible; (c) involving the children and interacting with them; and (d) creating a sense of intrigue rather than promoting a mundane approach to task completion. You do not want to curb children's enthusiasm, of course, but it must not be at the expense of an unsettled or, in extreme cases, a chaotic learning environment. Occasionally, a child suffers from spells of hyperactivity, which is a separate but related matter and calls for special treatment in liaison with the school's SENCO and, as appropriate, the parents.

As part of their class management, some teachers use positive incentives through rewarding good behaviour. For instance, you carry, or the assistant carries, a pad of 'blank' raffle tickets and in each lesson hands them out to children who are concentrating on their work and making a sustained effort. To ensure the system is not abused, the child's name is written on the back of the ticket. At the end of the day, or each week, you draw out a couple of tickets from the 'pot' and the winners receive a small prize, such as a pencil, an eraser or a plastic figure.

By contrast, and as a more immediate and punitive strategy, you might draw three boxes on the board and every time the noise level gets too high, you put a cross in the box. Three crosses result in absolute silence for (say) five minutes. A similar technique is to draw an empty cloud shape on the board and if a child, after being warned, deliberately disturbs the class, his or her name is written in the cloud. If another child becomes disruptive, the first child's name is deleted and substituted by the new name. Whoever's name is inside the cloud when the lesson ends is last to leave the room or misses a few minutes of playtime or has to straighten the classroom before being dismissed. If the child whose name is presently written inside the cloud settles down to work, his or her name is deleted. Ideally, the cloud should be empty by the end of the timetabled session.

Some teachers select one child to be the 'noise controller' for a period of (say) ten minutes. The child sits at the front of the room and writes on the board the name of anyone who is off-task or misbehaving. If the transgressor attends to his or her work, the controller rubs off the name after about one minute. The noise controller is not allowed to engage in dialogue – especially arguing – with any classmate; if the controller does so, another sensible pupil takes over. If it operates smoothly, especially during group activities, the system is more or less self-perpetuating, allowing you greater liberty to concentrate on teaching rather than being constantly distracted by noise. Children whose names have been noted during the day are barred from being noise controller during the following day. Choice of the noise controller can be used as an incentive for pupils with weaker self-control to be rewarded if they improve sufficiently to be considered, even if their behaviour is less than ideal.

To gain the attention of the class and combat off-task conversations, teachers of younger children can use simple chants to a well-known tune like Frère Jacques, such as: 'Are you listening? Are you listening?', whereupon the children sing back, 'Yes, we are; yes, we are'. The act of responding tends to reduce the amount of idle chatter and conveys subliminally to the children that the noise level is too high. If you use your imagination, the singsong approach can be employed in other situations, such as: 'Start to pack your work away; save it for another day' (tune: Twinkle, twinkle, little star) to which the children respond: 'We will start to pack away; save it for another day'.

With all pupils, it also helps to promote the concept of three types of pupil voice in the classroom: (1) *discussion voices*, in situations where children are collaborating and need to talk about the activity; (2) *table voices*, in situations where co-operation is needed; otherwise children work silently; (3) *head voices*, in situations where silence is a necessity. You can, of course, select other terms to use rather than the three suggested ones, but the principle of different voices is one worth pursuing. If any children refuse to respond to your request for silence, begin counting down from five to nought – it is normally effective with every age group.

Teachers who believe in rewarding peaceful behaviour and low noise levels view punitive approaches as being incompatible with good discipline. They argue that incentives (commendation or rewards) help to foster a harmonious and purposeful learning climate, as children enjoy being part of a well-behaved and motivated group that works together for everyone's benefit. The use of 'control techniques' such as those described above serves to calm situations without the need to resort to harsh sanctions or punishments. There are some teachers, however, who take a wholly different view. They consider inducement techniques as being 'bribes' that are offered by adults who are unable or unwilling to impose discipline on the class through other means. They argue that teachers should insist on, not negotiate for, a peaceful working atmosphere, and refuse to countenance any violations of rules. According to this view, a teacher must use the strength of her or his personality to enforce discipline and impose sanctions ('punishments') without compunction on pupils who refuse to comply. Under such an approach, rewards should be used sparingly, if at all, and – taking note of the pupil's capability – only for exceptional achievement.

It also has to be admitted that incentives and techniques using crosses, clouds, noise controllers or similar ideas require additional effort and can interrupt the smooth running of the lesson. Use of simple non-verbal signals is probably the ideal way of maintaining order, but occasional use of other strategies, whether gentle or fierce, is usually necessary from time to time, especially in the early days with a new class. (See also Challenge 4 in this chapter.)

Top tip

Despite sounding rather old-fashioned, the 'put your finger on lips' technique works well with younger children if used sparingly. If the noise ceases and children pay attention, you can then tell them to sit normally. Older pupils respond to a variety of strategies. For instance, sternly using 'Mr' or 'Miss' with the child's first name or surname instead of using the first name alone signals your displeasure. Again, the use of a loud 'clicker' carries a similar message: one click signifies the need to talk more quietly; two clicks indicate that a sanction is imminent, and so forth. Some teachers tell the noisy pupil to stand up, though this method can backfire if more than one pupil is involved or an individual shows off and becomes the centre of attention.

Activate your thinking!

While it should be a cardinal rule that pupils never talk or interrupt when the teacher is speaking, the issue of noise levels is much more complex when children are engaged in collaborative tasks and activities. A useful guideline is: 'Talk loudly enough for your friend to hear you, but quietly enough so that no one else can'. Obviously, collaboration cannot take place without talk, so you will need to show a degree of flexibility in the matter or you will be forever using the largely pointless 'shush'.

Additional reading for Challenge 1

Barnes, R. (2006) *The Practical Guide to Primary Classroom Management*, London: Sage. (See Chapter 5 for advice about managing noise levels in the classroom.)

Hayes, D. (2009) *Primary Teaching Today*, London: David Fulton. (See Chapter 6 for issues concerning behaviour and the modern-day child.)

Challenge 2: Protecting your own wellbeing

Being an enthusiastic teacher while avoiding the fatigue that results from continuous teaching.

Introduction

New teachers are often encouraged to be enthusiastic and convey to pupils their love for the subject or topic, lesson after lesson, day after day. While such commitment is commendable, it carries a risk of overexertion and strain. Every teacher is faced with the not-inconsiderable challenge of giving of their best without becoming exhausted and thereby losing their sharpness. The onset of ill health only adds to the problem, leading to distress and less effective teaching.

Scenario

Teachers work hard before, during and after school, such that conscientious ones can be more tired than the pupils by the end of the day. Over time, extreme weariness sets in; teachers find it difficult to keep going at the same pace and struggle to maintain a high standard of teaching. As a way to cope, teachers tend to utilise more of a direct teaching approach and 'paper and pencil' exercises, which allows them to dominate the class and exert stricter discipline (see Challenge 5 in this chapter). However, such an approach is itself both physically and mentally tiring and does not provide the conditions for high motivation and effective learning. Children initially enjoy the formality and the straightforward tasks, but gradually become restless and seek greater autonomy through requesting permission to employ alternative approaches, chatting to classmates about ideas and hurrying to finish in the hope of moving on to more creative types of activity. The teacher then employs stronger discipline to keep the situation under control, which absorbs even more energy and adds to the overall sense of fatigue. In addition, the regular responsibilities of planning, completing paperwork, marking, liaising with colleagues, responding to parents, evaluating practice by means of a diary or log and meeting deadlines combine to create conditions under which the job never ends. Teachers work later in the evenings and use time that should have been reserved for recreation and relaxation to keep pace with what can feel like a series of unremitting demands.

Factors for consideration

1. To be proficient, rather than sacrificial, in preparing lessons, teaching and assessing pupils' work, and communicating with adults.
2. To organise and manage classroom life in an orderly yet productive way that places increasing amounts of responsibility on pupils for their behaviour and achievement.
3. To teach enthusiastically without expending an excessive amount of energy in a single session.
4. To ensure that pupils work conscientiously and systematically without losing their creativity and power of imagination in the process.

Discussion

Less-experienced teachers tend to consume more energy in their teaching than their experienced colleagues for five principal reasons: (1) new teachers fear being labelled as uncommitted; (2) they have not yet learned how to channel their energies into efficient ways of working; (3) they take time to grasp the fact that pupil learning involves more than just good teaching; (4) they expect too much of themselves and too little of the pupils; (5) they expend a lot of emotional energy because of the need to satisfy their mentors/induction tutor/head teacher as they learn 'on the job'. (See also Challenge 3 in this chapter for advice about managing your time efficiently.)

Having high, but realistic, expectations of children must be used in conjunction with the fact that pupils should not only make an effort to do what a teacher says is needed but also try hard to achieve good results as a means of satisfying their *own* learning ambitions. Of course, every pupil has an 'off day' when poor health, boredom, anxiety or distractions create the circumstances for underachievement, but most of the time it is reasonable for you to anticipate that children will work consistently well. Naturally, even hard-working pupils are still dependent on adults for guidance, clear instructions and suitable resources to complete tasks. They also rely on a positive learning climate in which discipline is maintained, explanations are offered without rancour or disdain and mistakes are accepted as part of the learning process. By setting a high standard yourself through diligence, quiet enthusiasm, determination to see the job through, a questioning attitude and thoughtful reflection, you will gradually instil in children awareness that hard work brings its own reward without the need to be frantic in aiming to complete tasks. Although reaching this happy position takes a great deal of effort initially, it results in a more relaxed and affable climate that makes fewer demands of you to maintain.

Your teaching approach is a key factor in combating exhaustion. It will vary according to the age of pupils, subject content and desirable learning outcomes, but in every lesson or session it is helpful to have a spread of teacher-led talk and explanation, children's responses and activities that require a high level of pupil initiative. One useful strategy is to monitor the amount of time that you spend in undertaking one of four roles during the lesson: (1) organiser; (2) director; (3) expert; and (4) facilitator of learning, the terms being broadly defined as follows:

1. Organiser: providing information, explanation and instruction prior to an activity.
2. Director: unsolicited intervention during activities by demonstrating and advising.
3. Expert: solicited responses to pupils' questions and queries.
4. Facilitator: providing necessary resources such that pupils can largely work unaided and with minimal intervention during activities (i.e. teacher 'standing back').

As a rule, the greater your role as facilitator, the less strain you place on yourself, though it is worth noting that the concept of 'facilitating' has been less favoured by external policy makers than the other three roles, being seen (unfairly) as a soft option for lazy teachers. Nevertheless, it is in your interest to stand back occasionally and take stock of the roles you undertake.

Inexperienced teachers tend to talk too much during lessons and fail to drink adequate amounts of liquid; as a result, they can become dehydrated, with the inevitable damage to their vocal chords. An additional problem for trainee teachers is that they usually exercise weaker discipline than the regular teacher and compensate by using louder speech and raised voices to maintain control. The general rule is to speak less and listen more and to sharpen your explanations prior to allocating tasks so that pupils have less need to ask you questions of clarification.

On the days you have 'playground duty' or another supervisory responsibility and might get back to the classroom at the last minute, leave the children a simple task during the preceding lesson for when they return after the break; in that way, you will reduce the pressure on yourself to hurry back and, hopefully, walk in to a calm 'heads down' environment when you do. Teachers can sometimes liaise with the teaching assistant about assuming charge for the first few minutes.

It is possible to mistake busyness for effectiveness in learning. Smidt (2006) comments: 'We see how children everywhere develop a range of strategies as problem-solvers, and in doing this make hypotheses, try these out, analyse what happens, identify patterns, generate rules, use analogy, come to conclusions and move on' (p. 107). However, in the hurry-scurry of planning, teaching and assessing pupil progress, teachers can be caught on a treadmill of activity and intense concentration, ignore Smidt's shrewd observation and only succeed in wearing out the children and themselves. Although children enjoy sessions that have pace and vitality, they also need opportunities to pause, reflect and process the information.

It is not being idle to seek a work-life balance that provides you with a degree of freedom from the many duties that slowly exhaust teachers, with the inevitable impact on health and reduced effectiveness that result. On the contrary, you have a legal entitlement to regular periods of rest and opportunities to draw back occasionally during lessons to conserve energy and stay alert. Extreme weariness is a condition that affects all teachers on occasions, but learning to relax and keep lessons running smoothly by being well organised and thinking ahead minimises the effects. It goes without saying that the best remedy for tiredness is to enjoy your teaching and to know that the children are enjoying their learning. The best teacher is a fresh teacher – not a physical and mental wreck.

Reference

Smidt, S. (2006) *The Developing Child in the 21st Century*, Abingdon: Routledge.

Top tip

Work in partnership with the teaching assistant. Give her or him guidance but also plenty of flexibility to show initiative, make decisions and express her/ his talents. The happiest assistants are those who are trusted, supported and appreciated.

Activate your thinking!

Teaching should be like a steeplechase, with long periods of slow, but steady, running, interrupted by periods of sprinting, clambering over barriers, combating hazards and occasionally stopping to replenish supplies. Any distance runner attempting to go fast all the time without any breaks or sustenance would quickly collapse.

Additional reading for Challenge 2

Bubb, S. and Earley, P. (2004) *Managing Teacher Workload: Work-life balance and well-being*, London: Paul Chapman.
This book is a useful resource for new and experienced teachers to assist them in self-reflective practices to help cope with sources of stress and fatigue.
Troman, G. and Woods, P. (2001) *Primary Teachers' Stress*, Abingdon: Routledge.
The study is based on research involving twenty-five teachers, covering issues such as the perceptions and causes of stress; stressed schools; coping strategies; recovery; and health and safety issues.

Challenge 3: Fitting it all in

How to have sufficient time during the day to achieve all that is required of a teacher.

Introduction

School life is complex and requires a high level of organisation and dedication from every member of staff to ensure that things run smoothly. The basic structure of pupils being in classrooms with a regular teacher continues to be the norm, yet variations and innovations in school life have added to the multidimensional nature of the role, which can result in a sort of mental paralysis for teachers whereby there is so much to do that nothing ever seems to get done properly. Effective time management is a vital component of the process, but it is not only about the pragmatics of being well organised, prioritising tasks and working efficiently, it is also about being motivated and possessing self-confidence. In addition, it is noteworthy that a relaxed and confident teacher, who is normally capable of completing a job on time, will struggle to do exactly the same job if feeling under stress and anxious.

Scenario

Studies indicate that, contrary to expectation, workload reforms have not significantly reduced the burden on teachers in England and Wales. One of the reasons for this position is that successive Governments have taken a close interest in all aspects of education and produced what many school leaders and practitioners have viewed as an unreasonably large number of policy documents, stipulations, advice and interventions, which have threatened to overwhelm those who have to implement them. Attempts to respond to such a wide range of measures have led to what is popularly known as 'innovation fatigue'. Teachers appreciate the planning, preparation and assessment (PPA) time they have been given, but many argue that paperwork demands and expectations have risen steeply too, as head teachers seek to deflect any criticism that they have failed to implement rigorous and effective monitoring systems. For instance, it is not uncommon for annual reports to parents to cover as much as four sides of paper per pupil. Owing to time pressures, some important tasks can remain undone, some decisions are deferred and some deadlines are missed or barely met. The commitments can mount up until they hang like a dark cloud over a teacher's life. Corners are cut; preparation is reduced; lessons become strongly controlled by the teacher, with reduced pupil autonomy. The stresses and strains of the job rise as teachers convince themselves that it is virtually impossible to respond to the multitude of demands. The situation in different schools, and even within the same school, can vary considerably, such that, while some teachers become burdened and distressed by heavy work pressures, others cope with relative ease and, though perpetually busy, seem to have sufficient time to complete tasks and stay buoyant. So what is their secret?

Factors for consideration

1. To work more efficiently, rather than work harder.
2. To establish the relative importance of the varying demands placed on a teacher.
3. To try and ensure that teaching is a pleasure – at least for most of the time – rather than an ordeal.
4. To be realistic about what is achievable by one person, however talented, within a given period of time.

Discussion

As well as being centres of excitement and intellectual stimulation, schools can also be pressurised environments. Certain times of the school year are particularly hectic when, in addition to their normal workload, teachers have to cope with writing reports, parents' evenings, putting up displays and devising medium- and long-term plans with colleagues. (See also Challenge 4 in this chapter about coping with a new class.) Sometimes, the added responsibilities of organising extra-curricular activities, managing a drama production or supervising a sporting event create a state of continuous busyness and unremitting pressure. A detailed study of three hundred and twenty-six primary teachers in the early 1990s showed that less than three-fifths of a teacher's working day was spent in direct contact with classes; fifteen per cent of the day was spent in school, but without class contact, and a quarter of the day was spent entirely outside school hours working on teaching-related issues (Campbell and Neill 1994). It is interesting to estimate the equivalent figures for teachers in school today.

Although the reforms of recent years have made it possible for you to focus on teaching and learning without having to worry unduly about relatively minor matters, there has nevertheless been a corresponding increase in the administrative workload. Owing to budget constraints, the numbers of teaching assistants in school are falling, which has implications for organising and managing learning. Despite having assistance with displays, resources and general classroom organisation, you are still responsible for all that happens to your pupils, so delegation does not absolve you from managing children's learning experiences and safeguarding their welfare. The vast majority of assistants are keen to help and expand their expertise, so time spent in liaising and in developing relationships with them is worthwhile.

New and trainee teachers are often advised to 'pace' themselves and avoid what is popularly referred to as 'burnout'; however, such a worthy aspiration can be put in jeopardy for at least ten reasons:

1. Motivation for teaching: teachers are sometimes their own 'worst enemy' because they have such a passion for the job that they commit an excessive amount of time, emotion and mental energy to doing it. Research indicates that it is normal for teachers to work well in excess of forty hours per week, let alone the countless hours spent in cogitating over issues as diverse as where to store pencils and how to promote advanced thinking skills in non-core subjects. Trainee teachers, in particular, allocate a lot of additional time to detailed lesson preparation.

2. Commitment to the cause: teachers will often struggle in to school despite feeling unwell for fear of letting the side down, giving additional work to their colleagues or being regarded as workshy. They rightly see themselves as an integral member of the team and feel a responsibility to both pupils and colleagues.

3. High expectations: society expects a lot from its teachers. Parental involvement and greater accountability, together with a strong emphasis on pupil success in national tests, have intensified the need for academic and social achievement. A teacher can be nervous that, while she is away from her class, the children will fall behind in their work and standards of achievement will slip. For a similar reason, she devotes an immense amount of time to preparation, devising elaborate visual aids and detailed marking.

4. Close scrutiny of performance: all teachers are subject to performance management, focusing largely on their teaching competence. Trainee teachers are in the spotlight from the moment they enter their placement school until the day they leave. Every teacher is regularly assessed on teaching performance; inspectors base a significant part of their report on the quality of teachers as revealed by their observed classroom practice and discussions with parents.

5. Excessive paperwork: all teachers are obliged to set out lesson plans in some detail, keep copious records of pupil progress, write extensive reports for parents and, in the case of trainees, maintain a diary of critical events, an evaluation of their teaching performance and case studies of specified children. Although the golden rule is to record only those details that have a direct bearing on teaching and child welfare, teachers tend to write more than is necessary to ensure that they are above reproach in this area of work.

6. Pupil demands: it is generally accepted that children are less compliant and more demanding than was once the case. Equal opportunities legislation and policies to include all children in mainstream settings have added to the amount of effort that teachers and assistants have to make in planning for and responding to pupil needs. During the past decade or so, teachers have been encouraged to involve children in their learning, including setting achievement targets, offering ideas about school improvement and even interviewing prospective members of staff.

7. Class management complexity: years ago, there was one teacher and a class of thirty–forty children, who spent most of their time together in the same room. Today, it is common for there to be more than one adult with the bulk of the class in the main classroom area, a small number of children working independently in an annexe, computers in a corner of the room or in the corridor, and a computer suite for timetabled use, plus an environmental area located away from the classroom. Older pupils are likely to move from room to room as they go off to different 'sets' for mathematics or English. Children leave and enter the classroom as they attend music lessons and receive additional individual tuition from a dedicated adult or older child ('coaching'). Part of the teacher's role is to ensure that events run smoothly, which is a far from easy task, requiring close concentration and exceptional organisation. Simply keeping track of pupils' whereabouts, let alone resourcing their needs, liaising with assistants and monitoring learning is a demanding task.

8. High skill level: the expansion of knowledge is reflected in the growth of technology in schools such that, in addition to curriculum knowledge (information and facts), teachers need to be adept at handling and utilising equipment, be sensitive to health and safety, and provide opportunities for children to access information technology resources. A growing emphasis on teachers' subject knowledge has made it necessary for them to keep abreast of new insights into pedagogy, changes in our understanding of how children learn, and related issues about special needs attached to low intelligence, poor command of English and common misconceptions, especially in mathematics and science. Teachers are also expected to have a sophisticated grasp of interpreting assessment data, writing accurate reports for parents and, in many cases, providing leadership in a curriculum area or age phase.

9. Changes in societal structure: although it is still normal for teachers to relate to at least one parent (usually the mother) on a fairly regular basis, society is now multifaceted, both with respect to the make-up of family units, and also to the variety of first-tongue languages spoken and customs (see also factor 10, below). It is becoming less usual for the biological mother and father to arrive together for a consultation with the teacher and it is not unknown for brothers and sisters in school to have different fathers or for an 'extended' household to consist of several families. Arranging to see parents might involve separate meetings with the estranged parents; similarly, sending letters and reports home has to be done with great sensitivity due to legal complications and emotional entanglements. Teachers are not in a position to judge the moral conduct or suitability of home circumstances, but they have to handle the consequences of dealing with children from disrupted backgrounds.

10. English as a subsidiary language: increased mobility and the relative ease with which people from other nations have been able to enter the United Kingdom in recent years have led to a considerable increase in the number and range of nationalities in the country. The pupil composition in schools located in conurbations has changed dramatically, but even rural schools have been affected by the arrival of pupils for whom English is not

their first language. The presence of a single child with English language learning needs requires that teachers modify their approach, such as speaking more slowly and using a larger number of visual aids. There can also be additional considerations with regard to cultural sensitivities (e.g. food preferences), translation of letters into the parent's natural tongue and the presence of a teaching assistant in the room to support and coach the new pupil.

So what is to be done about the above factors? The following strategies will help to mitigate damaging effects and turn them to your advantage:

1. Motivation for teaching: high levels of motivation are essential for teaching, but there are other priorities in life: family, hobbies, holidays, religion, voluntary work, and so forth. Write a notice in large letters and place it somewhere appropriate, 'I teach because I choose to and not because I'm forced to!'

2. Commitment to the cause: team spirit can be uplifting and a source of considerable satisfaction; it can also be enervating and pressurising. This time the notice should read: 'I will never surrender my health for the sake of any pupil, parent, head teacher, worthy cause, government initiative or Ofsted inspection'.

3. High expectations: society expects a lot from you, but the main source of dissatisfaction comes from within your mind. The notice now reads, 'I will do my best, but doing the impossible might take me a little longer!'

4. Close scrutiny of performance: you are not an athlete on a running track trying to improve on your previous best time; neither are you a helpless victim of the system, awaiting your fate, as others decide what should become of you. Your note should read, 'I am a fellow professional, willing to learn, but not on trial.'

5. Excessive paperwork: over recent years, there seems to have been an assumption that more-comprehensive paperwork (on sheet or screen) inevitably leads to higher standards. There is a balance to be struck for, while you want to record essentials, you do not want your life to be consumed by it. This time, the note says: 'I will write down what is absolutely necessary for me to do my job efficiently, to be effective as a teacher and to demonstrate my capability, but not one jot more!'

6. Pupil demands: teachers are thinking and talking to others about their pupils constantly, so much so that they are sometimes in danger of wearying their listeners. On the other hand, you can only do so much, regardless of how many hours you work. Make up your mind that no pupil will be a burden on you or any other child in the class due to bad behaviour or any other reason. The mantra on this occasion reads, 'I will do my best for the children, but I refuse to attempt the impossible'.

7. Class management complexity: it is possible to confuse 'complexity' with 'complicated'. It is simply not worth operating an organisational system or attempting to manage learning by controlling everything tightly. Loosen up a little! You cannot learn *for* the pupils, you can only help them to do so. Write in large letters: 'I will concentrate my efforts on

assisting children to learn and use straightforward but effective means to do so'.

8. High skill level: you will continue learning, whether or not you make a conscious effort to do so. The important thing is *what* you are learning and its relevance for your work as a teacher. Keep asking yourself whether there are ways in which, in the circumstances, you might have done something better (e.g. introducing a lesson) or utilised something more successfully (e.g. incorporating visual images into your presentation). Your reminder on this occasion is, 'I will continue to learn from any situation, anywhere, any time or place, and from anyone'.

9. Changes in societal structure: it is simplistic and inaccurate to assume that pupils from dysfunctional families will inevitably suffer from behavioural problems or underachieve. Nevertheless, it is statistically true that such children are more likely to struggle in school and, later in life, find themselves in trouble with the police. There is, of course, nothing you can do about a child's background; you *can*, however, adopt a positive approach to the children such that, while you make allowance for their disadvantaged circumstances, you do not make it an excuse for low standards or agonise over life's inequalities. Write boldly, 'I will make every effort to help all children succeed and have high expectations for them to do so'.

10. English as a subsidiary language: it is increasingly unlikely that you work with a class in which all the pupils have English as their primary language. It is perfectly possible that there are several languages represented, with the attached cultural norms and customs. You can try to keep abreast of the different perspectives, priorities and expectations that each culture brings, but you are not paid to be a community worker and, apart from being sensitive, courteous and helpful, your job is to teach. The position can be summarised by writing, 'I want to be an excellent teacher, not an inadequate social worker'.

To make allowance for impending periods of work intensity, it is important to keep your work diary up to date so that you can plan your schedule and not be caught out by a tidal wave of demands. At the start of each term (or school placement if you are a trainee) it is well worth committing time to filling in your itinerary as far in advance and in as much detail as possible. Pay particular attention to significant deadlines, such as the occasion you will have to provide information about pupil progress to parents, and the period of time in which you have to mark or assess work and submit test results. Where possible, leave a small amount of leeway to allow for unexpected commitments and other distractions to avoid the onset of 'deadline stress'. Write phrases such as 'leave free' and 'no appointments' and 'one week left' and 'very busy' into your diary in advance. Despite its old-fashioned appearance, an annotated wall calendar is extremely valuable in keeping track of events.

It is helpful to remember that most lessons follow a regular pattern of introduction, question and answer, task allocation, task management and lesson review, so it is worth adopting such a straightforward model, rather than being unnecessarily elaborate. The best teachers use 'ordinary' content but present it in interesting and relevant ways, rather than trying to be constantly innovative. There are also plenty of lesson ideas in books, journals and on the Internet, so you don't have to think up something spectacular for every occasion. The production of visual aids, worksheets and computerised images is beneficial but also extremely time-consuming, so make sure that the effort invested is worthwhile. It is discouraging to have spent hours lovingly preparing an aid, only to find that you only use it once, briefly, and then consign it to the recycling bin or the 'delete' folder. Make it a firm principle that everything you create for lessons is reusable. Sometimes it is worth preparing a draft version initially and creating a permanent one after evaluating its effectiveness.

Planning, assessment and marking are wearisome tasks and can lead to teachers 'burning the midnight oil' – a situation that should be avoided if humanly possible. To avoid such a fate, remember that not everything needs to be assessed closely; older pupils can be trained to evaluate the quality of written work, both their own and, perhaps, that of a fellow pupil (a practice known as 'peer assessment'). Younger children can usually offer spoken comments about the quality of what they produce. You are understandably anxious that parents will complain if they see some work that is unmarked, but careful explanation about the purpose of the exercise and the value of discussing a child's output rather than covering the page with ticks and written feedback will usually provide reassurance. Nevertheless, a few large ticks to show that you have marked the work can be a useful public relations strategy, even if you are unable to assess it closely. As the professional, you have to make decisions about how best to utilise your precious time – grading pupils' work is not always at the top of the list, so don't become a slave to it or indeed to any other aspect of the job.

To stay on top of your work, you have to find various ways of dealing effectively with your time and keeping control over events, rather than the reverse, so consider employing some or all of the following strategies.

- Keep lists of jobs to be done and order them with reference to the deadline and/ or the task's importance; spend the minimum time over the least significant tasks.
- Complete a job at the earliest possible time and do not wait until just before the deadline to finish it.
- On the evening before a busy day, compile a checklist: (a) resources to take into school; (b) things to be done before school begins; (c) things to be done during the lunch break; (d) things that can wait.
- Don't do any work on Friday evenings and do only an essential amount over the weekend.
- Try to complete work while you are at school, rather than taking too much home to do.
- When working at home, use a timer and set it for (say) thirty minutes; work solidly for that amount of time before stopping and giving yourself a reward. Bear in mind that the first twenty minutes of every hour worked are normally by far the most productive.
- Prioritise with regard to the amount of work involved in completing tasks, as well as their deadline dates.

- Clarify the nature of the task, rather than wasting time and energy by doing it incorrectly.
- Put reminders about deadlines in the diary about one week before the due date.
- Take advice from more experienced colleagues about things that *really* matter and give them high priority.

In truth, and with the best will in the world, it is not always possible to adhere precisely to the above format, but it is worth considering its usefulness and value in coping with the avalanche of tasks that you have to manage as a teacher. If you are still in training, it is likely that you will take much longer to complete things that later you will become adept at doing rapidly; this process is unavoidable. However, unless you want to spend all your waking hours on classroom-related matters and give up any hope of a life outside school, you must find shortcuts and use well-tried methods and existing resources rather than reinvent them or plough a lone furrow. By all means aim for high standards in your work, but remember that self-sacrifice for the cause is optional!

Reference

Campbell, R.J. and St. John Neill, S.R. (1994) *Primary Teachers at Work*, Abingdon: Routledge.

Top tip

Make sure that the four parts of your 'person' are given the chance to recuperate: (1) your physical condition; (2) your mental state; (3) your psychological wellbeing; (4) your spiritual health. Don't neglect any of them.

Activate your thinking!

There are four principal reasons for poor time management: (1) you are attempting to do too much; (2) you are working inefficiently; (3) you are failing to prioritise your workload; (4) you are unwell or lacking confidence. In truth, time cannot be managed; it is only the *use* of it that is within your grasp. The secret is to seize control of events, plan ahead as far as possible and deny yourself the luxury of spending a lot of time on enjoyable tasks that don't contribute much to your success as a teacher.

Additional reading for Challenge 3

Purdy, S. (1999) *Time Management for Teachers*, Solvang, CA: Write Time Publishing.
One of the few books wholly dedicated to an exploration of this subject and the practical implications for teachers.

Thomas, W. and Hailstone, P. (2005) *The Managing Workload Pocketbook*, Southampton: Teachers' Pocketbooks.

The book provides practical advice on minimising stress and strategies for getting and staying organised, planning, declining invitations, coping with unreasonable demands and being assertive.

Challenge 4: Starting with a new class

The beginning of a new school year brings stresses and strains, but it is also an opportunity for a fresh start.

Introduction

The opening weeks of a new school year are hard for even the most experienced class teachers as they make the rapid adjustment from relaxing over the long summer holiday to an intensive, sometimes frantic attempt to get things up and running, while getting to know a new class, sorting out timetables and establishing routines. For a recently qualified teacher, the intensity of the time is coupled with emotional and psychological factors associated with an awareness that this is 'for real' and the protections offered by student status have been replaced by even higher expectations and more direct responsibility for the children's education. Every teacher wants to make a positive beginning without using up too much energy before the term has really got going. The opening few days are just the start of many more to come, so it pays to be wise about the way you handle them.

Scenario

At the opening of the academic year, and well before the pupils arrive in school, teachers have to be present for 'in-service' days and organising their rooms and resources. Despite the fact that they are busy attending meetings and dealing with a variety of practical tasks, such as rearranging furniture, checking technology and liaising with (equally busy) colleagues, there is a sense in which life seems to be 'on hold' until the first pupil day of term. However, from the moment that the children start pouring through the gate, it is not unusual for teachers to be in school from early in the morning until late in the evening, and then to take work home to complete.

One of the greatest challenges teachers face is to explain and then enforce ways in which they want children to act and behave; inevitably, this process takes time and is not the smooth kind of process that is portrayed by some writers and policy makers. It is also physically and emotionally tiring. The reality is that teachers have to hit the ground running, as they turn their attention to preparing the classroom; sorting out the timetable; gathering resources; drawing up group lists; meeting parents; finding places for equipment; and reminding children about procedures such as lining up, tidying the tables, returning items, when they can go to the toilet, have a drink, and sharpen pencils, where they put finished work, and so forth. During lessons, teachers have to introduce the topic; organise groups; distribute resources; respond to questions; guide the children about what to do if they are stuck; and reinforce rules about taking turns, being polite, and behaviour in and around the room. In fact, there is so much to do that teachers can feel overwhelmed and the recent holidays soon become a blur in the distant past. Welcome back to school!

Factors for consideration

1. Ways in which good preparation mitigates the heavy demands on teachers that a new school year brings.
2. Prioritising the many tasks that need to be completed prior to the opening of the term.
3. Ways to establish procedures and clarify expectations of pupils from the first day.
4. Being aware of the impact of a new school year on the children.

Discussion

There is no way of avoiding the intensity of the opening weeks of the school year. Regardless of your skill as a teacher, positive attitude to life and well organised mind, it is inevitable that the demands made by children, increased use of the voice, organising timetables, management of sessions, attendance at staff meetings and responses to a multiplicity of questions from pupils, parents, assistants and colleagues, make you feel that life is spinning out of control. Unless you are teaching the very youngest children, the whole class arrives on the same morning – twenty-five or more pupils, full of expectation, wide-eyed with anticipation and buzzing around you in a seemingly endless flow. You cannot 'freeze the moment' or modify the pace to a more acceptable level. You cannot tell parents to come back another day when you are less busy, though it is reasonable to arrange a more convenient occasion if they want to hold an extended conversation. You cannot inform the head that you'll complete your lesson planning when you've got more time. You cannot ignore your colleagues or miss meetings because you feel too tired to attend. Despite these 'cannots', there are a number of strategies and practices that can assist in making the start of term more enjoyable and less of an endurance test. And remember, it won't be this bad for long; within two or three weeks, life will settle down into a more manageable routine.

The completion of practical tasks is interspersed with numerous informal conversations with other staff, catching up on the latest gossip, sharing amusing anecdotes about everything and anything educational, usually laced with barbs of 'dark humour', and generally encouraging one another in the build-up to the opening day. Don't underestimate the significance of these personal and collegial interactions; they form the bedrock for a thousand and one encounters throughout the coming months. Knowing that your colleagues are sympathetic and supportive provides a vitally important source of reassurance and hope when you might otherwise feel unable to cope with the welter of demands and expectations. And, although you probably find it hard to believe, you fulfil a similar supportive role for colleagues, however much older, wiser and more capable they are or appear to be.

The new class will have different personalities and characteristics from ones you have previously taught. There might be a very unsettled pupil or a telltale or a genius or a compulsive liar or an abused child or a happy-go-lucky group of 'charmers' or a pupil with specific disabilities that require specialist intervention; or none of these types. Some classes seem to 'gel' almost immediately; others seem to bicker at the slightest provocation. In addition, there might be new children who are finding it difficult to adjust and missing their friends from the previous location. Pupils will take time to 'tune in' to your voice and can genuinely not hear what you are saying in the excitement and fervour of being back in the classroom. After weeks of relative freedom, children need opportunity to orientate to the school routine and be alert to your specific requirements. This need for explicitness explains why it is so important to be clear in your own mind about what you consider to be essential behaviour and what is relatively unimportant. It is important to set out your expectations early – but it becomes a more demanding task if you are unsure about them yourself. Playtimes offer children the opportunity to meet friends they might not have seen for some time; it is also an environment in which complex social interactions take place, friendships are re-kindled and norms of relating to new people are established.

If you are a brand new teacher in the school, it is probable that you have never met the children's parents. As they burst upon the scene in the early days of term, bear in mind six points. First, parents want you to succeed, not because they think you are personally worth it, but because it is in the best interests of their children that you do so. Second, the vast majority of parents are reasonable and caring, who trust you with the education of their most treasured possession – their children. Third, don't assume that the parents who are bright, cheerful and positive are necessarily the most approving; a small number could be trying to elicit your support for their own purposes; other parents can be experiencing tough times and compensate by being artificially jovial. By contrast, the majority of parents might appear relaxed, even a little indifferent, when in fact they are just happy to let you get on with the job. Fourth, don't assume that, because you don't see particular parents, they are uninterested in their children's education, as work and domestic commitments sometimes prevent them from appearing. Fifth, while you will want to be polite, pleasant and responsive, avoid being drawn into lengthy conversations. If a parent is genuinely troubled or needs to ask serious questions, arrange a time to talk that is convenient for both of you. Finally, you will often find that a parent who is initially inclined to be negative proves to be your greatest supporter, once won over by your charm, integrity and obvious competence, though from time to time you will meet a parent who seems almost impossible to please.

The first impression that you create for parents is significant. Even if you feel a little harassed and your nerves are jangling, do your best to communicate that all is well by maintaining soft eye contact and sounding cheerful and reassuring. Make sure that you are smartly (but not ostentatiously) dressed, preferably in bright rather than dull colours. Remember that they will be talking about you afterwards, so make sure they like what they see.

On the first day, instead of diving headlong into the regular routine of subject teaching, it is useful to start off with an activity that is straightforward to organise and easy to manage. This approach not only allows you a degree of flexibility to sort out administrative jobs and find your bearings, it also helps with class control. As they adjust to being in school and focus on the work, most children enjoy a straightforward lesson that allows them to 'get their heads' down, complete a task and gain approval. Although worksheets with blanks to fill, pictures to draw, and word games to complete might not be brimming with academic muscle, they are useful ways of settling the class during those first few heady hours. Make sure that you assess them instantly, either by putting a mark out of ten (older children love it) or writing a highly commending comment or giving a visual reward (such as a smiley face). You can then ask the children to devise a similar activity sheet of their own for a friend. Similarly, the first PE lesson should be fairly short, involve little or no equipment and tire them out as well as being fun. At the end of the morning or before they go home, you can read the class an exciting story and ask them to draw a map of the mysterious island; the face of the hungry monster; a 'before' and 'after' picture to show the effects of drinking the potion; or whatever is appropriate. Older and more capable pupils can elaborate their work in whatever way they choose. Send them home feeling that they have accomplished something worthwhile, even if it hasn't stretched them. It is also useful to give the whole class a simple homework task, such as working out how many paces/miles/roads it is from home to school – the next morning you can create a representation of the results in the form of a graph or draw some pictures with cartoon figures to show the journey. You can also give pupils the task of asking a parent or another grown-up for the name of their favourite children's book as a starting point for enthusing and stimulating ideas about reading. Keep things simple but, in doing so, set down markers for the future.

After the summer break, pupils will be keen to talk about their holiday experiences, so instead of dismissing their excited recollections of granny's melted ice cream, mum's karaoke singing and accounts of how they jumped down the vertical slide at the holiday park *on their own*, allow time for sharing and reliving these experiences. In turn, you might want to tell them about one of your special moments; if so, be careful not to make it too dramatic and avoid any mention of personal details, such as the names of close friends or members of your family. Be aware that it is highly likely that the children will ask you questions to find out more about the occasion; in addition, they will almost certainly relate what you say to parents when they get home, so exercise a little caution. When the children have selected their favourite (children often use the word 'best') memory or event, you can ask them to visualise that they are back in the situation and describe, write or draw (or all three) as if they were there, including what happened, what they heard and how they felt. Although you might view school as a 'separate' sphere from home, children tend to see life as a single experience, so finding ways to harmonise the two worlds is worthwhile.

Allow children a degree of flexibility to develop their ideas in creative ways, such as writing a short poem, designing cartoons, making up a simple board game based on a theme, acting out a scene using toys, or whatever is easy to manage and won't require a lot of preparation or create too much mess. Allow the activity to run for several sessions if necessary, possibly using it as a 'lead' into the formal curriculum and linked to a homework task. For instance, children can ask members of family to tell the children about something funny that happened on holiday when *they* were young. One way and another, send them home today so that they are eager to come back tomorrow.

Finally, there is no way of preventing the initial sense of feeling overwhelmed during the opening phase of the new year, but thorough preparation, good classroom organisation, uncomplicated lessons, seeking advice from colleagues and staying cheerful will preclude the worst excesses and see you through to the safe harbour of that dearly awaited half term!

Top tip

Don't expend all your energy during the first couple of days; a long year stretches ahead! Sort out reading books as a priority and, especially for younger children, hear them read as soon as possible, even if for a short time; parents will ask their children if you (or the assistant) have done so!

Activate your thinking!

Children, as well as adults, take time to adjust to the new school term. They, too, have to cope with nerves and can be fazed by the experience. Teachers should not be so caught up with their own concerns that they are indifferent to the emotional turmoil experienced by the pupils.

Additional reading for Challenge 4

Cowley, S. (2009) *How to Survive Your First Year in Teaching*, second edn, London: Continuum.
A book that offers a lot of practical advice for trainee and new teachers with the purpose of making your teaching experience as enjoyable as possible.
Fenwick, A. (2011) 'The first three years: experiences of early career teachers', *Teachers and Teaching*, 17 (3), pp. 325–43.
The study examines the transition period between induction and post-induction for early-career teachers and the consequences for their professional learning.
Read, C. (2007) *500 Activities for the Primary Classroom*, Oxford: Macmillan.
The book is full of practical ideas for teachers to employ, not least at the start of a new school term.

Challenge 5: Achieving a balanced teaching approach

How to use creative methods as well as formal teaching to enhance children's learning.

Introduction

The traditional view of a teacher is someone standing at the front of the class imparting knowledge to a passive group of pupils. To show the extent of their understanding, children are then expected to answer questions about the lesson content and complete associated exercises. While such an uninspiring episode is rarely a regular feature of modern-day classrooms, teachers are still faced with the challenge about the extent to which they use formal direct/transmission/ didactic teaching, followed by rigidly constructed tasks, as against how much they use strategies that foster pupil independence and encourage initiative and creativity. In fact, these differing approaches have both benefits and potential disadvantages.

Scenario

Curriculum requirements demand that teachers cover specific areas of knowledge in a given time (e.g. across a half-term), though it is the case, of course, that coverage is not necessarily equitable with 'having learned'. In a situation where there are two or more parallel classes and joint planning, the teacher must also keep pace with colleagues to try and ensure that pupils in both classes have a similar learning experience. The fastest method of imparting knowledge is through transmission teaching, teacher to pupil. Other approaches that involve close co-operation between children, such as collaborative problem solving and investigations – broadly described as discovery learning/enquiry-based learning – absorb more time and are more liable to deviate from the curriculum agenda and associated learning objectives, but have the potential to generate enthusiasm and deep learning. While teachers are often keen to promote group work and peer support through partnerships, they can succumb to the temptation of talking at length to the children instead of facilitating learning through activities that allow children to think for themselves, grapple with ideas and converse with one another.

Factors for consideration

1. The occasions when it is appropriate to use transmission teaching.
2. Ways in which co-operative and enquiry-based activities can be utilised to promote learning.
3. Keeping pace with curriculum coverage while activating pupil enthusiasm by allowing children to pursue their own interests to an extent.
4. Fostering independence in learning and greater pupil autonomy without deviating unduly from the principal lesson aims.

Discussion

You have a responsibility to your pupils, parents and colleagues to ensure that children are given the opportunity to make optimum progress and fulfil their potential by using whatever means appropriate. Sometimes, the pressure on you to demonstrate that pupils are achieving well and excelling in tests, especially in the crucial areas of reading and arithmetic, makes the 'route one' style of teaching very attractive; that is to say, a teaching approach that is heavily dependent on telling children things. On the surface, a direct teaching approach makes more efficient use of time and requires less organising. In practice, both telling and pupils finding out are important, as follows:

Telling pupils what they need to know and explaining what they have to do to learn more

↓

Allowing them opportunities to investigate, explore and discuss aspects of the topic

Ultimately, you want children to gain greater factual knowledge and conceptual understanding, and to master necessary skills to facilitate learning (e.g. using a dictionary; employing multiplication tables; utilising a computer program). The challenge is to strike a suitable balance between the two approaches – too much direct teaching becomes tedious, makes pupils overly reliant on the teacher and can lead to restlessness; too much enquiry-based learning can result in lack of structure and random learning.

Myhill and Warren (2005) warn that many teaching strategies and teacher–pupil interactions act as a heavy prompt or even what they refer to as a 'straitjacket' upon pupil learning. In particular, the teacher's desire to ensure that children are introduced to key concepts or topics sometimes means that the movement to independent learning is not achieved and the scaffold becomes a means of control, rather than of temporary guidance. The principle underpinning the strategy of 'standing off' from children as they struggle is that they need to be taught self-sufficiency rather than promoting their over-reliance on a teacher. It goes without saying, however, that you must avoid distressing an anxious child by refusing to offer guidance or leaving a pupil to flounder and become discouraged.

Depending on the ages and experience of pupils, a range of strategies are available to reduce the tendency to directly teach ('tell') too much and allow you the opportunity to stand back so that pupils have space to think for themselves and take some responsibility for their own learning. For example, you might consider using some or all of the following strategies:

- *Think, pair, share activities* in which you introduce ideas and content that are subsequently talked about by pairs of children and then shared more widely across the whole class. This approach relies heavily on each pupil's ability to discuss issues in a thoughtful, sensible way. It is particularly useful for problem solving and exploring moral dilemmas. In adopting this method, the time for peer conversation has to be strictly controlled; young children often only need a few minutes – time can be extended accordingly for older pupils. You play an important role in drawing the threads together and fashioning the 'next steps' in the learning sequence.

- *Research projects* in which the pupils select or are allocated a topic to investigate within the overarching theme (in an area of history, say). This approach allows children to use their initiative and often generates a great deal of enthusiasm; however, unless they are given careful guidance and specific objectives to achieve, the exercise can degenerate into poorly co-ordinated and superficial coverage of the topic. The research project is likely to run across several days or weeks and can form part of an on-going homework requirement. Some teachers conclude with in-class presentations or sharing with the whole school during an assembly.

- *Self and peer assessment* can be woven into the regular class routines, whereby children evaluate some of their own work or that of others. To succeed, two key components are vital. First, teachers promote the practice and provide clear instruction about the process. Second, the teacher offers pupils ample support in evaluating another child's work. Inexperienced teachers try to mark/grade everything that children commit to paper, but this attempt to keep on top of the marking is usually counterproductive, as it occupies a lot of time and energy for little reward. Children's learning is more likely to be enhanced by selective marking, ideally with the child in attendance. One way and another, pupil involvement is the key factor.

- *Use of mime, puppetry and drama* in small groups to present or represent information and knowledge, or to explore ethical problems. Mime is a much-neglected skill that is easily taught and demonstrated. It can be used with pupils of all ages and fascinates the whole class. It is most useful as a class-bonding exercise to fill odd moments waiting for the end of a session or before going home in the evening, during which pupils might otherwise be getting restless. The use of mime can then be extended into more formal drama and movement lessons.

The use of puppets, though normally associated with entertaining younger children, has immense potential for pupils of all ages as a means of transmitting information, sharing findings and raising questions. Puppets should be simple to make and easy to store, though occasionally you might want to incorporate a large, commercially produced puppet as a treat for the children to enjoy. They can be used to enhance a story by 'reading' sections for you in an appropriate voice; or to act as an 'interested onlooker' who asks you questions about the content; or to offer comments on aspects of the plot in a fiction book. In doing so, it is important to treat the puppet as if it were a living creature. You do not need to be a ventriloquist; simply use a different voice from your own and minimise lip movements. Even shy children respond well to a much-loved puppet in the classroom. Children with communication problems will sometimes spontaneously pick up a puppet and hold a 'conversation' with it.

Drama is most effective when children act out scenes and sequences that they have developed collaboratively. A large space is helpful but is not essential, as even quite small areas can be utilised if you insist on actions being 'in slow motion' and 'no touch' – which is essential to enforce or, inevitably, the boys in particular will find some way to include a physical fight scene into the proceedings! After the drama episode, which should never last more than a couple of minutes, a short discussion about the issues raised by the players is helpful. A similar approach can be adopted in PE, as pupils work in small groups to devise simple games using small equipment and later demonstrate them to the rest of the class. As with all such exploratory enterprises, you must specify the parameters; for example, the ball must not exceed waist height; the game must last no less than thirty seconds and no more than two minutes. (See also Chapter 3, Professional theme 42.)

To relieve the pressure on yourself during the lesson phase when pupils are busily engaged in allocated tasks, you can *make yourself unavailable* for short periods of time, which is a simple strategy whereby you 'disappear' from the proceedings without physically leaving the room. The technique works by arranging a signal (such as sounding a small bell or standing in a particular spot with arms folded) to indicate that you are now 'invisible' and out of communication contact. Ringing the bell or clapping three times tells the children that you are now available again. This strategy has three potential advantages: (1) it gives you time to catch your breath; (2) it allows you to observe what is happening in the room without distraction; (3) it forces children to look to their own devices or seek help elsewhere. Ideally, the 'invisibility' also applies to the teaching assistant; otherwise, children will simply direct their questions and queries to her/him rather than to you. If problems arise, you can, of course, revert to 'visible mode' in an instant. Children quickly realise that you are not going to respond to them during these moments and, after a surprisingly brief time, ignore you completely. Don't overuse the strategy – once a session is usually sufficient – or it will lose its potency, and less confident children can be unnerved by it.

The above strategies take time to establish and promote but, once in place, allow you to be more a manager of learning than the 'driver' and to encourage children to take more responsibility for their own education. The gradual increase in pupil autonomy not only leads to their greater self-confidence but also helps to control a tendency that you might develop to over-teach using didactic methods, which are better employed in fairly small doses. As with everything in teaching, you are, of course, the only person who can ultimately make decisions about the most appropriate teaching and learning methods.

Reference

Myhill, D. and Warren, P. (2005) 'Scaffolds or straitjackets? Critical moments in classroom discourse', *Educational Review*, 57 (1), pp. 55–69.

Top tip

Talk less; listen more; learn with the children; give them time and space to absorb and digest knowledge.

Activate your thinking!

No matter how brilliant your exposition or amusing your talk or dynamic your visual aids or technological your planning – there is a limit to how long children can concentrate on listening to your voice.

Additional reading for Challenge 5

Best, B. and Thomas, W. (2008) *The Creative Teaching and Learning Resource Book*, London: Continuum.

The authors present a large number of suggestions, ideas and practical strategies with an emphasis on inclusive learning experiences that engage learners and raise motivation levels.

Keeling, D. and Hodgson, D. (2011) *Invisible Teaching: 101 Ways to Create Openness, Energy and Focus in the Classroom*, Carmarthen: Crown House.

The book contains numerous activities that require little or no setting up and provide an antidote to formal teaching.

Challenge 6: Teaching mixed-ability, multi-age classes

Ways to organise and manage learning for two or more year groups in the same class.

Introduction

Teachers are often urged to 'differentiate' work as a means of ensuring that all children experience learning appropriate to their ages and abilities. In practice, differentiation is more complex and demanding than some educationists acknowledge, even when teaching a single year group. Strategies to cope with the variety of ability and complexities of organising learning in a *multi-age* class present teachers with particular challenges but also opportunities to develop peer support and social allegiances across a stratified age range. The many demands made of teachers with such a diverse group of pupils have led to some schools opting for dividing children into 'sets' on the basis of ability for mathematics and English. In a much smaller but growing number of cases, larger schools 'stream' pupils into ability classes – Class A, Class B, Class C – for most lessons.

Scenario

While pupil ability in a single year is normally wide, the situation of having pupils in the same class spanning two or more year groups creates a multi-age (mixed-age) class with even greater chance of academic variation. Other than in the case of a very small school (pupil roll below one hundred), the children in such a class are nearly always from within the same key stage, though combining reception-age children (five-year-olds) with the first year of Key Stage 1 (six-year-olds) is fairly common. Sometimes low numbers necessitate other age combinations.

Multi-age classes are more common in smaller primary schools where staff : pupil ratios make it impossible for classes to be single age. Occasionally, a school is organised on 'family groupings', which involves a cross-section of the school – older and younger children together – combining for specific activities. In a multi-age class, teachers are not only coping with pupils' curricular entitlement (year by year) but also with differences in maturity levels. While striving to engender whole-class cohesion, a teacher is conscious of the need to provide appropriate work for each individual. The situation for older pupils is likely to be more straightforward if they are set for mathematics and English (e.g. classified into top set, middle set, lower set, though not necessarily referring to the sets using those terms), in that teaching can be targeted towards a narrower range of ability, though the differing needs of mature and less mature children still need to be taken into account in terms of their concentration span, ability to handle critical feedback and social skills.

Factors for consideration

1. To plan lessons that provide tasks and activities, used in conjunction, for pupils spanning two different year groups.
2. To manage lessons in which a variety of activities are happening appropriate to the age and ability span of the children.
3. To ensure that children in each year group cover the required curriculum while promoting collaborative working practices across the years.
4. To promote social interaction and cohesion across, as well as within, year groups.

Discussion

There are three key differences between a single- and multiple-age class: (1) owing to the spread of ages, children in a mixed class usually exhibit a broader range of maturity needs relating to attention span, reliance on adults and coping with failure; (2) younger children tend to require greater use of 'hands-on' tactile experiences and learning aids than their older classmates; (3) planning for a mixed class is more complex owing to the need for curriculum coverage and avoiding repetition of material for the younger children when they become the older year group the following year. Perhaps the most positive way to think about the circumstances is that the spread of ability in a single-year class might not be appreciably different from that in a mixed-age class; thus, you are going to have some very able pupils and some strugglers in a single-age class as well as in a multiple-age situation.

A characteristic of mixed-age classes is the fact that teachers have the potential to differentiate work in such a way that the same task is sometimes suitable both for the more able younger pupils and for the less able older ones. Thus, the younger able children can be given the same or similar work that is being attempted by the less able older pupils.

Organising mixed-ability teaching is challenging for teachers, as it requires decisions about catering for the range of understanding and insight possessed by the pupils in each year group. In the majority of early years situations, children are placed in mixed-ability groups to work on tasks and activities initiated by the teacher and an assistant is present with the group for all or most of the time to teach, guide and encourage them. However, as pupils move towards the top of the primary school, there is more likelihood that they will be allocated to a group based on assessments of their progress in mathematics and literacy, with a subsequent narrowing of ability breadth within a group. In planning lessons, you must ensure that, regardless of year group, the more capable children are offered opportunities to forge ahead and not be constrained by the imposition of a fixed learning objective that does not take account of pupil initiative and creativity. One way in which this can be achieved is through structuring the lesson in such a way that the work pursued by less capable children parallels that of their more distinguished classmates but with either shorter components or less intellectually demanding ones.

For example, following an introduction to the whole class, the practical phase of the lesson might consist of work in pairs on a piece of text, recording ideas and answering set questions, and creating a visual representation based on the text. However, the level of difficulty of the text, nature of questions and expectations of the representation would be suitably adjusted for less academic children. If the same piece of text were used for all pupils, it might be appropriate for more capable ones to work individually and unaided, whereas less capable ones would gain support and confidence by working in pairs. Classroom assistants are a further source of support – you need to check that they spend at least a proportion of their time promoting learning for the brighter pupils and don't spend all their time with strugglers.

A characteristic of multi-age classes is that, in a cohort of (say) twenty-eight children, with roughly half the number from each year group (i.e. about fourteen per year), it is probable that there will only be about seven boys and seven girls from each year. This state of affairs obviously limits the number of friendship permutations within each year group, which can lead to an intensification of relationships and can sometimes increase the likelihood of children 'falling out'. Teachers of junior-age children often find that dealing with relational issues is just as demanding as organising and managing the curriculum. It is therefore essential that you foster cross-year unity by means of group composition in collaborative tasks, pairings and peer support. In doing so, teachers of junior pupils in particular must avoid giving the impression that older less able children are being given what they might perceive as 'baby stuff' to do compared to the 'grown-up' work given to capable younger pupils. Bear in mind that, if you have the equivalent mixed-age class in the following year, the younger children will have become the older group, with the accompanying risk of being given tasks and activities that they engaged with during the previous year when they were the younger cohort. Careful record keeping of activities is therefore essential.

It is worth noting that, in Montessori schools, all children are taught in mixed-age classes, namely, three–six, six–nine, nine–twelve, twelve–fifteen and fifteen–eighteen years. The teachers – also referred to as guides/ facilitators – observe each child individually and tailor their presentations of new concepts to individual children or small groups. A characteristic of the Montessori approach is that children watch and learn from each other, especially in mathematics and language. Older and more-able children work with and adapt session materials, while younger and less-able children observe what their older classmates are doing, reflect on the implications and are encouraged to try things for themselves. This approach is a useful model for all teachers, though it is worth noting that Montessori class sizes are normally smaller than those in the vast majority of schools, which allows for a higher degree of individual attention.

In mixed-age/mixed-year classes, a lot of reliance is placed on peer mentoring, such that every pupil has access to 'pupil-teachers' in the form of classmates and opportunities to recall, revise and consolidate their learning by working closely with another child. One way in which you can use such mentoring or 'buddy' systems is to encourage older pupils to link with younger ones and support them both in their academic learning (learning to read, for instance) and in their general wellbeing (e.g. during break times). Note that some schools initiate 'vertical tutoring' structures that are based on a mix of pupil ages, such that children can forge supportive relationships outside their own class and year group, a practice that reflects to an extent what happens beyond the school gate.

Mixed-age and mixed-ability classes therefore present both opportunities and challenges. On the one hand, you have to be aware of the different maturity, curriculum requirements, learning needs and expectations of separate year groups. On the other hand, it is right to relish the richness of interaction and relationships that can be explored in a cross-year situation. Careful record keeping is essential if you are to keep track of National Curriculum coverage, the varied activities undertaken by pupils and their achievements.

Top tip

Treat each child as an individual personality with unique learning needs, not simply as a member of a particular year group.

Activate your thinking!

How will you reassure a parent who expresses concern that her bright ten–eleven-year-old daughter might be disadvantaged by being in a class containing eight–nine-year-olds?

Additional reading for Challenge 6

Petty, G. (2009) *Teaching Today: A Practical Guide*, fourth edn, London: Nelson Thornes. Although secondary-orientated, the book provides an appendix in which differentiation strategies are summarised, each of which is explained in detail in the book.

Rowley, C. and Cooper, H. (eds) (2009) *Cross-Curricular Approaches to Teaching and Learning*, London: Sage. The editors use the humanities as a starting point on which to build case studies and explore the significance of values in the curriculum.

Stone, S.J. (1996) *Creating the Multi-Age Classroom*, Tucson, AZ: Good Year Books. Although the book is rather dated, the author examines all aspects of teaching two or more year groups, including environment, curriculum, planning, teaching and assessing.

Tomlinson, C.A. (2004) *How to Differentiate Instruction in Mixed Ability Classrooms*, Columbus, OH: Merrill Publishing/ ASCD. A short text providing guidance, principles and strategies for teachers who are interested in creating learning environments that address the diversity typical of mixed-ability classrooms.

Postscript: Letter to a newly qualified teacher

Dear Chris,

I trust that this letter finds you well. I'm sure that you are still 'coming down to earth' after the double-joy of graduating and also being appointed to your first teaching post. You have every reason to feel extremely proud of your achievements, which I know have taken a considerable amount of effort.

Your first year in teaching will be challenging, exciting, exhausting, frustrating, joyous, bewildering, exhilarating, depressing, uplifting and every other emotion and condition imaginable! So from that perspective it's not that different from being a student! If your experience is similar to most new teachers, your first term will probably follow a pattern similar to the following:

- An immense surge of excitement and adrenaline carries you through the first few days.
- Huge waves of emotion wash to and fro during the initial encounters with 'your' class and 'your' parents (at last!).
- A gradual settling takes place in the first couple of weeks as you 'find your feet', get to know your colleagues and discover 'the way it's done here' – but now as a fully-fledged inexperienced teacher, not as a trainee.
- The first meeting with parents is exhilarating and a bit scary – but nowhere near as bad as you anticipated; in fact, you rather enjoy it.
- Reality begins to rear its head as your energy level drops and the first flush of enthusiasm seeps away, not least because a few mischievous children have weighed you up! You also 'run out' of lessons that you have previously used; niggling doubts about your ability to cope tend to shake your self-confidence.
- Fatigue begins to creep through your body and mind due to the long hours you give to the job, the emotional commitment it requires and (perhaps) coping with one of the many 'viruses' floating around the place. Each Friday evening is like a foretaste of heaven!
- You begin to wonder if you'll ever learn to handle having so much to do in so little time. (This job is impossible! Why didn't I become a hairdresser instead?)

- You never thought you'd be so happy to reach half-term intact – a bit battered and bruised, but still hanging in there.
- Unbelievably, the job gets even tougher for a time after half-term, as what you thought was a heavy workload seems to grow heavier. The long dark evenings don't help.
- You grit your teeth and begin to make changes to your practice and actions that you were a bit reluctant to risk doing previously, but which now help you become more effective. You really are a 'proper' teacher now and don't have to get permission to be innovative!
- By the beginning of December, planning for Christmas gives you a lift; life seems a lot brighter; and you get your 'second wind'.
- The run-up to Christmas is impossibly busy but enormous fun, and you somehow stagger to the end of term covered in tinsel, glitter and glue; making silly hats and reindeer antlers; organising the children to perform at the concert; and hoarse from countless singing practices.
- Your spare moments are spent writing Christmas cards to all the children in your class and you feel a tingling sense of joy in doing so, as you realise just how much each child has begun to mean to you.
- It's the last day of term. You've made it! You wobble back into the classroom after saying your final farewells to parents and starry-eyed pupils. The staff gathers to celebrate, swap stories and laugh hysterically about the silliest little incident. Your sense of belonging and camaraderie with colleagues has never been stronger; even the head teacher seems human!
- Soon you can collapse into an armchair with dignity, but first there's a lot of tidying and catching up with record keeping and related matters that have been neglected recently.
- Christmas flies past and, although you couldn't wait for the end of last term, you now can't wait for the start of the new one.
- By the time you return to school in January, you feel like an old hand at the job and realise that your decision to spend your working life as a teacher was right after all.

Well, that's what commonly happens to new teachers. Your experience might be different, of course, but probably not that different. Studies show that the morale of new teachers tends to follow a sine curve: it starts very high, dips midway through the term and edges its way back up towards the end.

Throughout the initiation process it's useful to 'let off steam' or share concerns/joys with someone who is removed from the situation but knows something of what you are experiencing. The deep emotions attached to teaching are seriously underestimated by those outside schools – but not by those who work in them. Here's what one teacher wrote after working in the classroom for a few years.

> Teaching is a great job but undoubtedly hard work and time consuming. There is a lot of paperwork, much of which seems pointless; thankfully, schools are now introducing easy to use software that makes recording information much more straightforward. We teachers watch as external initiatives come and go with their fresh set of demands then get on with the job much as we did before. I love the interaction with children and seeing

them learn, develop new ideas and increase in confidence, which helps their creativity to grow.

I love the opportunity to be innovative in the classroom and to make learning exciting. Against that, there are lesson observations and occasional inspections by OFSTED when your feet don't touch the ground. It seems that you are under constant scrutiny as a teacher and being given advice from all quarters about how to make your lessons outstanding. It is possible to feel that you are never good enough. If you aren't careful, you lose your evenings and weekends, too. I always try to stop by 9 pm so that I can relax and clear my head. Good time management and not getting obsessed with the job are essential qualities that you must learn quickly.

Despite all the challenges, you have the compensation of knowing that every day is different, that you build up brilliant relationships with your class, and that most time in the classroom is good fun, especially when your teaching is going well. Being a teacher has brought me close to tears when I've been under pressure from colleagues, had to deal with difficult parents or been faced with what seems to be an impossibly heavy workload. But I've cried for a different reason when the children tell you how much they enjoy being in your class and even more when they move on at the end of the year – even the naughty ones seem lovely! It's thrilling to receive kind words from parents, who let you know you have made a positive difference to their children's lives. The disappointments and frustrations are always present but they are far outweighed by the pleasure of doing a job that really counts for something.

Hope you have a great time teaching. Remember to put your own wellbeing at the top of the agenda. It is all very noble to sacrifice yourself for the sake of the children, but you must stay healthy and optimistic if you are to succeed in becoming a **top teacher**!

Your friend,
Prof

Index

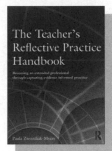